A2

ENGLISH LANGUAGE for AQA B

Ron Norman
Anne Watkiss

Published by Heinemann Educational Publishers,
Halley Court, Jordan Hill, Oxford OX2 8EJ
A division of Reed Educational and Professional Publishing Ltd

OXFORD MELBOURNE AUCKLAND
JOHANNESBURG BLANTYRE GABORONE
IBADAN PORTSMOUTH (NH) USA CHICAGO

First published 2001

05 04 03 02 01
10 9 8 7 6 5 4 3 2 1

ISBN 0 435 132261

Acknowledgements
The Publishers would like to thank the following for permission to use copyright material:

Extracts from 'GP axes doomed cancer sufferer' by John Coles, from The Sun, 28th April 2000. Copyright © News International Newspapers Limited. Reprinted with permission; Extract from 'Radio 4 News read by James Naughtie' 1st October, 2000 taken from 'Today'. Reprinted by permission of Today, BBC; 'Preview of Films on General Release' from Independent, August 1999. © The Independent. Reprinted by permission; Extracts from *The Staples Christmas Book 'Suddenly: Millennium Stories* Staples 1999 edition. Reprinted by permission of Axiom Communications; Blurb from the back cover of *Dark Vision 3: The Nightmare: The Passion* by L. J. Smith published by Simon & Schuster Inc; Blurb from the back cover of *Darker* by Andrew Matthews published by Scholastic Limited. Reprinted by permission of the publishers; Blurbs from the back covers of *Hit and Run* by R. L . Stine and *Let Me Tell You How I Died* by Sinclair Smith, published by Scholastic Inc. Reprinted by permission of the publishers; Blurb from the back cover of *The Forbidden Game* by L. J. Smith, published by Scholastic Limited; Extracts from *Microsoft Encarta 98 Encyclopedia.* © Microsoft (R). Reprinted by permission of Microsoft Corporation; Extract from *The Young Scientist Book of Stars and Planets* by permission of Usborne Publishing, 83-85 Saffron Hill, London EC1N 8RT. Copyright © 1977 Usborne Publishing Limited; Extract 'birth of a black hole' by Professor Stephen Hawking found at 'www.ampt.cam.ac.uk/user/gr/public/bh.Intro.html. Copyright © Professor Stephen Hawking. Reprinted by permission of the author; Extract from *The Twitter Machine* by Neil Smith, published by Blackwells 1989. Reprinted by permission of the publishers; Extract from *The English Stage: A History of Drama and Performance* by J. L. Styan, published by Cambridge University Press, 1996. Reprinted by permission of the publishers; Extract from *The Language Web, The Power and Problem of Words - The 1996 BBC Reith Lectures* published by Cambridge University Press, 1996. Reprinted by permission of the publishers; 'A language all of its very own' in The Young Guardian, supplement 13th November, 1990. Copyright © The Guardian, 13th November, 1990. Reprinted by permission; Extract from *A History of the English Language* by A. Baugh and T. Cable, published by Routledge 1951; Extract from *The Cambridge Encyclopedia of Language* by David Crystal, published by Cambridge University Press. Reprinted by permission of the publishers; Extract from *Exploring Pennine Countryside and Lancashire's Hill Country pamphlet* published by Northern Spirit Limited. Reprinted by permission of Arriva Trains Northern Limited; Extract from *Words and Rules* by Simon Pinker, published by Weidenfeld & Nicholson 1999. Reprinted by permission of The Orion Publishing Group Limited; Extract from *Blake* by Peter Ackroyd, published by Sinclair-Stevenson. Reprinted by permission of The Random House Group Limited; Extract from *The Oxford Children's Book of Famous People* published by Oxford University Press. Reprinted by permission of the publishers; Extract from *The Rolling Stone Encyclopedia of Rock and Roll* edited by Jon Pareles and Patricia Romanowski. Copyright © 1983 by Rolling Stone Press. Reprinted by permission of Simon & Schuster, New York; Extract from *The Children's Picture Pre-History of Dinosaurs* by permission of Usborne Publishing, 83-85 Saffron Hill, London EC1N 8RT. Copyright © 1977 Usborne Publishing Limited; Extract from *The Illustrated Dinosaur Encyclopedia* by Dougal Dixon, published by Hamlyn Children's Books. Copyright © 1988 Octopus Books Limited. Used with the permission of Egmont Books Limited, London; Extract from *First Interest - Long Ago* published by Ginn. Reprinted by permission of REPP; Extracts of text and some illustrations from *Pirate Adventure* by Roderick Hunt and Alex Brychta, published by Oxford University Press. Reprinted by permission of the publishers; Extracts of text and some illustrations from *The Toys' Party* by Roderick Hunt and Alex Brychta, published by Oxford University Press. Reprinted by permission of the publishers; Extract from *Pol and Pax in the Salty Red Sea* by J C M Truijens © text JCM Truijens 1989, published by Nelson. Reprinted by permission of Nelson Thornes Limited; Extract *Teen speak: the definitive Lexicon 2001* compiled by Sophie Wilson, editor of J17 magazine, found in The Observer 18 March 2001. Reprinted by permission of Sophie Wilson, J17; Extract letter *Slang is Slung* from Middlesborough Evening Gazette. Reprinted by permission of the Middlesborough Evening Gazette; Definition of 'meat' as used in *The Oxford English Dictionary CDROM* from *The Oxford English Dictionary* (2nd Edition 1989) published by Oxford University Press. Reprinted by permission of the publishers.

Nicola, Chris and Harry Biddulph for Harry's talk; Lynn Coxell and the children of Spotland Primary School, Rochdale for their stories; Tim Shortis for many helpful suggestions and observations; the students of Ashton Sixth Form College who have already trialled some of this material; and Geraldine Norman for additional research and forbearance.

The Publishers have made every effort to trace the copyright holders, but if they have inadvertently overlooked any, they will be pleased to make the necessary arrangements at the first opportunity.

Typeset by TechType, Abingdon, Oxon
Printed and bound by Bath Press in the UK

Contents

Introduction	iv
Module 4: Language Investigation	1
What is a language investigation?	2
Preparing for your investigation	5
Some sample investigations	46
Commentaries	54
Module 5: Editorial Writing	73
What is editorial writing?	73
Working with sources	79
Producing new texts	93
Some editorial experiments	120
Preparing for the examination	126
Commentaries	132
Module 6: Language Development	147
Children's language acquisition	148
Preparing for the examination	187
Commentaries	188
Changing English	196
Preparing for the examination	231
Commentaries	232
Glossary	242
Further Reading	244
Index	246

Introduction: Approaching A2 English Language

Where we start from

Welcome to the second part (A2) of your English Language A level course. If you are reading this, we assume it means several things – that you have achieved at least a grade E in the AS English language examination, you have found the work involved in that course sufficiently interesting to wish to carry on your studies to a higher level, and you are now aiming to achieve at least as good an outcome from the A2 part of the examination.

This book follows on from our companion volume, *AS English Language for AQA B*, to which we make reference from time to time when it seems useful for students to revise concepts, approaches and terminology introduced in the AS course. The Glossary we include in this volume includes all the terms listed in the AS book along with new items introduced for the first time in the A2 Units. However, we hope you will find this A2 volume useful whether or not you have used the AS book before.

The book is organised in ways that will make most sense in terms of the AQA Specification B; however, we hope that the content of the book may also be of some value whichever A2 English Language specification you may be taking.

The A2 Course

A2 does, of course, build on the skills and knowledge developed over the 3 AS Units, but is designed to extend your studies into new areas and develop analytical, research and writing skills of a higher order.

The table below summarises the AQA B A2 Units, and their relationship to the knowledge and skills developed in the AS Units:

A2 Unit	Weighting as % of total A level	Content	Links from AS
Unit 4: Language Investigation	15	Coursework. Students carry out a research project into a linguistic area of their own choice, collecting and analysing data, and presenting findings in a report of 2000–4000 words	This will draw heavily on many of the concepts and analytical frameworks developed in Units 1 and 2 (*Introduction to the Study of Language* & *Language and Social Contexts*).

A2 Unit	Weighting as % of total A level	Content	Links from AS
			The final report is also a specialised kind of writing to inform (as in Unit 3, *Original Writing*)
Unit 5: Editorial Writing	15	Examination ($2^1/_2$ hours) Students use a variety of source materials provided on a given topic to produce a new text according to a specific assignment brief. This involves the careful study, and appropriate editing, reconstruction and transformation of the material.	This builds on the writing skills developed in Unit 3 (*Original Writing*), and the understanding of how texts are constructed implicit in much of the work in Units 1 & 2.
Unit 6: Language Development	20	Examination (2 hours). Students develop knowledge and understanding in two areas – the acquisition of language by children, and the nature of language change in English. In the exam, students respond to linguistic data from each of these areas. This is the so-called synoptic module for this course – see below.	The approach to these areas will draw on the basic linguistic concepts and frameworks introduced throughout the AS course, especially in Units 1 & 2. Your examination answers will also be assessed for your writing skills, as developed in Unit 3.

The Sequence of the A2 Units

In practice, the three A2 units overlap considerably, and although the contents of this book are laid out according to the sequence in the specification, it is unlikely that your teachers will simply take you through them one-by-one. Some centres may start teaching Unit 6 first, in order to encourage and support students in tackling an area of Language Development for their Language Investigation. Many teachers will wish to start working on the skills you need for Unit 5 at the same time as you are working on your Investigation and/or Unit 6.

So – you should always look for ways in which your work for one of the Units connects to either of the others. We have tried to indicate some of the main points of cross-reference by flagging these up in the text.

Unit 6: The 'Synoptic' Module

This Unit is so-called because it is designed to assess **all** the skills and major areas of linguistic knowledge developed over the whole two years of the course. You should, therefore, prepare for this Unit particularly thoroughly – you will note that it counts for 20% of the total A level, or 40% of the marks available from A2 – and revisit your AS work as you do so.

The difference between AS and A2 study

A2 is more than just a repetition of AS in new areas of study; it is designed to represent a significant step up in terms of challenge. This extra challenge takes several forms:

- your own **writing skills** are expected to have developed in accuracy, maturity and sophistication from AS
- the **linguistic concepts** encountered in some of the work may seem more advanced
- the degree of **depth and detail** required in your knowledge and understanding will be greater
- you will be expected to study and **research language issues more independently**, making extensive use of additional resources beyond the ones introduced into the classroom by your teachers.

The importance of Independent Learning

The last point above is crucial – here are just some of the ways in which you should extend your reading and research during this course:

Unit 4: Language Investigation: Collecting your own data, either by tape recording spoken language and/or by searching in libraries, bookshops and local archives for appropriate written texts; studying your chosen topic in depth by reading some of the academic research available.

Unit 5: Editorial Writing: Researching a wide range of possible genres and formats in which you might be required to write. This will involve gathering examples of many different types of informative texts, including spoken forms such as Radio documentaries and Audiotape guides.

Unit 6: Language Development: There are large bodies of information and research available on both Language Acquisition and Language Change. You will need to extend your work in class by reading around these areas. Your school/college libraries should have (or be able to obtain) many, of not most, of the titles we refer to in this book.

So: we certainly cannot pretend, and neither should you expect, that this book – or any other single resource of this limited scope – can offer a 'one-stop-shop' for A2 English Language. Instead, we hope it will serve as both a launch pad and a point to which you might wish to return. Throughout, we have tried to refer you to some of the most useful and informative resources we are aware of, and to so many of which we are ourselves much indebted. We very much hope you will follow some of these trails and continue to enrich and deepen your English language studies.

Good luck!

Ron Norman
Ann Watkiss

Examples of key websites are suggested. Although these were up to date at the time of writing, it is essential for teachers to preview these sites before using them with pupils. This will ensure that the URL is still accurate and the content is suitable for your needs. We suggest that you bookmark useful sites and consider enabling pupils to access them through the school intranet. We are bringing this to your attention as we are aware of legitimate sites being appropriated illegally by people wanting to distribute unsuitable or offensive material. We strongly advise you to purchase screening software so that pupils are protected from unsuitable sites and their material.

MODULE 4 Language Investigation

This module counts for 15% of the total A Level marks.

ASSESSMENT OBJECTIVES

The skills and knowledge that you develop and demonstrate in this module are defined by the Examination Board's Assessment Objectives. These require that you:

AO1 communicate clearly the knowledge, understanding and insight appropriate to the study of language, using appropriate terminology and accurate and coherent written expression ($2\frac{1}{2}$%)

AO2 demonstrate expertise and accuracy in writing for specific purposes and audiences, drawing on knowledge of linguistic features to explain and comment on choices made ($2\frac{1}{2}$%)

AO3ii understand, discuss and explore concepts and issues relating to language in use ($2\frac{1}{2}$%)

AO4 apply and explore frameworks for the systematic study of language at different levels, commenting on the usefulness of the approaches taken (5%)

AO5ii analyse and evaluate variation in meanings and forms of spoken and/or written language from different times according to context ($2\frac{1}{2}$%)

This module is organised into the following sections:

What is a language investigation?

Preparing your investigation

- Getting started
- Planning and collecting your data
- Gold dust or garbage?
- Sifting, sorting and counting
- Transcribing and annotating spoken English
- Asking the right questions
- Researching the topic
- Drawing conclusions

- The write-up
- Assessment Objectives in focus

Some sample investigations

Mark scheme

Commentaries

What is a language investigation?

In this section we will be looking back at:

- 'The "science" of language study' (*AS English Language for AQA B*, p.2)
- using analytical frameworks for language study:

  'Stylistic analysis: using a framework' (*AS English Language for AQA B*, p.11–31)

  'Characteristics and functions of speaking and writing' (*AS English Language for AQA B*, p.32)

  'Lexis, grammar, phonology, semantics and pragmatics' panel (*AS English Language for AQA B*, p.58)
- key topics from *AS English Language for AQA B*, Module 2, 'Language and Social Contexts'

During your preparations for the AS English Language examination, you have already learned a good deal about many aspects of language in use. Many of your discoveries should have resulted from actively exploring language for yourself, either in the classroom or outside it, and learning to ask the right kinds of linguistic questions. These should lead to interesting insights into the samples of language you study.

So, you should now be familiar with the notion that as students of language (*AS English Language for AQA B*, p.2), you should use a systematic method for examining the spoken and written words which surround us.

This means you have learned to:

- collect and gather specimens of spoken and written language – **data**
- describe, classify and analyse it using different 'frameworks' and terminology
- ask relevant questions about your data and test your ideas about how language works.

The Language Investigation module gives you the opportunity to take this process of exploration much further by applying what you have learned to an original language research project of your own. As with the coursework Module 3, Original Writing, the development of your project is likely to be spread over a considerable period and will result in a submission of 2,000–4,000 words (excluding data). You are not entirely on your own, however; your supervising tutor will take an active interest in your investigation, and make constructive suggestions about the directions it is taking.

You will find it helpful to break down such a substantial piece of work into the ten steps mapped out below.

*Your language investigation**

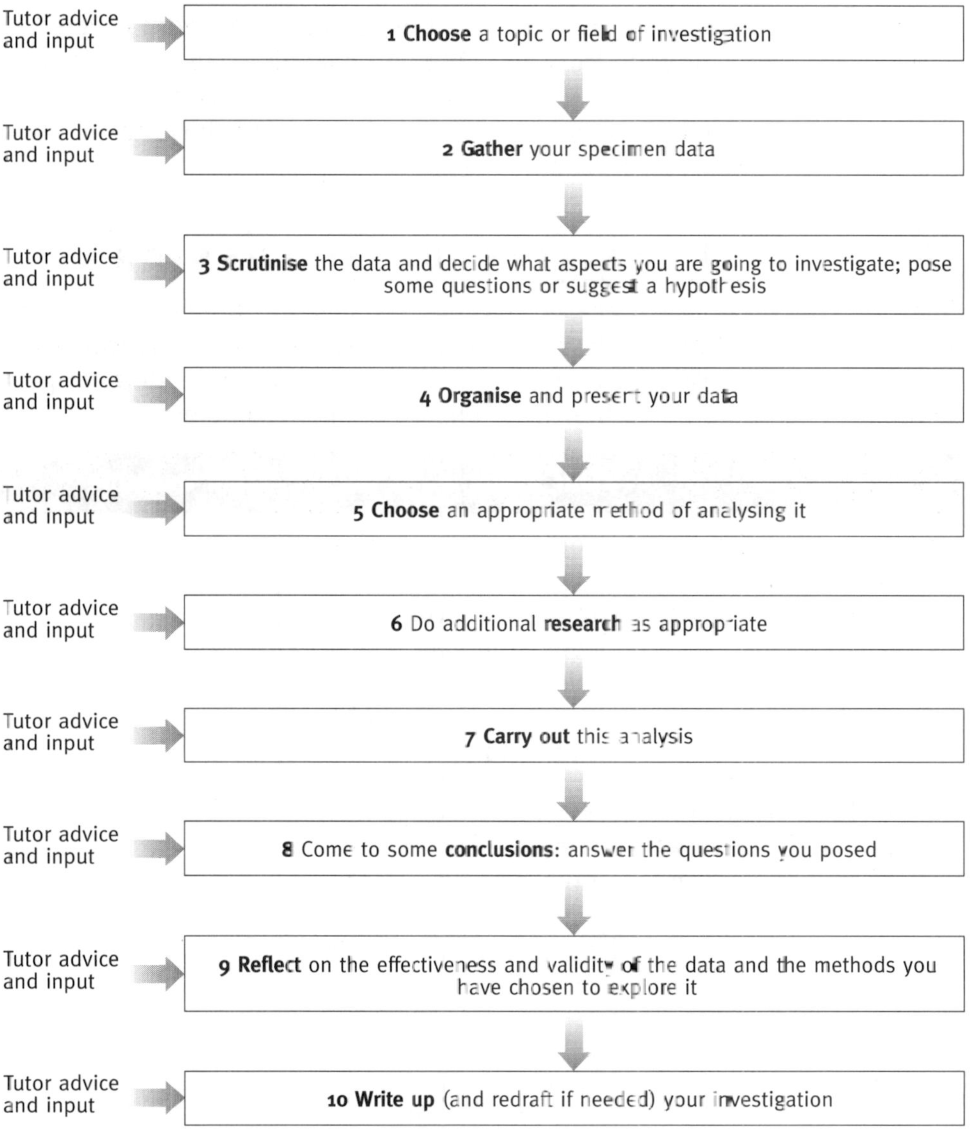

* I am indebted for many of the approaches proposed here to a book to which students are also strongly commended, *Researching Language* by Angela Goddard, also available from Heinemann.

At first sight, this process can appear daunting, but for many students, the investigation can also prove to be the most absorbing piece of work you do on your A Level course.

The activities in this module are designed to help you prepare to carry out your investigation step-by-step.

Suitable subjects for investigation

You can choose to pursue virtually any topic of linguistic interest that appeals to you. Your tutor will advise and guide you in your choice, but the initial selection of a topic should come from you.

The topic you choose is likely to arise from some of the work covered in Modules 1 and 2 of your AS course, but you may also like to tackle a subject that leads you towards the areas of Language Development (such as the development of children's language or the changes that have taken place in English) to be covered in Module 5.

Activity 1. Pair/Group discussion

The Examination Board suggests possible investigation topics under eight broad headings, as listed below. We have suggested some possible specific examples of the kinds of investigation you might tackle under each heading; in pairs or groups, try to come up with at least one additional example:

	Our example	Your example
a. A study of the differences between spoken and written language	You could compare any kind of oral narrative (e.g. an anecdote, or even someone telling a fairy tale or joke) with a written version of the same story	
b. A study of examples of a regional variety of spoken English	You might compare the speech of two speakers from different regions in which each speaks about a similar incident or topic	
c. A study of examples of the English spelling system	You could examine the spelling in the early written work of one or more younger children	
d. Observations of the speech (or writing) of individuals in the	You could record the speech of one or more children, comparing the	

process of language development	way they use language at different ages	
e. A study of norms and variations* in uses of English	Possible examples include the study of various names (of pop bands, breakfast cereals or cafés and restaurants) or surveys of short texts such as greetings cards, diary entries, book 'blurbs' or small ads	
f. A study of a passage of everyday discourse	Building on your work on analysing talk, you could record (with permission!) and examine a typical piece of classroom conversation between teacher and students	
g. A description of some characteristics of the written and/or spoken English of a distinct occupational, professional or other social group	If you have a special interest or hobby, you could collect examples of specialist publications and/or record conversations between like-minded enthusiasts	
h. An exploration of stylistic features of popular media	You could survey and examine a range of advertising slogans, or compare the language used in magazines catering for different audiences	

* Norms and variations: this term is often given to a study of a range of examples of language used in a very specific context. So, for example, if we look at the language of horoscopes, we know the texts will make predictions and offer advice – but there may be many interesting variations between the ways this is done in different magazines.

Now compare your suggestions with the ones in the commentary on p.54.

Preparing for your investigation

In a way, all the small-scale investigations and explorations that you carried out as part of your AS course have helped to prepare you for the task ahead.

However, before jumping straight into the investigation itself, you need to consider the various research and analysis skills which, according to the Examination Board, are required for a successful investigation.

ACTIVITY 2. SKILLS AUDIT

For each of the following skills defined in the exam specification, in the second column of the table below, write in your own words what you think the skill actually means, then, if you think you have learned this skill already, give yourself a tick in the third column.

The Examination Board says you need to be able to:	In other words you can . . .	OK? (tick)
a. establish an appropriate context for investigation		
b. collect and identify data in a principled and sensitive way		
c. identify significant features in data or texts		
d. record observations and describe data accurately		
e. transcribe and annotate spoken English as appropriate		
f. apply a knowledge of systematic frameworks to data in a sustained, reflective and practical way		
g. apply and evaluate different approaches and methodologies for the study of language		
h. draw conclusions to show an awareness of the limitations and value of investigations into data		
i. organise material coherently and use an appropriate style of writing		
j. present findings in an accessible format, ensuring accuracy and relevance		
k. use standard conventions of spelling, punctuation and grammar		

Now compare your responses briefly with the commentary on p.54.

Getting started

An appropriate context for an investigation.

Choosing your topic:

Before tackling this section you may like to look back at the section 'Language all around us' in *AS English Language for AQA B*, pp. 4–5.

It can be daunting to have to choose a subject from a bewildering range of possibilities. The starting point may well be the same as the way you began your language explorations at the beginning of the AS course – by considering the many different types of language usage you encounter every day.

ACTIVITY 3. SUGGESTING A FIELD OF INVESTIGATION

The aim of this activity is for you to propose to a partner some possible subjects for their investigation and/or sources of interesting data arising from their lifestyle and interests. S/he will do the same for you.

In pairs, interview each other about your lives and interests. As you make a note of your partner's responses, try also to jot down some ideas for language study/data that might arise from the circumstances in which s/he frequently finds him/herself.

For example, if you discover that s/he has an interest in computers, you could suggest that the language of e-mails or chat-rooms might be worth studying; or if s/he babysits for younger children, the development of their spoken and/or written language may strike you as a possible topic.

Finding possible subjects and data

(i) Explore your partner's school or college routines. Do the subjects s/he is taking offer any possibilities? What about interactions with other family members? Are there members of his/her family whose language/dialect differs significantly from his/her own?

(ii) Ask about your partner's activities outside school or college. Might a part-time job offer scope for an investigation into an occupational variety of English? Or the language used by people who share a common interest or hobby?

(iii) Consider your partner's use and knowledge of the media. What kinds of TV programmes, films, radio stations, newspapers and/or magazines does s/he regularly view, listen to or read?

(iv) Which aspects of the AS course does s/he remember enjoying most and finding most interesting? Many of the short activities and exercises you carried out last year could be the starting point for a longer investigation.

(v) Try to suggest three possible areas for your partner's investigation and record them in the panel below. As you consider your suggestions, remember that the topic and the data need to be:

- **linguistic** – they must be able to pursue questions about language
- **practical** – the data has to be obtainable using reasonable and legal methods
- **manageable** – the data should provide scope for language analysis but there should not be vast quantities of it.

Suggested areas of language usage for investigation	Suggested sources of data
1.	
2.	
3.	

Planning and collecting your data

In this section it is helpful to look back at the section 'Guidelines for recording and writing down "live" speech', in *AS English Language for AQA B*, p.9.

When scientists set out to carry out an experiment or analyse data, they have to be confident that the data they collect will allow them to reach valid conclusions. In a language investigation, exactly the same applies.

There are several different approaches to collecting your data. These include:

- a case study – studying the language from a single source (a single speaker, organisation or publication
- a longitudinal study – studying the language from a particular source over a set period of time
- a contrastive study – studying the language used in directly comparable contexts
- sampling – taking a sample from a much larger potential data source

This means that the examples of language which you examine must be:

- **real:** the data you collect should arise from a genuine context; as a researcher, you should not manufacture data either by writing it yourself or by actively participating in a conversational situation which you are taping. You may, of course, set up the situation yourself, but should not participate in it. It would be legitimate to use your own written language only if it was originally produced for some purpose other than this investigation.

- **pure:** you should not edit, censor or distort the data. This is especially important when researching spoken language. Transcripts must be as accurate as possible a record of what was actually said.

- **representative:** any data you choose to analyse will inevitably be a small sample of all the possible language of that type which is used and produced. Before you can arrive at any conclusions, it is important to establish that your data is a fair sample. This will usually mean using some kind of random sampling method. So, if, for example, you are looking at the spelling mistakes made by a class of 11-year-old pupils, you could either take your work sample from every third pupil on the class register, or ask the teacher to use assessment data to provide you with a representative sample of the full range of the pupils' ability.

- **comparable:** in many investigations, you will be making comparisons between different sets of data. Where you do, it is clearly vital to compare like with like. Try to ensure that the data was created in similar circumstances, or that the material concerns a similar subject.

- **legal and ethical:** you must make sure your method of data collection is both legal and ethical. This means always seeking the permission of anyone whose speech/writing you are aiming to study (and obtaining the consent of parents and/or teachers of any children involved). You should protect the confidentiality of any such arrangement by making your data anonymous and deleting/changing any names/references which might cause it to be identified. You should also honour the confidentiality of the data by sharing it only with your supervising tutor.

Activity 4. Data validity

For each of the following examples of investigation proposals, suggest how you would ensure the validity of the data you collect.

a. *A study of the differences between spoken and written language*
Proposal: to investigate the different ways people tell stories in speech and writing

b. *A study of examples of a regional variety of spoken English*
Proposal: to investigate the characteristics of a regional dialect speaker known to the investigator

c. *A study of examples of the English spelling system*
Proposal: To investigate the differences in spelling errors made by two groups of students aged 11 and 15

d. *Observations of the speech (or writing) of individuals in the process of language development*
Proposal: To compare the writing skills of children at different stages of their primary education

e. *A study of norms and variations in uses of English*
Proposal: To investigate the distinctive features of language used in Valentines messages published in newspapers on February 14th

f. *A study of a passage of everyday discourse*
Proposal: To test the idea that males and females use language differently in social talk

g. *A description of some characteristics of the written and/or spoken English of a distinct occupational, professional or other social group*
Proposal: To investigate the distinctive language uses of football commentators and pundits

h. *An exploration of stylistic features of popular media*
Proposal: To investigate the differences between the presentation of a particular news item in the press and broadcasting media.

Now compare your suggestions with the commentary on p.55.

Gold dust or garbage?

Identifying significant features in data or texts; selecting your data and identifying its potential

As you are looking around for possible raw material for your investigation, you need to be able to recognise the potential in data for linguistic exploration. It is possible to run out of steam on an investigation where the data has some initial appeal but then fails to sustain a really far-reaching analysis, or is simply too flimsy to allow you to meet the demands of the Assessment Objectives (see p. 53).

On the other hand, language which you may not think is terribly serious or 'difficult' can often prove surprisingly rich.

In this section we will look at two sets of data gathered by students for potential investigation and try to assess their potential value.

Activity 5. Happy Birthday!

Below is a potential data sample for a 'Norms and variations' investigation into the language of birthday cards. You are going to consider this data and carry out a 'feasibility analysis' of its potential for further analysis.

To do this, try working through the following tasks:

- study each item carefully, and note any features (such as the use of rhyme, for example) which seem to be typical of this genre or an interesting variation on it
- when you have studied all the items in the data, note the features that keep cropping up. Use these as headings under which to group or link together two or more of the items. For example, if you noted down 'rhyme schemes' for several of the items, this might give you one of your headings
- now try to formulate some questions arising from this classification. These enquiries would be the starting point for your investigation (e.g. *What are the most common rhyming words/patterns used in these greetings?*) Make sure your questions focus on a linguistic issue

- compare your work with the commentary on p.56
- you are now ready to take any one of your headings/questions and write a full response to it/them.

Data: birthday greetings
Source: birthday cards in stock at corner shop
Basis of sample: random collection from available stock, with non-specific ages

Note: It has not been possible to reprint here these greetings with all their original graphological features such as font, colour, layout etc. Such features in themselves may, of course, prove a worthy aspect of the data to study when carrying out such an investigation. You should also consider the relationship between text and any accompanying images.

1. *Hope your birthday*
   is filled with all the things
   you most enjoy
   Because you really deserve it.
   WITH BEST WISHES

2. *JUST TO SAY*
   have a wonderful birthday

3. WISHING YOU ALL OF
   LIFE'S BEST AND FINEST THINGS TODAY

4. *I bet you'll use your birthday as*
   an excuse to drink and carry on!!
   Not as daft as you look, are you!!
   HAVE A GREAT BIRTHDAY!

5. **HAPPY BIRTHDAY**
   With Love

6. With loving *thoughts* and *wishes*
   On your very special day,
   that every kind of *happiness*
   will always come your way.

7. As far as cool brothers go
   You're really rather neat.
   You're such a bloomin' sweety
   'cept for your cheesy feet!

8. *For today –*
   a happy birthday
   For tomorrow –
   dreams come true,
   And for always –
   so much happiness for you!
   HAVE A HAPPY TIME

9. **Here's wishing all the**
   things that make
   a perfect day for you . . .
   And then a year to
   follow that is just
   as happy, too.
   HAPPY BIRTHDAY

10. Wishing you every happiness
    And wishing for you, too
    All the very special things
    That mean the most to you.

11. *May your birthday be*
    A joyful celebration
    Of all that you are
    And all that you dream to be.

12. **Hoping your birthday**
    Is really special
    In every way for you!
    HAPPY BIRTHDAY

13. *May your day*
    Be as happy
    As you make
    Every day for me.
    HAPPY BIRTHDAY

Activity 6. Working with spoken language: classroom discourse

In this activity, it will be helpful to look back at the section 'Language and power in action: analysing conversation' in *AS English Language for AQA B*, pp.76–83.

As you saw in the AS course, classroom discourse offers a readily available and linguistically interesting source of data for investigation. With the permission of teachers/lecturers it is usually possible to tape and transcribe sections of lessons, and a number of different kinds of investigation can suggest themselves. You may choose to carry out a study of an excerpt from a single lesson and compare lessons taught by different teachers, or of different subjects, or to students of different ages. You may choose to focus on specific discourse features such as the teacher's use of questioning and management of students' responses, or you may be interested in the way s/he uses language to explain/explore specific concepts with learners.

- Look closely at the following transcript drawn from a Physics lesson with Year 10 pupils and identify some potential focuses for a full investigation. Note also any potential problems which you see in using this data as presented here.
- Could the investigation be made more interesting by extending its scope? Suggest any additional data which you might want to collect to extend the nature of your investigation.
- Compare your observations and suggestions with the commentary on p.58.

Data: classroom discourse – Physics lesson and Maths lesson
Source: recordings made in September 2000, High Gill Secondary School
Basis for sample: openings of lessons

T = teacher
P 1, 2, etc = pupil

T: Just a quick word about the practical sessions (.) erm (2) seemed to go alright (.) everybody seemed to know what he or she were doing (.) The (1.) idea of having a break at ten to three is specific (.) er (.) particularly in this sort of weather is to (1) to keep your concentration up (.) but having a break at ten to three does mean that (.) you know (.) you have to stay here longer than you would have done (.) you know (.) but it's probably going to be more effective time (4) now (.) what we haven't yet done is show how we can represent electric fields on a diagram (.) what an electric field looks like (.) of course it doesn't look like anything (1) er (3) (laughs) you have actually drawn a different sort of field (.) plotted it (.) magnetic field (3) anyone (.) done that (.) have you (.) (2)

P's: (several): Yeah

T: And either sprinkled iron filings (3) all that (.) or maybe put a compass around it and plotted it (.) anybody seen that done (.)

P's: Yeah

T: It points towards the pole and away from the pole (.) (4) has anybody not seen the difference in the iron filings (.) (2) you tend to see it (.) fairly early on don't you (.) (1) maybe in primary school

P1: Mm

P2: Yeah

T: So you're used to the idea of sketching that (.) the shape of the field (.) Any idea what kind of a path they will have (.) what sort of (.) how they will trace (.) will they (.) will they go in a straight line upwards (.) or (.) or at (.)

P3: A parabola

T: A parabola (.) Yeah very good. Why (.)

P3: It's just the same as a gravitational field (.)

T: It's very very similar to a projectile (.) in gravitation (.) as you know (.) a horizontally projected mass has a parabolic path

Sifting, sorting and counting

Organising and quantifying your data.

Once you have collected your samples of data and decided that they offer plenty of scope for investigation, you will need to carry out a process of sifting and sorting, breaking down your data into manageable and meaningful categories.

As with other classification exercises that you may have carried out as part of your AS course (e.g. Activity 4, in *AS English Language for AQA B*, p.5), there is no single 'correct' way of doing this, but the categories you use for your classification should eventually lead you towards specifically linguistic analysis.

Activity 7. Café names

Reprinted below are the names of all the cafes listed in the 'cafés and cafeterias' section in a regional edition of Yellow Pages. There are 93 items in all.

Begin with the basic question, 'What trends do you notice in the choice of names for these establishments?'

(i) Your task is to suggest a number of linguistic categories within which you can group together several examples from the data.

For example, you could decide that one category might be names that attribute ownership to a named person (as in *Goodbody's Café*, etc). Your categories may overlap, of course, and the same item may occur in more than one category.

Data: names of cafés
Source: Yellow Pages
Sample: all entries under cafés

A Bite to Eat
Alison's Kitchen
Alliance Café
Aunty Richards
Bait Box Café
Beckindales
Blue House Café
Bon Lea Café
Bowes Museum Café
Bramblewick Café
Bridge Café
Brunches Café
Café Brisco
Café Caffae
Castle Café
Central Café
Chelsea Snack Bar
Circus Café
Clarkes Café
Classic Cuisine
Coach & Horse Café
Cobblestones Cafe
Cook's Gallery
Crusty's Café
Debs Place
Drop Inn Cafe
Fat Rascal's
Food for Thought
Friarage Café
Goodbody's Café
Grubbs Diner
Harley's Diner
Honey Pot Café
Johnny's Café
Kay's Café
Kirkorah's
Kwicksnax
Le Tiffin
Londonderry Lodge
Marine Café
Meals R Us
Monks Haven
Mrs Mac's
Mrs Pumphrey's
Nibblers
Number 4
Oxbridge Café
P.I.E.S.
Pendrys Eating House
Penny Garth
Peyote Café
Porthole Café
Portrack Café
Quick Snacks
Riverside Café
Roya's Pantry
Slipway Café
Stray Café
Sue's Kitchen
Tempest Café
The Battery Parade Café
The Bay Tree
The Bayleaf
The Beachside
The Bistro
The Court Express
The Crumbs Café
The Diner
The Grape Vine
The Honey Pot
The Hot Plate
The Pantry Café
The Shepherd's Kitchen
The Shoppers Rest
The Topiary
The Upper Crust
Three Squares Café
Trainstop Café
Trinity Café
Virgo's
Woodside Café
Zetland

(ii) Once you have set up your categories, you can then take your sorting further by counting up the numbers of items they contain as a proportion of the whole data (e.g. 18/93 include reference to a named person) and then making further distinctions between the items they contain.

For example, these eighteen names can be subdivided into those referred to by first names, surnames, and nicknames, or could be distinguished in terms of gender.

It is often helpful to present this kind of statistical information using tables or diagrams such as pie-charts.

(iii) Finally, for each of the categories, comment in detail on what you have discovered about the different ways language has been used to identify the establishment and attract potential customers. Speculate on the possible reasons behind the variations you find – and suggest how you could extend this investigation to test some of your ideas.

Now compare your work with the commentary on p.59.

Transcribing and annotating spoken English

In this section, it may be helpful to look back at the following sections of *AS English Language for AQA B:*

'Collecting your own data', p.9

'Speaking and writing', pp.30–33, p.52

Activity 2, a transcript, p.60

You have already seen that when transcribing recorded speech-data, you need to use a different set of conventions from everyday written English. For most purposes, the methods set out in the AS course are adequate, and will allow you to carry out a detailed and systematic analysis of many aspects of spoken English.

However, as you have seen (in *AS English Language for AQA B*, Activity 23, p.31) the transcripts you have looked at so far still do not offer a complete or accurate record of all aspects of spoken language.

ACTIVITY 8. TRANSCRIPTS AND SPEECH

Below is a short passage from the transcript of a conversation between two students, taped as part of an investigation. Remind yourself of the familiar transcript conventions.

- What are the aspects of the communication which the transcript does *not* supply? Check the commentary on p.62.
- Now (in pairs) try to recreate the dialogue as a pair of actors might when putting a piece of dialogue on the stage. This will mean restoring these missing aspects. Rehearse and present your version of the dialogue to the rest of your group.

A: So who's your boss anyway at the minute (2)
B: This bloke called Brian
A: Brian (.) Brian what(.)
B: Brian West but everyone just calls him Brian
A: What's he like then (.)
B: Oh he's all right really (.) you know (2.) //he leaves you alone most of the time
A: how long . .
How long has he been there (.)
B: Ages (.) about ten years
A: Bloody hell (.) I can't believe people staying in the same job that long (5)
B: Nah (2.) pretty boring really (3)
A: What you doing Saturday (2.)

Making a more detailed transcript

When investigating spoken language, it is important not to ignore these **prosodic** and **paralinguistic** aspects, and if you are hoping to investigate the specifically phonetic aspects of conversation, you will need to develop a more sophisticated method of transcription.

Ideally, you should try to capture your original data on video tape, as you can then note important paralinguistic and contextual details on your transcript.

Various attempts have been made to create notation that enables prosodic features to be indicated, though there is always a balance to be struck between accuracy and complexity – an absolutely comprehensive record of every shift in intonation, stress and volume would be virtually impossible to decipher!

However, a relatively simple code would be to indicate a significant rise or fall in the pitch of the voice with an arrow, and to indicate a notably stressed word in **bold:**

e.g.

A: So who's your boss anyway at the minute (2)

B: this bloke called Brian

A note about the International Phonetic Alphabet and Phonemic Transcriptions

If you are especially interested in the pronunciation of particular words by different speakers (as in a study of regional speech, for example), you may also need to make use of the **International Phonetic Alphabet** (or **IPA**). As you saw in *AS English Language for AQA B* (p.33) there are many more phonemes in English than there are individual letters of the alphabet, so the conventional English spelling system cannot be a purely phonetic one. So, if you wish to study a speaker's pronunciation of particular words/phonemes, you need to use a different system that allocates a single symbol to a single phoneme – and this is just what the IPA does. In fact, it aims to offer linguists the means of transcribing accurately the sounds of any given language or accent (producing a **phonemic** transcription).

The IPA is a specialist tool for advanced phonemic studies. It includes hundreds of different symbols corresponding to the many different phonemes that occur in different languages and the various accents within them. The basic version which is usually reproduced in textbooks (and which is shown opposite) gives only the sounds for Received Pronunciation; this is fine if you are studying the speech of an RP speaker, but not as useful if you wish, for example, to discuss the particular vowel sounds used by a northern speaker, whose phonemes may be very different.

At A Level, students are usually advised to concentrate on lexical and grammatical aspects of regional speech; however, the IPA is likely to be useful in investigating spelling (see pp.35–37 below) and language development studies (see p.147).

Ambitious students with an interest in developing a more specialist knowledge of phonetics and the use of other IPA symbols to describe non-RP accents of English should consult the relevant titles recommended in the Further Reading Section on p.244.

Activity 9. Using the IPA

Below are the symbols used in the IPA to represent the phonemes found in RP. Note the examples of various spellings which are used in English to express these sounds in writing.

- practise speaking each phoneme in isolation, and writing the appropriate symbol. Note that IPA symbols are written between slash lines / /
- transcribe your own name (as if spoken in RP) using the IPA.

Remember:

- the most common vowel in English is the unstressed sound called **schwa,** represented as / ə /. This often occurs instead of the vowel sound which the spelling of a word indicates when a vowel is an unstressed position, e.g. banana = / bənɑ:nə /
- many phonemes represented by more than one letter in English require only a single IPA symbol (e.g. ʃ)
- on the other hand, sometimes words are spelt with letters that do not actually correspond to additional phonemes. (e.g. in RP cart = /kɑ:t/ letter = /lɛtə).

So, when using the IPA, concentrate on the sounds of the words spoken, and forget how they are usually spelt.

Received Pronunciation using the IPA

Vowels		**Consonants**	
Sound in RP	*IPA symbol / /*	*Sound in RP*	*IPA symbol / /*
sea, **he**, **fie**ld	i:	**p**ub, li**p**	p
b**i**g, nois**y**, w**o**men	I	**b**oy, lo**b**	b
b**e**d, h**ea**d	ɛ	**t**oe, ea**t**	t
s**a**t	æ	**d**o, bea**d**	d
*p**u**n, s**o**n, m**u**ch	ʌ	**c**ook, lo**ck**	k
f**a**ther, c**ar**t, p**al**m	ɑ:	**g**ive, pi**g**	g
h**o**t, c**ou**gh	ɒ	**ch**ur**ch**	tʃ
s**aw**, **a**ll, b**ore**	ɔ:	**j**eep, ju**dge**	dʒ
*p**u**t, g**oo**d, st**oo**d	ʊ	**f**our, cou**gh**	f
m**oo**n, d**o**	u:	**v**an, o**f**	v

Sound in RP	*IPA symbol / /*	*Sound in RP*	*IPA symbol / /*
b**ir**d, t**ur**n	ɜː	**th**in, ba**th**	θ
th**e**, b**a**nan**a**, **a**bout	ə (**schwa**)	**th**is, loa**the**	ð
eight, b**ay**	eɪ	**s**ix, la**s**t, mi**ss**	s
wh**y**, l**ie**, h**igh**	aɪ	**z**ip, boo**ze**, lo**se**	z
b**oy**, bu**oy**, p**oi**se	ɔɪ	**sh**ip, ba**sh**	ʃ
s**o**, sl**ow**, t**oa**d	əʊ	**g**enre, rou**ge**	ʒ
m**ou**se, **ou**t	aʊ	**h**elp	h
w**eir**d, p**ier**, n**ear**	ɪə	**m**op, li**mb**	m
st**are**, **air**, w**ear**	eə	**n**ot, **kn**ot, pi**n**	n
p**oor**, man**ure**	ʊə	ri**ng**	ŋ
		lip, pi**ll**	l
		rot, pa**rr**ot	r
		wet, **wh**at	w
		you	j

* in some regional accents of English, the phonemes represented by these two symbols may, in practice, be identical.

Asking the right questions

Applying knowledge of systematic frameworks to data in a sustained, reflective and practical way; applying and evaluating different approaches and methodologies for the study of language.

In this section, it will be helpful to remind yourself of the following sections in *AS English Language for AQA B*:

'Using the stylistics framework: levels of description' (pp.13–31);

'A framework for analysing talk' (pp.34–35) and 'Language and power in action: analysing conversation' (pp.76–83);

'The power of language: some common techniques' (p.75)

In your AS course, you will have looked at many different kinds of texts, both spoken and written, and analysed them at some length. In many cases, your teacher (or your AS textbook) may have suggested for you the kinds of analysis to carry out on a particular piece of language.

However, one of the important skills with your investigation is to make that decision yourself, and ask those linguistic questions that are likely to produce the most interesting and productive analysis of your particular data.

In the conclusion to your investigation, you need to be able to reflect critically on your choice of approach to your data to meet Assessment Objective AO4 (see p.53 below).

Another way of looking at this is to return to the analogy with scientific investigations and experiments. Faced with a collection of data and experimental or observational evidence, a scientist may formulate a hypothesis, or provisional theory about the data, whose validity further analysis and observation are designed to test. The quality of the investigation will depend on the intelligence and appropriateness of the initial hypothesis and subsequent investigation.

At this point, therefore, you need to consider again the various analytical frameworks available to you, and their possible application to a range of data.

Which framework?

You can think of the different kinds of question that can be asked about language as being different 'levels' of analysis under the following headings:

Framework	Linguistic questions to ask
Discourse structure	How is a text arranged, sequenced and organised?
Graphology	How is a (written) text visually presented on the page?
Pragmatics	What actual and implied meanings do texts have in the particular contexts in which they are produced?
Syntax	What is distinctive about the sentence structure and word order in a text?
Morphology	What is interesting about the structure of individual words in a text?
Lexis and semantics	What is distinctive about the vocabulary used in a text?
Phonology	How are the meanings and connotations produced in a text? What is interesting about the sounds involved in a text?
Orthography	How is a (written) text spelt and punctuated?

In this section, we will briefly consider how each of these frameworks can inform your investigation of a range of texts.

Framework 1: discourse structure

In this section, it will be helpful to look back at the section 'Discourse structure', in *AS English Language for AQA B*, pp.13–18.

As you may remember from your AS course, to consider the structure of a piece of discourse you should look at:

- *written texts*: the underlying sequencing, logic and organisation within a text
- *spoken texts*: the 'invisible' structure to the conversation or interaction.

In slightly more linguistic terms, this means studying a text's **coherence** (how the text is sequenced and organised) and **cohesion** (how it is joined together).

Activity 10. Making sense

Reproduced below are the various paragraphs which made up a news report which appeared in the *Sun* (28/4/00). However, they have been reprinted here out of sequence. In other words, the text is presently not **coherent**.

- first, in groups, rearrange the paragraphs in their proper sequence so that they make sense
- once you have successfully reconstructed the text, make a note of any clues that helped you to do so.

You may find it helpful to trace the various connections within the text by highlighting them or drawing pencil lines to show these (e.g. if you find that the word 'he' refers to a named, male person in the previous paragraph).

Compare your work with the commentary on p.63.

GP axes doomed cancer sufferer

A. But now health chiefs have told the mum-of-two the GP wants her taken off his list – and she must find another doctor.

B. A cancer patient has been cruelly dropped from her doctor's list just a month before she is expected to die.

C. Laura sobbed: 'This is such a terrible blow. I have just sat and cried since getting the letter.'

D. South Essex Health Authority says: 'This is a national system.'

E. Soon afterwards she moved to Leigh-on-Sea, Essex, hoping to benefit from the coastal air. She signed up with Dr Imran Nathoo.

F. He said: 'She moved to us as a temporary allocated patient and the normal procedure is we only have to keep them for three months. We're only a small practice.'

G. Former dancer Laura Thompson, 45 – who has cancer of the pancreas – was given six months to live in November.

H. Pakistan-born Dr Nathoo, 49, denied his decision had anything to do with the cost of treating Laura.

How texts make sense: cohesion and coherence

You can now build on your work on the previous activity and summarise some of the most important ways in which texts are constructed and cohere.

These links may help structure the text as a whole or just help join together elements within a single sentence:

Cohesive feature	Example	Notes
Logical connectors:	Words/phrases which indicate the underlying logical relationship between different parts of a text	Note that in each category, there are many different ways of expressing the relationship according to the register of the text in question, ranging from very formal to colloquial
Addition	and, also, too, in addition, furthermore	
Result	so, because, thus, as a result, consequently	
Comparison	similarly, likewise, just as	
Contrast	but, however, whereas, and yet, on the contrary, on the other hand	
Passage of time	later, then, next, now, soon, afterwards	
Enumeration	firstly, next, finally	
Example	such as, that is, for instance, for example	
Summary	in conclusion, on the whole, at the end of the day	
Grammatical connectors:	These items connect one part of the text with another	

Pronouns and their referents		
Demonstrative pronouns	this, that, these, those (i) You lied to me. That was unacceptable. (ii) This is what we're going to do. We're going to fight to the end. (iii) How much are those?	These may refer to something earlier in the text (= **anaphorically**) (as in (i)) or . . . to something later in the text (= **cataphorically**), as in (ii) Sometimes – especially in speech – they refer to things outside the text which are part of the context in which the words are spoken (as in (iii)). Such reference is known as **deixis**
Lexical/ Semantic connectors: *Synonyms and antonyms*	These items create links in meaning between different parts of a text (i) *Health Chiefs* have told the mum-of-two . . . South Essex *Health Authority* says . . . (ii) *She signed up* with Dr Nathoo . . . *the GP wants her taken off the list*	Words/phrases which relate semantically to each other either because of their similarity ((i) synonyms) or contrast ((ii) antonyms)
Repetition of word or phrase	In the example text, the words *Dr/GP*, *list* and *cancer* recur	Sometimes, this repetition may take the form of a slight variation in the form of a word – decide/decision, for example

So, when examining any set of linguistic data, one interesting question to ask is 'What is distinctive about the ways in which this text/these texts are organised and cohere?' In Module 5, 'Editorial Writing', you will be asked to put into practice your understanding of the principles of textual cohesion when you create new texts from a number of different source materials.

ACTIVITY 11. RADIO 4 NEWS

As an example of the kinds of analysis this might produce, you can now use this framework to carry out an analysis of textual cohesion in the following extract. This is a Radio 4 News bulletin, broadcast at lunchtime on Sunday October 1st, 2000.

Start by describing the overall text structure and sequence of the text (see 'Discourse structures', *AS English Language for AQA B*, pp.13–18) before going on to examine the fine detail of its cohesive features.

Data: Radio News Bulletin

The Tories are gathering in Bournemouth for their annual conference, the last probably before a General Election. Today they've gone on the attack, promising to match and better any Labour promises on pensions, a pledge dismissed by the Social Security Secretary Alistair Darling. We'll be examining whether the Tories really believe they can beat Labour. The Conservative Party Chairman, Michael Ancram, will be joining us live. The car maker Rover says it's in talks with another manufacturer about a possible collaboration and the Sydney Olympics have ended with Britain winning its biggest medals tally for 80 years, something for British sports fans to cheer about at last – but is it good enough? The Sports Minister Kate Howie, just arrived back from Sydney this morning and she joins us live. The News is read by Corrie Caulfield.

Now compare your analysis with the commentary on p.66.

Framework 2: graphology

You should first refer to *AS English Language for AQA B*, pp.18–19

In written texts, the physical and visual appearance of the text on the page can be an important feature, contributing significantly to their effectiveness in communicating meanings to their audience. On your AS course you briefly surveyed some of these possible variations in textual graphology. Some of these key variables can be summarised as follows:

Graphological dimensions of a text

Feature	Questions to ask	Notes
The physical arrangement of text on the page, whether using columns, short or long paragraphs, headings, sub-headings, numbered or bullet points, panels (white or coloured/ shaded) and tables	What do these features contribute to the character and effectiveness of the text in communicating to its audience? In what ways are these appropriate to its context and purpose, and distinctive of its genre?	It may be worth pursuing the question – what kinds of text favour which of these features, and why? Informative texts, for example, are likely to use a range of devices to present information, especially where there is also an element of entertainment or where the audience is relatively young or inexperienced
The relation and proportion of text to images and white space	In what ways do these aspects of the text contribute to its	The amount of white space. Images on a page can affect its perceived

	character, and impact on its readers?	accessibility and readability. Even relatively dense textbooks, such as this one, will have margins, paragraph breaks and other spaces; in any text, the amount of space left white or given over to images may vary according to the nature of the audience and purpose
Size and typeface(s) used in the text: font style, use of bold or italic, and upper or lower case	In what ways does the choice of font and other typographical features relate to the text's context, tone, purpose and audience?	Font selection can contribute to the 'feel' or tone of a text, from formally serious to fun-filled and frivolous. **The typeface on an Irish souvenir shop front** is likely to be different from that in **an advertisement for a young people's holiday**, for example **Bold** and *italic* can be used simply to create emphasis and simulate the stress patterns of speech

If you decide to work with written texts, it may be useful to include some discussion of the graphological dimension in your analysis. In some studies (e.g. a norms and variations investigation – see below), you may decide to make this a key focus for your investigation by surveying a range of related texts to determine precisely how these features vary according to audience, purpose and context.

Framework 3: pragmatics

Look again at the sections 'Speech in conversation: analysing talk' (pp.33–35) and 'Language and power in action: analysing conversation' (pp.76–83) in *AS English Language for AQA B.*

When you started to examine conversation on your AS course, you will have learned to note the many ways meanings are conveyed in speech. The main ones are summarised below:

- conversation works because the participants follow some basic rules regarding turn-taking and topic management (e.g. the 'Maxims' of H. P. Grice)

- there are strong connections between the way people participate in talk and a range of social factors affecting their relationships

- meanings in talk are both overt – what is actually said – and covert – what is implied and understood:

(i) one set of these underlying meanings relates (perhaps unconsciously) to the status and relationship of the participants; everything about the way we behave in a conversation is sending signals about our attitudes towards the other speakers and our understanding of our own status and role

(ii) another set of meanings may be equally implicit, but more conscious – when, for example, we pass the time of day using phatic talk to develop a relationship, or deliberately say one thing in order to imply something else.

Pragmatics asks how these implied meanings are created, in written texts as well as in speech.

ACTIVITY 12. BETWEEN THE LINES

For each of the short pieces of data below, suggest what possible discrepancy (if any) there may be between the overt and covert meanings of the text:

(i) 'Excuse me. I think you'll find that this is a no smoking area.'

(ii) Gillian has found this course challenging, but has been making every effort.

(iii) A: What are you doing tonight?

B: Dunno. Staying in, I suppose (.) I've got stuff to do.

(iv) I regret to have to inform you that due to rationalisation of the company's production methods, your employment will be terminated as from January 1st 1999. May I take this opportunity of thanking you, on behalf of the company, for the service which you have given over the last four years.

(v) Do not empty your dog in front of my garage.

(vi) 'I'm afraid Mr Harrison is unable to take your call at the moment. May I take a message?'

Compare your suggestions with those in the commentary on p.66.

Pragmatics is a tricky area; it seems that out of a need to protect ourselves from too many unpleasantly direct confrontations, in many situations involving both spoken and written language, we use a variety of strategies to maintain an insulating layer of politeness – though at times, we *may* choose to do the opposite.

It is also an area of uncertainty and ambiguity; if what is said may not be the same as what is actually meant or understood, you may need to research the actual meanings *understood* by speakers or correspondents. This will mean not only analysing texts yourself, but also quizzing/interviewing the people involved about their intentions, implied meanings and understanding of the utterances.

Framework 4: syntax

Look back at the section 'Sentences: length, construction and function', in *AS English Language for AQA B*, pp.20–22.

In your AS course, you began to consider the kinds of sentence used in particular contexts in terms of their length, construction and function. **Syntax** is largely concerned with the construction and word order used in sentences, and at this level of analysis there are many linguistic issues in your data that may be worthy of investigation.

This section will look briefly at some important linguistic concepts and outline the kinds of grammatical and syntactic questions that may be relevant or revealing to ask when examining various types of data. For a fuller treatment of this subject, students are referred either to David Crystal's book *Rediscover Grammar*, or to the titles listed under the appropriate section of the Further Reading list (see p.244)

To begin with, consider the process whereby words are assembled into sentences.

ACTIVITY 13. SENTENCE-BUILDING: GROUPS/PHRASES

A sentence consists of different groups of words (or phrases) that combine together in particular ways. Here we will consider the three most important. For each one, add your own examples to the column on the right.

1. The Noun Phrase	• Take a noun	The very simplest **Noun Phrases (NP)** consist of just that – the noun	*cats*	
	• Add a **determiner/ quantifier** a/an/the/these/ those/each/some/ few/many/six	Not all nouns can accept these – but most do	*six cats*	
	• Precede the noun with some extra information using adjectives (this is called **pre-modification**)	The amount, and the type, of pre-modification will vary according to the kind of language and context	*six nasty black cats*	

	• Follow with yet more information – called **post-modification**		*six very nasty black cats with sharp teeth*
2. The Verb Phrase	• Take a verb	A simple **Verb Phrase (VP)** may consist of this single word	*attack*
	• Include any other words that are needed to form the complete tense of the verb	However, many more complex verb phrases exist	*may be going to attack*
3. The Adverbial Phrase	• Take a single adverb or	Again, a one-word **Adverbial Phrase** is possible	*tomorrow*
	• Take a phrase that provides information about how, where or when the action occurs	You can include several bits of this sort of information	*in the park* and/or *after lunch* and/or *in a frenzied rage*

Activity 14. Combining phrases into clauses

When we combine a Noun Phrase (NP) with a complete Verb Phrase (VP) we produce a **clause;** in some cases this may already be a sentence, but in others we may feel that something is still missing. If so, complete the sentence by adding either another NP or an AP as in the example:

NP	VP	Sentence ?	NP	AP
Cats	attack	Yes	–	–
Six nasty black cats with very sharp teeth	may be going to attack	Yes	–	–
My favourite Martian	has already consumed	No	two buckets of hay	since yesterday

In each of these examples, the first Noun Phrase is functioning in the clause as the **subject,** (i.e. the agent of the verbal action) and the second is the **object** (The receiver of the action).

Activity 15. Combining clauses into sentences

A sentence that consists of a single clause (like the ones above) is known as a **simple sentence**; however, clauses can be linked within a sentence in various ways to produce multi-clause (or **multiple**) sentences.

The easiest way of creating such multiple sentences is by using the conjunctions *and, or* and *but* (**co-ordinating conjunctions**), and the resulting sentences are known as **compound sentences.** They are easy to construct and can go on virtually endlessly:

I went home and I sat down to read the paper but there was a knock at the door and then I got up but Jimmy got there first . . .

More complicated structures are created by using a different set of conjunctions which includes *because, when, who, which, that, after* and *since*. These produce **complex sentences:**

When I got home, I switched on the TV.

This may look simple enough, but the word *when* effectively makes one part of the sentence – the getting home – less important than the other (the switching on of the TV), and so *I switched on the TV* becomes the main focus of the sentence. The lesser, or so-called **subordinate clause** (*When I got home*) can no longer stand by itself, and is said to be dependent on the **main clause.**

This process can be taken much further, as in the following:

When I got home, the man who had said he that would be coming to read the meter had left a note which told me that it would no longer be possible for him to do the job.

- Try to find the subject, verb and object which form the main clause at the heart of this complex sentence
- Identify the other subordinate clauses, and the conjunctions which have been used to link them to the main clause.
- Suggest why this sort of sentence is awkward to construct, and potentially difficult to read and understand.

Compare your notes with the commentary on p.67.

Looking at syntax in your data: some suggestions

Once you start trying to apply this kind of approach to your data, it can be all too easy to get bogged down with meaningless grammatical analysis. Instead, you need to use your linguistic common sense to decide what *kinds* of grammatical analysis are useful for the data you are looking at.

The table below may help:

Types of data	Some syntactic points to investigate
Spoken data; written texts in a colloquial register	Proportion of simple/compound sentences Use of question tags (*isn't it? are you?* etc.) Sentences in which parts of the structure seem to be left out (**ellipsis**) as in *Hope to see you soon* instead of *I'm hoping to see you soon* Repetition of the subject (and even the verb) at the start and end of a clause, as in *He's all right is our Jack*
Verses, poems, rhymes and lyrics	Non-standard word-order, either to achieve rhythmical and rhyming effects, or to take readers by surprise and throw the focus onto a particular word
Learners' English	Any early attempts to use complex structures? Preferences for relatively simple phrase and sentence structures?
Headlines/ captions	Ellipsis – which elements of the clauses are omitted?
Texts perceived as 'descriptive' or 'complex'	Is the complexity at phrase or sentence level? i.e. are the noun phrases extended by a lot of pre- and post-modification, or are the sentences using complex patterns of subordination?
Persuasive texts such as adverts and speeches	The repetition of successive phrases with a similar structure *(Call it Spearmint. Call it Wrigleys. Call it Gum.)*

Framework 5: lexis and semantics

Look again at the section 'Words and phrases', in *AS English Language for AQA B*, pp.22–26.

As you will have found when learning to apply a framework for stylistics analysis, there are many questions to ask about the choices made by speakers and writers at this level. Some of the ones you may have looked at on your AS course are:

- How does the lexis convey meanings, opinions, ideas, feelings and facts?
- What register(s) or dialectal variety does the lexis belong to?
- What degree of personality/impersonality does the lexis bring to the text?
- To what degree is the lexis in a text used literally or figuratively?

Activity 16. Working with word classes

As you examine your selected data, it is likely that you will need to extend some of these queries. As with the section on syntax (above), we offer here a brief summary and overview of the kinds of enquiry which may be useful. See the suggested titles in the Further Reading list (p.244) for a fuller treatment of this aspect of English grammar.

The panel below suggests some additional linguistic issues which may arise from an investigation of the use of major word classes in different kinds of data.

The final column offers some suggested texts on which you can practise applying these questions.

Word class	Additional questions to ask	Possible applications to data	Suggested data to investigate
Nouns	Proportion of concrete to abstract?	A higher proportion of abstract nouns is likely to characterise language which is perceived to be difficult, complicated, literary or 'educated'.	**The writing of children of different ages**, even when writing about a similar topic, might show interesting differences. Perhaps also investigate two similar articles from **a tabloid and a broadsheet newspaper**.
Adject-ives	Frequency and number attached to nouns Factual or opinion-ative? Number, colour, appearance, texture, taste, etc?	Some highly factual language may include very few adjectives, or be limited to pre-modifiers which convey additional information or qualification to the nouns. Language which you might be tempted to label as 'descriptive' (a term whose vagueness makes it unhelpful in linguistic analysis) may include a larger number of adjectives which provide judgements or other subjective descriptions.	An **official** or **legal report** of an event or occurrence is likely to differ in this respect from either an **oral eyewitness account** or a more sensational **press report**. **Travel brochures** may offer an extreme example of adjectival proliferation! Compare the way the brochure writers use adjectives with the adjectives used about the same location in a **Geography textbook**.

Verbs	Tense?	There are many tenses in English; the present can be shown by both *I sail* and *I am sailing*, (the **simple** and **progressive** forms) although both these forms can also indicate the future (*I sail tomorrow/I am sailing on the 10.15 ferry*). Both simple and progressive forms are also used about the past (*I was sailing/I sailed*) with different meanings, though in many oral narratives (especially jokes) speakers may tend to use present tense forms even when referring to past events (*this bloke comes up to me and says . . .*)	Any kinds of **oral** or **written narratives** are worth examining here; watch also for the ways speakers may slip between different present/past forms in the course of telling an **anecdote** or **joke**.
	Modal verbs?	Then there are the **perfect** forms (*I had sailed, I had been sailing, I have sailed, I have been sailing, I will have sailed* etc . . .) and the forms which use one of the **modal verbs** to express different attitudes towards the possibility of an action or event: consider the differences between *I can/could/shall/will/would/may/might/must/ought to/need to/. . .sail*	The **present perfect** has drifted into use in a particular kind of oral narrative – accounts of sporting highlights given to interviewers by participants – where it might be more usual to use the simple past. Record such **sports interviews** and watch out for accounts such as *He's got the cross in* and *the lad's put it straight in the back of the net.* Modal verbs can often be used either to soften or strengthen commands and judgements (*Could you open the window? You must open the window!*) as well as to express degrees of conviction about actions past or present. They may feature interestingly in **teachers' language** (in classroom discourse and reports) and wherever the language of authority (**instructions/warnings**), persuasion (**adverts, political speeches**) and prediction (**horoscopes**, etc) is employed.

	Active/ Passive voice?	Verbs in English exist in both **Active** and **Passive** forms – this means we can say: *The monkey ate the banana* (Active) or *The banana was eaten by the monkey* (Passive) Active forms make for easier reading because they present the doer of the action as the subject of the sentence, as we expect, but the passive has its uses when we may not know, or may not wish to say, who is responsible for an action: *The banana was eaten.* (Mystery! Who did it?) *Yes, mistakes were made.* (Who made them? Did you?!)	Passive forms are acquired later by learners and so may appear gradually in the **language of learners** at different stages of development. The complex syntactic manipulation involved may lead to errors. Similarly, texts aimed at readers with different reading ages may be distinguished by the varying frequency of such forms. Some genres may favour passive forms because they avoid the personal – look at **legal documents**, **scientific reports/articles,** and at the selective use of active and passive forms in **news broadcasts/reports.**
	Phrasal verbs?	English has hundreds of verbs such as *get up, get up to, get down, get away with, get into,* which consist of a verb + preposition(s) and whose meaning is impossible to predict just by looking at the words that make them up. These are called **phrasal verbs.** These idiomatic phrases are a very important part of colloquial English, and are more likely to be found in larger numbers in informal language. There may often be equivalent single-word verbs with similar meanings (*look into = investigate, look up = research,* etc) but the style and register of these are usually quite different.	The language of non-native speakers of English (**letters, speech**) can often appear stilted because of the absence, or incorrect usage, of phrasal verbs. A comparative study of similar texts in contrasting registers may reveal greater use of phrasal verbs in the more informal context, and a comparison of spoken and written language may reveal a higher proportion of phrasal verbs in speech.
Adverbs	Frequency and type?	As with adjectives, the frequency of qualifying adverbs may account for a perception	The language used in **cookery** or **DIY TV programmes** is likely to have a high proportion of

	Time, manner, place?	of a text as 'descriptive', but the kind of adverbs will reflect the nature of the text.	'how' adverbs, as are their written-text equivalents. *In practice, it may be more useful to consider adverbial usage at the phrase level (see p.27 above)*
Pronouns	Which person (if any)?	The presence or absence of 1st-person pronouns from a text significantly affects how it is read and perceived. Whereas *I* foregrounds the individuality of the speaker/writer, *we* can have various uses (*all of us/this company/my family/my wife and I* etc.), according to context. 2nd-person *you* (and *thee* in some contexts) is equally striking in its directness of approach to its audience. Few texts will avoid the 3rd-person pronouns, but their infrequency in some texts, or the use of *one* in some registers, is worth noting.	Any passage of **informal talk** is worth looking at here. The shifting meanings of *we* and *they* can be intriguing (as in the anonymous collective *they* in *they say he's gone off sick* . . .). Similarly, *you* can be used to refer to the self or to a more general collective in informal contexts (*Why didn't you go in?/You don't like to interrupt, do you?*) The impersonal 3rd-person pronoun *it* can also be an interestingly slippery customer in such common uses as *It's raining/It's too late.*
Conjun-ctions	What kinds?	This is best discussed in terms of sentence structure – see p.28 above.	

Framework 6: morphology

The previous framework is concerned with the study of the functions and meanings of words; morphology, on the other hand, asks the question *how are words themselves constructed?*

At a very basic level, words are, of course, made from letters and sounds (phonemes), and our most simple words consist of single units of meaning which result from the combination of these sounds/letters:

d + o + g = dog	s + a + d = sad	t + a + k + e = take
/d/ /ɒ/ /g/ /dɒg/	/s/ /a/ /d/ /sad/	/t/ /eɪ/ /k/ /teɪk/

However, we can easily add other combinations of phonemes/letters which also act as 'units' of meaning, and thus change the meanings of the basic words:

dog + s = dogs	sad + ness = sadness	re + take + ing = retaking

These separate 'bits' of meaning that go to make up a word are called **morphemes**.

So we can see that each of these new words consist of two or more 'bits' of meaning. Some of these meanings are *semantic*, and others are *grammatical*:

	Semantic	Grammatical
dogs	dog = four-legged canine	s = plural
sadness	sad = not happy	ness = the state of being (as in happi*ness*, sweet*ness*, etc.)
retaking	re = doing again take = seize	ing = progressive action

Activity 17. Morphemes

For each of the following complex words, identify the separate morphemes which contribute different 'bits' of meaning, and define what those meanings are:

impossibilities   unthinkable
destabilising   John's

Now compare your analysis with the commentary on p.68.

In completing this activity, you will begin to discover that we can classify the different sorts of morphemes from which words are built:

Base/stem: the 'core' meaning of a word. These can exist in a simple form on their own or can have other morphemes attached to them. These base forms are sometimes referred to as **free morphemes**.

Affixes: the 'attachments' that are tagged onto the base/stem forms. As they can only ever exist when attached to free morphemes, these are called **bound morphemes**. They may be of two types:

<table>
<tr><td rowspan="3">Prefixes (attached to the front of the word as in unthinkable)

e.g. un, in, anti, ante, de, re,</td><td colspan="3">Suffixes (attached to the back, as in unthinkable)</td></tr>
<tr><td rowspan="2">Some change the word class from the base form:

sadness
freedom
equalise
lucky</td><td colspan="2">Others give grammatical information about a word:</td></tr>
<tr><td>Verbs – tense/ person

I walk
he walks
I walked
I am walking</td><td>Nouns – number/ attribution

keys
children
John's</td></tr>
</table>

The ways in which these, and many other, morphemes operate within English are fascinatingly complex. If you decide to carry out your investigation into some aspect of the process of language development, this framework is likely to prove especially useful as you consider how a language user learns to apply accurately these principles of word-building.

This is covered in more detail in Module 6, Language Development, p.147.

Framework 7: phonology and orthography

Look again at the sections 'Speaking and writing' and 'Sounds and spelling' in *AS English Language for AQA B*, pp.30 and 32) and the International Phonetic Alphabet (pp.17–18, above).

At this level of analysis, we ask questions about the sounds of spoken language, the conventions of spelling and punctuation in written language, and the relationship that exists between these two systems.

So far on your course, you should have discovered that:

- The English sound system uses 44 phonemes; only 26 letters are available in the written alphabet, but some of these are combined into pairs like sh- or ch- (known as **digraphs**). In English, the relationship between spelling and phonemes is complex.
- Much of the meaning in speech is conveyed by paralinguistic and prosodic features with no direct written equivalent. Punctuation of written texts mainly indicates the grammatical structure of sentences, but some elements of punctuation (such as !) can correspond to certain phonological features.

If your investigation involves comparing spoken and written texts, you will need to ask how these different systems each convey equivalent meanings.

We can begin to explore this question by examining the writing produced by a six-year-old girl, Sophie. She is just learning to find written equivalents for the spoken language she is already confident in using.

ACTIVITY 18. SOUNDS AND SPELLINGS

Here, Sophie tells the story of a little girl who goes for a walk in the woods with her grandad and sees a squirrel. Look closely at Sophie's writing, transcribed with uncorrected spelling and punctuation below. Try to comment closely on some of the spellings in her text, and offer some explanations of what you find there.

You will be drawn at first to focus on Sophie's errors, but try also to consider positively what she has already learned about the writing system and how it relates to the spoken language.

Jesse and har grandad went too the woods thay saw a scviral Jesse seb I wud layck too ciPe a scwiral but Jesse you cannt cipe a scwiral wer is hiy goingt too sLiPa I will make him a bed in my roome hang on grandab I thinck I can si a worta foll But Jesse wispard granddad it is too waylb I now if is sed Jesse you siy one of tose dock over ther phaps hee niyds loccing after

Now compare your work with the commentary on p.68.

It is not only children whose spelling deviates from the norms of Standard English. Your data may include examples of other, more deliberate misspellings. Commercial firms, shop owners, pop bands, writers trying to represent regional accents, senders of text-messages and anyone using other note-forms are all likely to manipulate the usual spelling conventions for their own purposes. In these cases you can investigate exactly how the *phoneme:grapheme* relationships work.

Functions of punctuation

It is easy for experienced writers to take punctuation for granted, but the data you investigate may include examples of the deliberate manipulation of punctuation for specific purposes. The table below summarises the usual functions of the most common punctuation marks, and suggests some of the ways in which different texts might vary their use.

Punctuation mark	Function	Relationship with speech	Variations to look for
. (full stop)	Marks syntactically complete sentences	Spoken language is more likely to consist of longer, loosely connected sentences	Children may apply the full stop more uncertainly as they work out what the concept of the written sentence is. Adult writers may create short or minor sentences for effect – or create a 'stream of thought' effect by not using stops for lengthy passages
, (comma)	Separates phrases and clauses within a sentence, or items in a list	May *loosely* correspond to the pauses and breaks in speech	In learners' writing, may commonly be used incorrectly instead of either full stops/semi-colons or conjunctions
? (question mark)	Indicates a question	May indicate a rising tone in questions such as *You coming?*	Multiple question marks may be used to indicate degrees of extreme surprise, shock etc, sometimes in combination with exclamation marks, as in (what do you mean ?!?)
! (exclamation mark)	Indicates a command or exclamation	Usually indicates a strident tone or emphatic stress	Some texts as diverse as informal notes and advertisements may use these extravagantly for rhetorical or humorous effect. Popular, youth-orientated journalism may insert these (!) in parenthesis as an editorial comment on the content of the text

– (dash)	Connects two related elements of a sentence	May correspond to a short break preceding an emphatic climax	Journalism, especially, may use this to postpone the end of the sentence containing a piece of vital information – for dramatic effect
; (semicolon)	Connects two syntactically distinct but semantically related sentences	No direct correlation	Likely to be used more in more formal texts
's (apostrophe)	Indicates attribution /possession	No direct correlation	Often misused and sometimes deliberately omitted (e.g. on shop fronts)

Which framework?

We now need to consider some different data sets and make some decisions about which frameworks are likely to provide the most fruitful analytical results.

Activity 19. Which frameworks?

For each of the data samples below, carry out a thorough brainstorming of any linguistic issues which strike you as interesting, and then identify the most appropriate levels of analysis which you would propose to undertake if this were to become a full-length investigation.

Try to frame your responses as a series of questions or hypotheses to pursue.

Afterwards, compare your work with the commentaries on p.69.

A. Data: film previews
Source: the *Independent*

Austin Powers: The Spy Who Shagged Me (12, 99 mins)

Old-rope sequel in which Austin Powers (Mike Myers) travels back in time to 1960s London to recover his 'mojo' from the evil Dr Evil (Mike Myers). There's a lot of fun to be had in Myers' twin creations but bad jokes that advertise themselves as bad jokes are still simply bad jokes.

***Belly** (18, 95 mins)*

Hype Williams' expletive-stuffed début feature (after a decade in pop video) is a dud, a turkey, a triumph of style over substance.

***Bride of Chucky** (18, 89 mins)*

The latest graduate from the *Scream* school of self-referentiality, *Bride of Chucky* strings together a series of humorous asides and knee-jerk shock tactics.

Cruel Intentions *(15, 97 mins)*

A transplantation of *Les Liaisons Dangereuses* to Manhattan in a toxic little tale of two scheming half-siblings (Sarah Michelle Gellar and Ryan Philippe) who embroil their peers in all manner of sexual machinations.

The Matrix *(15, 139 mins)*

If you can accept that Keanu Reeves is the Messiah sent to save our souls from extra-terrestrial robots, then there's much to relish in this virtuoso slice of sci-fi nonsense.

The Mummy *(12, 115 mins)*

The Mummy is this year's *Godzilla*: a cheesy monster-mash that has Brendan Fraser and Rachel Weisz uncovering a lost city and battling a bandaged bogeyman.

My Favourite Martian *(PG, 93 mins)*

After *The Brady Bunch Movie* and *The Beverly Hillbillies*, Hollywood must be hunting hard for old TV shows to cannibalise. Forgive them, then, for alighting finally upon *My Favourite Martian*, surely the last stale crumb in the bucket.

The Red Violin *(15, 130 mins)*

François Girard's daisy-chain of historical vignettes follows the course of its cursed violin down the centuries. Girard's broken-up and bitty narrative leaves the film labouring in third gear throughout.

Rogue Trader *(15, 92 mins)*

The magic movie mill moulds weaselly Nick Leeson into princely Ewan McGregor and his half-arsed rise and fall into an Icarus-like assault on the British class system.

Star Wars Episode 1: The Phantom Menace *(U, 132 mins)*

George Lucas sets about telling his tale in a languid, ruminative fashion. Yet one can never forget that Lucas's prequel is merely a protracted introduction as opposed to an organic whole.

B. Data: advertising slogans from the 1970s
Source: personal research

1. A Mars a day helps you work, rest and play.
2. Bloo, the blue loo cleaner
3. Call it Wrigley's. Call it Spearmint. Call it Gum.
4. Cook ability – that's the wonder of gas.
5. Designed by a computer. Silenced by a laser. Built by a robot.
6. Domestos kills all known germs – dead!
7. Don't just stick it – Bostik it.
8. Don't say " brown". Say Hovis.

9. Drinka pinta milk a day.
10. Eight out of ten owners said their cats preferred it.
11. Every bubble's passed its fizzical.
12. Give your hair a touch of spring.
13. Go to work on an egg.
14. Go well. Go Shell.
15. Guintelligence test.
16. Have a break, have a Kit-Kat.
17. Heineken refreshes the parts other beers cannot reach.
18. Hermesetas – little things to make life sweeter.
19. Hermestetas – the sweet alternative.
20. Inter-City makes the going easy (and the coming back).
21. It wouldn't be the weekend without Woodpecker wood it?
22. Let colour go to your head.
23. Mr Kipling makes exceedingly good cakes.
24. My goodness! My Guinness!
25. NEI4DD?
26. Nothing acts faster than Anadin.
27. Our sages know their onions. (*The Times*)
28. Oxo gives a meal man appeal.
29. Persil washes whiter and it shows.
30. Say it with flowers.
31. Sch . . .you know who.
32. Schweppervescence.
33. Seven million a day and still going down. (Guinness)
34. Something cooler happens with Canada Dry.
35. Switch to Michelin and make it for life.
36. The prose without the con. (*The Times*)
37. There's no Camparison.
38. There's no present like the time. (Zenith watches)
39. Think once. Think twice. Think bike.
40. We take no pride in prejudice. (*The Times*)

Researching the topic

Once you have decided on the subject of your investigation and the kinds of questions you are going to be pursuing, you need to extend your knowledge of any relevant research that already exists in your chosen area. The Further Reading section of this book (see p.244 below) contains some suggestions for getting started. When you find some relevant material, you can make use of it in several ways:

- Use it to refine/amend the questions you are setting yourself about your data. You may, for example, be able to test the findings reported elsewhere in your own data. Beware of 'cocking' your data, however, so that it leads you to the conclusions you think you ought to find – it may well be that your data leads you to different conclusions from those in the research you have read.

- Use it as a source of comparisons with your own study. You can refer to it at appropriate points in your investigation – perhaps in your introduction, or just in passing as you proceed with your analysis. It is certainly useful in your conclusion to show that you are aware of the work that other researchers have carried out, and to discuss your findings in relation to these (see 'Citing your sources', p.42 below).

Presenting findings

As you started your investigation by asking some questions about your data, or by setting out to test a theory or hypothesis, your analysis should lead you towards some answers to these questions.

However, a good scientist will keep an open mind about the investigation, not allowing prior assumptions to influence their conclusions. It is quite likely that you will find something surprising, or even *in*conclusive. Don't worry. Remember, it is the quality of the process of investigation which matters. So, in drawing your conclusions:

- be open-minded; don't make the data fit your preconceptions
- be cautious: how true a sample, and how representative of all the possible material you could have collected is your data?
- be tentative: use expressions such as –

  there is a tendency for . . .
  on the whole, this seems to be . . .
  we can perhaps conclude . . .

- be self-critical: how effective and revealing have your chosen methods of analysis been? What are the limitations of your data, and the methods you have used to collect and analyse it?

The write-up

The last stage of your investigation will be to write it up ready for submission. The text you produce is a rather specialised piece of informative writing, which should be written according to the appropriate academic conventions.

The relevant writing skills identified by the Examination Board include:

- *organise material coherently/present findings in an accessible format.*

– this means you should plan and present your report systematically, using conventions such as a contents page, headings and sub-headings, bibliography and appendix. A typical text-structure is suggested below:

Investigation report: suggested text structure

Section/heading	Content
Cover page	The title and scope of your investigation, and your name
Contents	A list of the main section headings and page numbers
Acknowledgments	Briefly acknowledge the sources of your data, and any other assistance you have received in the preparation of your investigation
Introduction	Explain your reasons for choosing to explore the topic you have, how you set about collecting and sampling your data, and the initial questions/hypothesis about your material which have provided the starting point for your investigation
Data	Present your data clearly labelled and sourced. It is useful, also, to provide line numbers for ease of reference in your analysis sections
Analysis (with sub-sections)	The bulk of your investigation. You will need to create sub-section headings according to the different levels of analysis you are carrying out. Use this section to present analysis of the data in verbal and diagrammatic form, using tables, bar charts and any other graphic devices that seem appropriate
Findings	See above (p.41)
Citing your sources	At the end of your submission, include a bibliography, list the author, title and publisher (with date of publication) of any text to which you have referred in the course of your study. Similarly, give the full address of any websites you have consulted. Within the body of your report, you should identify any sources you refer to by placing the name of the author and the date of publication in brackets immediately after your reference, e.g. (Jones, 1976). Readers can then pursue the reference from your bibliography.
Appendix	Use this final section to include any additional materials that may be relevant to the investigation (such as data collected but not included in your sample or questionnaires which you used as part of your research)

- *use an appropriate style of writing*

– your report is a fairly formal academic report and analysis whose purpose is to share understanding and information between people with a specialist interest in language. So, maintain an appropriately formal style, making appropriate use of specialist terminology.

- *ensure accuracy and relevance/use standard conventions of spelling, punctuation and grammar*

– this speaks for itself; as an A Level student, you are expected to maintain the highest standards of accuracy in your writing. The grammar, vocabulary, spelling and punctuation of Standard English should be used consistently throughout.

Use your tutor!

Throughout your investigation, you should expect to meet your teacher/tutor regularly to report on your progress and discuss your findings. It is expected that s/he will make a significant input to your learning; although the investigation must remain your own piece of independent research, you should ask your supervising teacher to comment on your work as it develops in each of these areas:

- the feasibility of your proposed investigation
- the quality, validity and scope of your data
- the appropriateness of your approach to your analysis
- the accuracy of your analysis
- suggestions about further reading and research
- the validity of your findings
- the organisation of your final report
- the presentation of your work for assessment.

Your tutor will keep a record of these consultations. The typical record sheet reproduced below reveals the ways in which the tutor's input has helped to keep the investigation on track:

Language Investigation Record

Student: Alastair Bilton **Supervising Tutor:** M. Briggs

Investigation Topic: The language of sports coverage

Date	Consultation	Action
July 01	A's first thoughts on the language of sports commentary. Wants to compare BBC/Sky coverage. What to concentrate on – one sport or several? Match commentary or previews/interviews? Contrastive study of commentators? Case Study of one programme or more? Discussed range of options.	Suggest he reads Adrian Beard's *The Language of Sport* over Summer, and anything on spoken language/discourse. Will need to decide a clearer focus/hypothesis and tape some good data when new football season starts in August

Sept.01	Some progress – has got hold of Beard but is still dipping in. Plenty of stuff taped – far too much, in fact. One possible focus has emerged – the 'in the tunnel' interviews with players and managers. Lots of discourse analysis possibilities. Alternatively has good data from Premiership games involving commentary/'expert' 'conversation' during game.	Must now (a) decide precise focus and (b) select own data appropriately. Continue reading Beard – also Wardhaugh's book on Conversational Analysis.
Oct 01	Has decided: after the match interviews it is. Still too much data – has over 20 examples taped and transcribed. This includes several different interviewers and players. Focus: both on management of interviews by the interviewer(s) – possibly comparing questioning techniques – and on discourse features of players. Suggested breaking this down into narrative, comment and personal analysis/ reflection by player. Discussed e.g.s of deviance from SE and various kinds of non-fluency.	Must now agree final selection of data and a structure for the analysis. Discourse framework most obvious, but plenty at grammatical and lexical/semantic levels too. Probably leave out accent issues.
Half term	Has shown me proposed structure for analysis – looks OK. Two main sections – the discourse of interviews and 'footballer speak'. Lots of subsidiary issues include some survey/ qualification of question types; analysis of AMU for different footballers; use of present perfect tense to narrate action: I suggest 1 or 2 others.	Nitty gritty time. Next meeting will be to discuss a complete first draft. Needs some help with grammatical issues – referred to Crystal's *Rediscover Grammar.*
Nov 01	First draft submitted. Structure a bit chaotic – needs proper formatting etc. but content sound. Some interesting discoveries starting to emerge – the range of figurative language used by footballers, for instance, exceeding his expectations re. clichés etc. Mechanics need attention, as does 'Findings' section which is insufficiently evaluative at present.	To re-draft, and format properly with appropriate headings/sub-headings etc. Final section needs particular attention – evaluation of methods, data, and findings – must hit AO4!
Dec 01	Final draft submitted!	

Assessment Objectives in focus

As you are working towards your investigation, you should, of course, consider how your approach to your data will enable you to meet the Assessment Objectives for this module, as set out on p.53.

As you prepare your work for submission, use the panel below to check that you have done so – and consider the 'tips for success' suggested below.

The specification says:	This means you must:	Tip for success
AO1 communicate clearly the knowledge, understanding and insight appropriate to the study of language, using appropriate terminology and accurate and coherent written expression (2½%)	Organise the presentation of your investigation helpfully, using appropriate headings, sub-headings, section headings and other means of presenting information such as bullet points, charts, tables and diagrams Use the proper linguistic terminology to define the features of language you are discussing	See the write-up of your investigation as a specialised kind of informative writing (see *AS English Language for AQA B*, pp.128–32). Think of yourself as writing for a fellow-student of language, whom you will lead through your investigation Review your language glossary to revise the appropriate terms
AO2 demonstrate expertise and accuracy in writing for specific purposes and audiences, drawing on knowledge of linguistic features to explain and comment on choices made (2½%)	Maintain a high standard of accuracy in terms of spelling, punctuation and Standard English grammar	Ensure you proof-read your work thoroughly before it is submitted If you can, use a suitable word-processing package to present your work professionally
AO3ii understand, discuss and explore concepts and issues relating to language in use (2½%)	In the questions you ask about your data, and in the analysis you carry out to answer them, apply the relevant knowledge about language that you gained throughout your AS/A2 course	Revisit some of the major topics and approaches you undertook as part of your AS course. Ask yourself 'could any of this be usefully applied to the data I am now working with?'
AO4: apply and explore frameworks for the systematic study of language at different levels, commenting on the usefulness of the approaches taken (5%)	We have covered the question *Which framework?* (p.38 above) In your conclusion, make sure you discuss how useful you have found your chosen approaches to be	In your conclusion, explain why you chose to organise your selection of data and its analysis in the ways you did. Briefly suggest other approaches you could have taken (e.g.

		placing more emphasis on the analysis of lexis than on phonology) and consider whether these approaches might have yielded equally interesting results
AO5ii analyse and evaluate variation in meanings and forms of spoken and/or written language from different times according to context (5%)	Relate your linguistic analysis of the data to the contexts in which they are produced	Don't just feature-spot; keep asking yourself – how have any of these factors influenced the ways language is used in this data: • the time it was produced • the place it was used • the situation in which it was used • the purpose for which it was used • the relationship between the participants

Some sample investigations

Look back at the ten stages of an investigation as set out on p.3 above. For each of the following sets of data, steps 1 (*Choose a field of investigation*), 2 (*Gather your specimen data*) and 4 (*Organise and present your data*) have already been completed. Your task in this final set of activities is to work systematically through the remaining steps to carry out a small-scale version of the investigation you will yourselves complete.

You may wish to work through both sets of data, or to be more selective. As this data has been provided for you, this work cannot legitimately be submitted as part of your examination assessment, but the process of working through at least one of these data sets will give you important experience of applying a systematic investigative methodology, before you embark on your own independent work.

In the Commentaries section on p.54, for each step you will find suggestions about approaches and lines of enquiry which may prove interesting. These are, of course, neither exhaustive or exclusive.

Activity 20. Children's stories

Data: children's narratives; response to Childline competition to write a story in 90 words
Source: 'Suddenly . . .' – 99 short stories for the Millennium (STAPLES, 1999)
Basis of sample: one from each age group represented in the anthology

1. Suddenly a volcano erupted and down the volcano came big eggs and big flames as well. When the volcano had stopped one by one the eggs hatched. Out came big dinursors but some were quite small, the monsters were big and fat and green and some were orange they used the little straw houses as their diner and the people for tea and for supper the cars and vans, then they went to bed and the next day they ate the fruit trees, bushes, shrubs and flowers and so the dinasors took over the world instead of the people.

   (Thomas Heenan, 6)

2. Suddenly . . . I woke up and looked at my clock, it's midnight, I said to myself. I couldn't believe it, tonight is the millennium. I ran into my mum and dad's bedroom and jumped on their bed and woke them up. What's the fuss about said my parents. It's the millennium, I told them, and please can we have a party. Later on said my parents. Okay I'll go back to bed then. I just couldn't believe it was the millennium, but my parents didn't want to celebrate yet. I closed my bedroom door and had a party with my teddies.

   (Gemma Dean, 7)

3. Suddenly, an enormous eruption happened! Things changed amazingly, no killing just smiles of happiness, children laughing, parents crying with joy! I myself knew what had happened. Millenium joy had covered the Earth. It was like a new world. But the strangest thing was, if someone felt sick or ill he would not be! Animals from the rainforest were enjoying themselves. The nasty spirit that killed and fought was now part of the old world, as if it had been locked up in jail. One day it will be released but everybody will have learnt to say no to it!

   (Thomas Rowland 8)

4. Suddenly the door burst open and there stood Henry the eighth with Florence Nightingale, behind them Queen Victoria, Sir Winston Churchill and Robin Hood. 'This is a great way to celebrate the last thousand years', said Walter Rayleigh, to Emmeline Pankhurst. Everyone at the party had dressed up like someone from the last millennium and were having fun acting like the person they had dressed up to be. There was food and drink. There was even a competition for fun. At midnight as the clock began to strike the hour they all raised their glasses, 'to the new millennium'.

   (Kristina Fleuty, 9)

5. Suddenly the door opened. The books on the shelves gasped. Not many people visited the library, less still on New Year's Eve. Since the invention of computers, televisions and leisure centres, nobody seemed to want to read books any more. One

particular book on the bottom shelf loved to be borrowed, to visit new homes, to see how humans lived and sometimes, unfortunately, get treated rather roughly. Today, he willed himself to be picked, to spend the millennium in a festive home and as the woman approached, he thought Yes, and looked forwards to the next exciting three weeks.

(Dan James, 10)

6. Suddenly William was in his podracer. The race to determine the driver of the Third Millennium was about to start. William pressed down the accelerater and felt the push in his back as he started off. Around the course he hurtled. He felt dizzy and sick.

   'Seven laps, eight laps.'

   Then he made a disastrous turn and tumbled out of control.

   He woke up to find himself in his bedroom, his mother looking very concerned. 'William, you've come out in a rash and you're very hot! You must have caught the Millennium Bug!' she exclaimed to his utter amazement.

   (David Hutchings, 11)

7. Suddenly I was face to face with 'Old Father Time'. It was as though I walked into a Victorian Child's story book. I should have been at my friends millenium party but somehow I lost my way in the sea mist which hung over our village. As the village clock chimed midnight on this special eve, I was with this amazing old man. He spoke in a whisper 'Happy New Year!' I smiled and asked 'What about the future for mankind?' he shook his head and walked away muttering, 'Use the earth's resources wisely if you want another millennium!'

   (Suzi Keating, 12)

8. Suddenly a crash filled a cottage. 'Ssh, be quiet' a man whispered. 'Sorry, I tripped' a second man answered back. It was one hour to the new Millenium. 'Come on guys, he'll be home soon. Now let's get to work' the first man ordered. The time was perfect, everyone was out celebrating the Millenium. The figures worked silently until eleven fifty when a noise outside made them freeze. A man and a woman walked in the door. The woman walked in the door. The woman flicked on the lounge light. The man opened the door and was met with thirty people shouting 'Happy Birthday Brian!'

   (Joanna Taylor, 13)

9. Suddenly the clocks struck midnight, the world cheered, the Earth was singing; and the people remembered what had been. The invention of the wheel, the industrial revolution, the poppy fields of remembrance and one small step for man, one giant leap for mankind.

   Then they looked forward to what will be; the cure for cancer, a non racist society and peace for mankind. As the chimes stopped, the whole world came to a halt, and everyone thought of that precise moment and why they were there; a baby born into a cruel world, who died for them. JESUS CHRIST.

(Clare Martin, 14)

10. Suddenly . . .the ground before him shook, and the heavy gates rose to reveal the object of his quest: the sand-timer. He had passed all the tests: war, famine, disease, and even death. It had taken him another thousand years, twenty more metres to his beard, but he was here at last . . . and just in time. As the last grain fell, he reached forward and turned over the timer . . . Then, he heard the voice of the Overlord!

'Well done, Man. You have made it to the new millenium. But I foresee worse obstacles ahead. Will you make it again?'

(Chris Edmonds, 15)

11. Suddenly, the clouds parted and the watching stars illuminated the sky. This was a special night, when all of creation watched with interest. Trees whispered tales of another night like it, many years before. Animals everywhere sniffed the air. They could feel the anticipation in the gentle breeze and the very roots of the earth. In a small town, humans waited to experience something feared by many, but, they couldn't stop the new dawn. And, as the sun glinted on the horizon, the world held her breath as its radiance gave birth to the dawn of a new millenium.

(Gemma MacInnes, 16)

12. Suddenly an icy wind blasted Jack's face. Huddled within the dark shadows of the shop doorway, inside his blanket of newspapers, he listened to the noisy celebrations. He wondered whether his mother ever thought of her runaway teenage son, he felt the intense pain of loneliness. Just before midnight he closed his eyes tightly, opening them with anticipation to view the new millenium. This, he decided, was a new beginning. A chance to build bridges over the troubled waters of teenage years. Bridging the rivers of quarrels and pride. Beyond the street party he saw the phone box.

(Clare Forster, 17)

13. Suddenly, and with solemn authority, the chimes struck twelve. Shouts of exultation echoed through dark skies, adorning the night. Nature breathed new life; every familiar sense felt different somehow. Full of promise. The celebratory beams of carefree rejoicing roared up into the night sky like great spotlights, crashing and banging, proclaiming the earth as a stage on which great actors took their bows, proud of this majestic theatre that had stood the telling test of time. And much like an audience, the world applauded and cheered, touched by the wonderful play; praising the breathtaking realms of time and space.

(Jennifer Baines, 18)

Activity 21. Horror books

Data: horror book back-cover 'blurbs'
Source: paperback horror novels
Basis of sample: random selection from local library

1. Be warned.

The untold terror is out ...

Abernant's a dead town. Dead boring. But not this summer. Because Abernant's hidden history – Abernant's *dark* history – is about to reawaken...

Nick feels it coming. The weather turns hot, close, brooding. Kids become restless and aggressive – joy-riding, thieving and mugging.

And that's only a beginning. For within the violence something ancient lurks. Watching. Preparing to feed...

2. Play at your own risk . . .

When Jenny buys the game from Julian, the gorgeous stranger with dangerous blue eyes, she little realises the stakes involved. Because this is a game like no other, and soon she and her friends are playing for their lives . . .

Trapped in a house of horrors, running from the Shadow Man; this game is for real. The rules are Julian's and Jenny is the prize. And if he wins, she is his forever . . .

3. Eddie, Scott, Winks and Cassie. Four best friends go out in a car one night to practise their driving. Especially Eddie.

But then Eddie has a terrible accident and now the four friends share a horrifying secret.

Because Eddie has hit someone and killed him.

Or has he?

4. Was she going to die . . . again?

Delia can't stop reading the old diary which mysteriously appears in her locker one day. Little by little, she starts to become more like the girl whose words she reads – even having her memories and seeing the world through her eyes. Dead girl's eyes. Soon, Delia is convinced that she was the girl who wrote the diary – in a past life.

But the terror is about to come alive once more. For the girl who wrote the diary was murdered. And the killer is after her again . . .

5. "Goodbye, my dear. Pleasant dreams"

The door was open and they were forcing her inside. She couldn't help it, she was going into this *thing*. This thing that they were going to close on her, that they were going to bury her in alive. As the dark metal walls rose around her and the water came up to meet her, Kaitlyn's nerve broke. She did scream. Or at least, she tried. But the thing in her mouth muffled it like a gag .. There was only silence as water enveloped her. And darkness. Then the metal door clanged shut. It was the last sound she was to hear ...

Planning your investigation

The key to a successful investigation is to manage your time carefully over a long period, so that your work does not end up being a last-minute rush.

ACTIVITY 22. YOUR PLAN

Use the chart below to help you plan. Always start at the bottom of the chart – pencil in the deadline your teacher/tutor has given you for the final submission of the project, and work backwards from there, building in time for 'slippage', accidents and mishaps along the way.

Your investigation mark scheme

Stage	Complete by: (date)	Done (tick)	Approved by tutor (tick)
Choose your topic/field to investigate			
Gather data			
Organise and present data			
Ask key questions/propose hypothesis			
Choose appropriate method of analysis			
Carry out this analysis in rough notes/annotation			

Do additional reading/research as appropriate			
Write up and organise your analysis			
Arrive at conclusions			
Reflect on the effectiveness and validity of the data and the methods you have chosen to explore it			
First draft of write-up			
Final draft of write-up			
All materials packaged and presented for submission			
Deadline set for final submission to Centre			

On page 53 is the mark scheme to which your teacher and the external moderator will work when assessing your investigation. Keep this in front of you as you write up your final report, and make sure your work fits the criteria and the descriptions below for the grade you are aiming to achieve.

Assessment Objective	Marks gained					
	0–5	6–10	11–15	16–20	21–25	26–30
AO1	Evidence of the skills represented by the four Objectives present in limited ways. There will be very little awareness or understanding of causal relationships. Candidates will typically be engaged in unsystematic feature-spotting, showing only everyday general knowledge of language.	Shows limited linguistic knowledge of the data	Shows linguistic knowledge of chosen data	Shows linguistic knowledge of chosen data	Shows perceptive linguistic knowledge of chosen data	Demonstrates full, perceptive and detailed linguistic knowledge of chosen data
AO3ii		Uses one or two frameworks for investigation Makes limited comment on the approaches taken	A limited number of frameworks for the investigation of language data in evidence Comments with some validity on the different approaches taken	Some effective application of different frameworks for the investigation of language Some sensible/valid comments on the approaches taken	Systematic application of frameworks for the investigation of language Comments appropriately on the effectiveness of the approaches taken	Systematic application and exploration of relevant frameworks for the investigation of language Comments with pertinence and insight on the effectiveness of the approaches taken
AO4		Makes occasional comment on concepts of language in use in relation to chosen task	Comments with some success on concepts of language in use in relation to chosen task	Some discussion of concepts of language in use in relation to chosen task	Effective discussion of concepts of language in use in relation to chosen task	Insightful, clear and succinct discussion of concepts of language in use in relation to chosen task
AO5ii		Shows awareness of one or two contextual factors Attempts to apply contextual variation to data	Some consideration of relevant contextual factors Limited application of contextual variation in significant areas of the data	Analysis of some of the relevant contextual factors Applies contextual variation to the data with some success	Analysis of a range of the relevant contextual factors Clear appreciation of contextual variation in significant areas of the data	Perceptive analysis of relevant contextual factors Clear appreciation of contextual variation in significant areas of the data

Commentaries

Activity 1. Pair/group discussion

Don't worry if you didn't come up with the same examples as the ones the activity suggests – it would be highly coincidental if you had – but these may start you thinking about the kinds of topics that might interest you:

a. Perhaps compare a live commentary with a written news report on the same event.

b. If a member of your family, or a friend or neighbour, has a distinctive regional speech, collect and study examples of their speech.

c. You could collect and examine the words you have misspelled in your school/college work over the past few months (or years).

d. Perhaps examine the various kinds of mistakes made by one or more foreign learners of English in their speech and/or writing.

e. Other examples might include the opening lines/titles of a particular set of song lyrics, or the comments written by teachers on school/college reports.

f. The social talk between friends, or at the family dining table, or around the TV, would also be possible subjects.

g. If you have a part-time job, this may bring you into contact with specific uses of language associated with it. The language of courtesy when serving in a shop, perhaps?

h. You could look at the contrasting linguistic styles of different broadcasters (e.g. BBC 1 compared with Channel 5), as reflected in their news, sport or weather reports.

Activity 2. Skills audit

Don't worry if some of the wording puzzled you, or if you were unable to put a tick in each box. The following section of this module is designed to consolidate your skills in the crucial areas.

a. = Decide what would be an interesting and valid topic, and plan a suitable method of collection your data.

You may need to consolidate your ideas about this in the next section.

b. = Record, transcribe and collect your data in a way which serves the purpose of your investigation without offending people's right to privacy or breaking the law. See *AS English Language for AQA B*, p.9 for basic advice on recording; you will consider how to assure the **validity** of your data in the next section.

c. = Notice interesting aspects of your data, and ask relevant questions about them without always being prompted by a tutor.

d. = Use linguistic terminology to define precisely (and correctly) the distinctive characteristics of a particular piece of language.

e. = Use suitable conventions to represent aspects of spoken language accurately on paper.

f. = Use a systematic approach in your analysis, so you are not just 'feature-spotting' in a random way.

g. = Decide on the method of analysis that will produce the most interesting insights, and discuss explicitly the reasons for your choice of approach.

This is a high-level skill and one which you may well feel very uncertain about at the start of your A2 course. It will be covered later in this module.

h. = This really follows on from points (b), (f) and (g). It means being able not just to say what you think your study has revealed, but also how successful and valid it has been.

i., j., k. = Produce a final report of your investigation which is a professional and polished document appropriate to its purpose, audience and register.

This is an extension of the writing skills developed in your AS course.

Activity 4. Data validity

a. The issue here is to eliminate variables other than that between speech and writing. So, you could perhaps set up a situation in which the same individual tells the same story, but once on paper and once orally. At least, you should ensure that the theme/subject matter of the story told is the same in each case and that the author/speaker of the text are of comparable age and verbal ability.

b. To achieve 'natural' data here, carry out your interview without telling your subject it is a language investigation into his/her dialect! Instead, perhaps suggest you are doing an oral history project, and invite your subject to reminisce about their experiences of early childhood where they were brought up.

   Transcribing regional pronunciations can be a very specialised business (see 'Using the Phonetic Alphabet', pp.17–18). You are likely to encounter fewer problems if you focus mainly on dialect features (i.e. lexical and grammatical variation from Standard English). If so, you may need quite a lot of data to work with.

c. With this investigation, two issues arise: making sure that there is some comparability between the types of writing from which you draw your data (e.g. a piece of autobiographical writing from both classes) and ensuring that the sample of students selected is similarly representative (using either a random sample or a selected cross-section of ability).

d. Similar issues arise here as with (c). Ensure comparability of the work collected, and a similar representation. Check also for a fair balance of male and female students, and make sure you are aware of pupils whose first/home language may not be English.

e. In this case, the scope of the investigation could include a comparison between the ads carried in two different styles of publication (tabloid and broadsheet) or could concentrate simply on one source. In either case, the sheer volume of data will probably require some sampling – a random 1 in 5 selection, perhaps. Alternatively, some kinds of investigation may wish to use all the data for some basic statistical analysis (e.g. investigating the proportion of the total number of ads which include an animal reference as a pet name!).

f. Here, several models are possible. A common one is to set up informal, social contexts for conversation involving (i) an all-male, and (ii) an all-female group, ensuring as far as possible that the two groups are of similar age, professional status and social class. You could tighten this up further by setting up comparable conversational contexts, for example by creating the same group-work or problem-solving activity for both groups.

g. Various possibilities suggest themselves here. For comparability across different media, select the commentary on a particular incident in the same match, which you tape simultaneously from Radio (Radio 5 Live) and TV. To investigate the language of punditry, compare the dialogue of the studio presenter and experts during half-time discussions on two different channels, ideally discussing the same match. Alternatively, tape and study a number of interviews with players after the match to focus both on interviewing style and the discourse of the players themselves.

h. Clearly, you need to focus on the main news of a particular day – probably the same news story – and you may choose to compare bulletins within one medium (on television, BBC, ITV, Channels 4 and 5, different radio stations or newspapers) or even carry out a multi-media study of the coverage of just one news story in several different news bulletins and reports.

Activity 5. Happy Birthday!

(i) Here are some initial observations on three of the items for you to compare with yours:

You may have noted in Item 1 the use of verse-like layout, but in this case the lines fragment the sentences and do not produce any rhyming. The address to the reader *you* is made three times and culminates in one of a small number of possible variations on the 'Happy Birthday' theme, 'WITH BEST WISHES'. Grammatically speaking, there is something missing from the beginning of the item – the 'I' of the sender (as in *I hope your birthday . . .*), and this gives the text a slightly colloquial tone. (Such omission is known as ellipsis, see p.29 above.) The text consists of a single sentence, though it does have a fairly complex structure. Lexically, the text is quite simple; all the words are either of one or two syllables and belong to the register of everyday usage. The impact is simple and straightforward but sincere.

Item 4, on the other hand, uses humour. There is a two-part structure to the joke; the first part sounds as if the reader is being insulted (any 'excuse' for irresponsible behaviour!) but in the second part it is clear that the sender approves of drinking and 'carrying on'. If anything it is more colloquial than Item 1, with its use of the contraction *you'll,* a rhetorical question tag *are you?,* the common formula *I bet . . .,* and informal vocabulary like *carry on* and *daft.* The illusion of speech is reinforced by the series of dots and double exclamation mark which implies a raised tone of voice and the second sentence which, like Item 1, begins with an ellipsis (*not as daft . . .* instead of *You're not as daft . . .*). Joke over, it finishes with a direct imperative – HAVE A GREAT BIRTHDAY – with the implication that *great* = including lots of drink and *carrying on.*

With Item 6, we see again the simple sincere message, but this time couched in a typically rhythmical and rhyming form. There is alternate line rhyming of lines 2 and 4 and metrically, each line has regular beats or stresses (With **lov**ing **thoughts** and **wish**es **on** your **ve**ry **spe**cial **day**). The vocabulary seems typical of the genre – abstract nouns such as *thoughts, wishes* and *happiness* and a direct address to the reader (*your way*). The sentiment is typically one of banal and overstated optimism that ***every*** *kind of happiness will* ***always*** *come your way.*

Item 7 uses a very different register, starting with apparently 'hip' language such as *cool brothers* and *neat.* This language seems to be targeted at a particular age group. As with several of the other items, the text seems to flatter the reader, but the words *neat* and *bloomin' sweety* contrast with the more staid compliments of the more conventional greetings.

The text also delivers a humorous punch line, which subverts the tone of what has gone before – still in a colloquial register (reflected by the token attempt at phonetic spelling in *'cept,* as with *bloomin'*) but now rather insulting of the reader's *cheesy feet.*

(ii) Some of the common strands which may emerge from these initial observations on the data include:

- the different phrases used directly to say 'Happy Birthday', 'Best Wishes', etc.
- the various uses of rhyme and rhythm
- the mixture of apparent sincerity and humour in the data
- other variations in tone and register
- the different ways in which optimistic sentiments are expressed
- the references in the data to the present day, the past and the future
- the direct address to the reader
- the use of abstract nouns
- the number, length and type of sentences used.

(iii) Some possible questions might be:

- What devices are used to achieve humorous effects in the data?
- How does the register/tone vary according to the age of the intended recipient?
- What devices are used to create the illusion of spoken language in these written texts?
- How is language used to address/flatter/insult the recipient?
- What variations are found in rhyme and rhythmic patterns, and how is word order manipulated to achieve these?

Overall, this data, although quite simple in many ways, could nevertheless be the basis of a very successful investigation.

Activity 6. Classroom discourse

It is sometimes tempting to be drawn to the superficial non-fluency features (such as the fillers, hesitations and pauses in speech) and to consider making these a focus for study. In practice, however, these are seldom the most interesting or fruitful features for investigation. Once you have identified them, it is not always easy to go on and say anything particularly revealing or illuminating about them.

On the other hand, the data *does* offer at least the starting points for some more penetrating analysis. The teacher is clearly 'managing' the discourse, and at times, explicitly underlines the purpose of his/her utterances (*just a quick word about the practical sessions . . .*). S/he is also the manager of the session itself, and some of his/her speech is designed to structure the session clearly for the pupils – first by making clear the topic and objectives for the session (*what we haven't done is show how we can represent electric fields on a diagram)*.

The teacher is obviously being fairly careful to assess the pupils' understanding, recap on previous knowledge and build on it. The various methods s/he uses to do so include **closed questions** aimed at the whole class (*anyone done that have you, anybody seen that done*), **question tags** (*you tend to see it fairly early on* ***don't you***), reassuring reminders (*as you know*) and more open questioning (*any idea what kind of a path they will have . . .*), as well as what you might call a leading question (*will they go in a straight line upwards or at a . . .*).

You might also have noticed the variation in the use of pronouns in the discourse. The teacher moves between *we, you* and *anyone*, when questioning the class.

In the beginnings of the explanation, you might also have noted the classic teacher-student interaction pattern of question–response–repetition–reward–extension (*P3: A parabola / T: a parabola Yeah very good. Why*) and the reinforcement of pupils' use of the appropriate subject-specific vocabulary such as *gravitational field*.

However, in many of these areas, examples are limited and in the given data there is only limited scope for investigating the key features of classroom discourse.

So, if this data may not offer sufficient scope by itself, you could extend the investigation in a number of ways. If you still had the tape of the lesson, you might need to transcribe a slightly longer section, or look at sections from the middle and end of the lesson as well as the beginning. Alternatively, if you wished to make a particular study of lesson beginnings, also look at the first few minutes of a lesson with the same students but in a different subject area – or with students of a different age in the same subject area.

There again, if you wished to focus on very specific linguistic detail, such as the way teachers pose questions and respond to pupils' replies, you may need to collect data from two or three more lessons – but don't overdo it. Trying to work with too much data is likely to lead to superficial surveys rather than detailed analysis.

Another limitation with this data is the absence from the transcript of a distinction between male and female pupils. If we had more evidence of the pupils' contributions to the lesson, an interesting line of enquiry could be to explore what differences, if any, existed between the contributions of male and female pupils, or indeed in the way that the teacher addresses and responds to them, referring back to the 'Language and gender' section of *AS English Language for AQA B* pp.84–90.

Activity 7. Café names

(i) Here are some suggested categories – many others are, of course, possible:

- attribution of ownership. 18 of the 93 items appear to identify the owner of the establishment, though these names may, of course, be fictitious rather than actual
- you could also look at how the establishments themselves are defined. They are variously described as cafés (36 items), diners (3 items), kitchens (2 items), pantries (2 items), and assorted alternatives
- there is another significant group of names drawn from the semantic field of eating and food (e.g. *A Bite to Eat, Nibblers, Brunches, Grubbs Diner, P.I.E.S.* etc.)
- you may also have noted that a number of these names refer to rural or natural elements (e.g. *The Bayleaf*)
- another linguistically interesting group consists of plays on words, spelling and sound (such as *Meals R Us, Kwicksnax, Upper Crust*)
- many names also refer to a location (e.g. *Londonderry Lodge, Slipway Café*, etc.).

(ii) To consider three of these possible categories:

a. Names of attribution: 17 items

Forenames	Surnames	Nicknames	Non-English	M	F	Non-specific
Alison's Kitchen Johnny's Café Kay's Cafe Kirkorah's Deb's Place Harley's Diner Roya's Pantry Sue's Kitchen	Aunty Richards Beckindales Mrs Mac's Mrs Pumphrey's Pendry's Eating House Clarkes Café Cook's Gallery Grubbs Diner (?)	Mrs Mac's Crusty's Café	Kirkorah's Roya's Pantry	2	9	5

b. Nouns of identification

When presenting statistical data, it is often most effective to use a bar-chart, pie-chart or other similar diagrammatic representation:

*(Londonderry) Lodge
(Monks) Haven
(Chelsea) Snack bar
(Pendry's) Eating House
(Cook's) Gallery
(The) Bistro

c. Plays on language

Puns	Alliteration	Phonetic spelling
P.I.E.S.	Kay's Café	Kwicksnax (c.f. also Quick Snacks)
Drop Inn Café	Crumbs Café	Meals R Us
Food for Thought		
Grubbs Diner		
The Hot Plate		
The Upper Crust		

(ii) Commentaries

First, we may consider the differences between the uses of first names only with other kinds of naming. This will usually imply some kind of friendly familiarity, particularly when the forename is abbreviated as in *Deb's Place*. Names themselves may have different associations; the monosyllabic *Kay* and *Sue* sound down-to-earth and unpretentious, whereas *Harley's* perhaps has a more cosmopolitan, American feel. *Kirkorah's* and *Roya's* hint at a more exotic, less traditionally English style of cooking, perhaps!

Within the surnames, there are also interesting distinctions. Some sound ordinary enough – *Pendry's, Clarkes* and *Richards* – but the alliterative familiarity of *Mrs Mac's* (like the other nickname, *Crusty's*) may imply a greater down-to-earthness than, say, *Beckindales*. *Mrs Pumphrey's* is a name suggestive of an older, homelier, even Victorian or Dickensian world. Some names – *Cook's* and *Grubbs* (or the nickname *Crusty's*) may have been chosen not because they are really the owners but because of their punning potential.

There is also some quantifiable variation in the use or omission of the possessive apostrophe.

(iii)

The majority of those names including a noun of identification describe themselves as *cafés*. Even here, though, there are some distinctions to be made between the standard syntax of *name + café* (*Kay's Café*, etc.) and the reversed word order found in *Café Brisco* and *Café Caffae*. You might conclude that this essentially un-English syntax hints at the same continental flavour and sophistication implied by their attached names of *Brisco* and *Caffae*.

The alternative nouns used have distinct connotations which may reflect the different style of provisions offered and the different target market. *Kitchen* is certainly homely, and may be designed to imply that the food is home-made, served, as it were, as an extension of the owner's own domestic cooking. *Pantry* is similar, but more old-fashioned; how many houses nowadays have a pantry? This may hint at values of traditional unfussy cooking with wholesome ingredients. *Diner*, on the other hand, sounds distinctly American and is associated with neon-lit aluminium fittings, burgers and French fries.

The other alternatives range from the basic *snack bar* (perhaps even more basic than café?) and the functional *Eating House* to the more sophisticated, continental-sounding *Bistro* and the slightly arty *Gallery*.

The use of humour, in the form of plays on words, is used in a minority of cases to attract attention, and the very lack of seriousness this implies may suggest that these are unlikely to be particularly pretentious establishments. Straightforward alliteration is used to give the name memorability (this is sometimes visual alliteration, as in *Crumbs Café*, or purely phonetic alliteration, as in *Kay's Café*). The use of non-standard spelling patterns is confined to a single example – interestingly, another café with exactly the same name has chosen to retain conventional spelling. What is the difference? The K's and X of *Kwicksnax* seems sharper, but is perhaps also a touch 'down market' from the more proper-looking '*Quick Snacks*'.

Otherwise, you find the use of puns in the names *Drop Inn, The Hot Plate* and *The Upper Crust*. The latter jokes with the idea that it might have an upper-class appeal, of course – unlike *Grubbs Diner*, whose use of the slang 'grub' seems to root the café and its food firmly at street level.

Overall, you have started to explore the linguistic choices in terms of the commercial identity and target market of these establishments. The investigation could be extended by subjecting some of the menus from a selection of these cafés to linguistic analysis, and/ or carrying out a survey of the customers who use them.

Activity 8. Transcripts and speech

First, of course, we need to know something of the *situational context* for the dialogue – where the conversation takes place, what the speakers are doing, how they are positioned in relation to each other. All of these factors will affect what is said, how it is said, and the meanings the speakers are conveying to each other. There are also many *paralinguistic features* absent, which may have contributed significantly to the meanings in the conversation. Gestures, eye-contact and other body language all play a vital part in the language of conversation.

Even if we just consider the verbal aspects of the conversation, our transcript at present offers few clues about the *prosodic features* – the intonation, stress, tempo and dynamics (i.e. volume) of the speech – let alone the accents of the speakers. Certainly the *pragmatic meanings* of the dialogue – what is really going on beneath the surface as far as the speakers' feelings, attitudes and intentions are concerned – remains a matter for conjecture.

Activity 10. Making sense

- The correct sequence for the report is: B G E A C H F D
- The reproduction of the text below illustrates many of the internal connections that you are likely to have recognised as clues to its sequence. In reconstructing this text, you may well have looked first for the opening sentence. As you discovered when looking at the discourse structure of news reports (see *AS English Language for AQA B*, p.15), this is likely to contain a summary of the key facts – and sentence B does just this. It also refers back closely to the headline; note the synonymous relationship between the two sets of phrases, those in the headline being briefer and more dramatic:

  cancer patient → cancer sufferer
  doctor → GP
  dropped from lists → axed
  expected to die → doomed

However, this opening sentence also announces the main elements of the story which are to follow; such forward-looking references are known as **cataphoric** connections.

The remainder of the article expands on these basic elements. One clue to the sequence of the paragraphs might be the various ways in which the subject of the story is referred to in each one:

A cancer patient has been cruelly dropped from her doctor's lists just a month before **she** is expected to die.	The first reference defines the subject in general terms – quickly followed by the appropriate pronoun (substituting pronouns for nouns is a process called **prenominalisation**).
Former dancer Laura Thompson, 45 – who has cancer of the pancreas – was given six months to live in November.	Then comes a full statement of her name, occupation and age.
Soon afterwards **she** moved to Leigh-on-Sea, Essex, hoping to benefit from coastal air. **She** signed up with Dr Imran Nathoo.	Subsequent references to *she* and *Laura* clearly refer back to something previously mentioned in the text – a feature known as an **anaphoric** reference. The word/phrase it refers to (i.e. *Laura Thompson*) is known as the **referent.**
But now health chiefs have told **the mum-of-two** the GP wants her taken off his list – and **she** must find another doctor.	Additional information is provided, but here the definite article (*the*) also refers anaphorically to previous references.

Laura sobbed: 'This is such a terrible blow. **I** have just sat and cried since getting the letter.'	The familiar *Laura* can also only occur once the full name has been given.
Pakistan-born Dr Nathoo, 49, denied his decision had anything to do with the cost of treating **Laura**.	
He said: **'She** moved to us as a temporary allocated patient and the normal procedure is we only have to keep them for three months. We're only a small practice.'	
South Essex Health Authority says: 'This is a national system'.	

You could, of course, similarly trace the references to the doctor or to the Health Authority.

Another such chain of references is the string of words in the semantic field of suffering:

cancer sufferer **cancer/cruelly/die** **cancer** **sobbed, blow, cried**	The word *cancer* in itself has strong connotations of suffering, but the other words here all refer to the impact of the doctor's actions rather than the disease, thus conveying the strong sense of disapproval.

On the other hand, the words *benefit* and *coastal air* imply a contrasting field of relief and relaxation which has been denied to the patient.

There is another type of clue which you may have followed – the early references to time and sequence (known as **temporal** connectors):

1	**A month before . . . expected to die**	The opening sentence announces what has just happened, with the second giving a six-month flashback. *Soon afterwards* clearly refers anaphorically to a preceding temporal detail, and the sense of the sentence prohibits it following the opening one. In paragraph 4, we are returned to the same time as the opening sentence with *now.*
2	**Six months . . . in November**	
3	**Soon afterwards**	
4	**Now**	

Other groups of words also offer vital clues as to the cohesion and coherence of a text. Like the personal pronouns *she/her,* the word *this* in paragraph 5 (known as a **demonstrative pronoun**) must refer to something else. Here, the sense of the piece means it must refer to *The GP wants her taken off his list*. The referent of the final *this* is less clear; the *national system* is, we assume, the procedure outlined in the preceding paragraph.

In any text, the role of conjunctions (such as *but* at the start of paragraph 4) is also vital in signalling the underlying logic of its sense and sequence. We know as soon as we see this word that what follows (the action of the 'Health Chiefs') will in some sense contrast with what has gone before (the actions and hopes of the patient).

The following diagram traces some of the cohesive connections we have examined:

GP axes doomed cancer sufferer

A cancer patient has been cruelly dropped from her doctor's lists just a month before she is expected to die.

Former dancer Laura Thompson, 45 – who has cancer of the pancreas – was given six months to live in November.

Soon afterwards she moved to Leigh-on-Sea, Essex, hoping to benefit from coastal air. She signed up with Dr Imran Nathoo.

But now health chiefs have told the mum-of-two the GP wants her taken off his list – and she must find another doctor

Laura sobbed: 'This is such a terrible blow. I have just sat and cried since getting the letter.'

Pakistan-born Dr Nathoo, 49, denied his decision had anything to do with the cost of treating Laura.

He said: 'She moved to us as a temporary allocated patient and the normal procedure is we only have to keep them for three months. We're only a small practice.'

South Essex Health Authority says: 'This is a national system'.

Laura	Relief
Dr.	Temporal connectors/references
Health Authorities	Conjunctions (logical)
Pain/suffering	Demonstrative pronouns

Activity 11. Radio 4 News

Overview: the text is organised as a list consisting of three distinct elements: the stories about (i) the Tories' conference, (ii) Rover cars and (iii) the Olympics. There is no semantic link between these items, but the Olympics and Rover stories are grammatically connected by 'and'. The function of the whole passage seems to be a trailer for what is to follow, and as such, it refers cataphorically to the rest of the news. This is specifically true for phrases such as 'we'll be examining whether . . .', 'she joins us live' (meaning – later in the programme) and 'The News is read by Corrie Caulfield' (meaning – not as a general truth but announcing what is to happen next, introducing the newsreader who is to speak).

Within each of these three stories, various cohesive features are used. The Conservative Party is variously referred to as *the Tories, the Conservative Party* and *they*. This raises interesting questions about these terms – although rooted in the historical origins of the party, the word 'Tory' seems to have rather stronger pejorative overtones in the mouths of their opponents. A chain of semantically related terms refers anaphorically to the initial *attack,* which apparently consists of a *promise/pledge* to match Labour Party promises – note the repetition of key words here, in varied form *(promises/promising). Labour* and *the Tories* function as contrasting opposites in the text, setting up an antonymous connection.

There are many examples of types of cohesion within single sentences. '*Something* for British sports fans to cheer about' and the subsequent prenominalisation *it* refer anaphorically to the whole of the previous phrase *Britain winning its biggest medals tally* and the *at last* is temporally connected to *80 years.*

The keyword *Sydney* occurs twice. The repetition of the word *Sports* serves as the lexical cohesion between the sentence ending with the unanswered rhetorical question *Is it good enough?* and the following *The Sports Minister Kate Howie . . . joins us live.* We are left to infer that the purpose of her doing so is to provide an answer to the question.

Activity 12. Between the lines

(i) The *literal* sense of this utterance is that of a statement and a prediction – *I think . . . you'll find* – but what is likely to be their underlying purpose? There is little point in them unless they are directed to someone in the act of smoking, whom the speaker wishes to stop. However, the use of a statement and the qualifying hedge *Excuse me. I think . . . you'll find* softens the request to an acceptable degree of politeness. The underlying meaning, though, is – *stop smoking*!

The range of such strategies which we use to achieve a degree of politeness in discourse can be a rich subject for investigation.

(ii) As we saw in the AS course (see *AS English Language for AQA B*, pp.90–92), school reports often use coded euphemisms to soften criticisms. That Gillian finds the course *challenging* is likely to be literally true, but a rather blunter judgment about her ability or intelligence may also be implied.

(iii) This could, of course, be a relatively innocent enquiry, or simply part of a phatic exchange. However, there are other possibilities! The whole business of asking someone out for a date is fraught with difficulties and ambiguities; behind the question asked may lurk another – would you like to come out with me? – and another – do you fancy me? The response could also be ambiguous. Has B simply read the question literally, and so is only responding to the overt meaning? Or has B understood the covert request and is offering a 'soft landing' to the knock-back? Or does the *I suppose* and the vagueness of the answer (*stuff to do*) still leave room for A to persist?

(iv) Here the overt and covert meanings are closer – it is clear enough that the recipient of the letter is being sacked – but the wordy preamble and the expressions of regret and appreciation (whatever their degree of sincerity) seem intended, again, to soften the blow.

(v) Of all the ways to ask dog-walkers to prevent their pets fouling the pavement, this one (seen on a garage door in Grassington, North Yorkshire) is possibly the bluntest. However, the phrase *empty your dog* requires a moment's thought for translation; far from being a softener or understatement, it seems designed to cause deliberate offence to dog-owners and conveys a strong sense of the proprietor's anger and contempt.

(vi) Saying 'no' in any form – turning down an invitation or refusing a request – is often couched in less direct language. Here again is the hedge *I'm afraid* and a non-specific excuse (*unable to take your call . . .*). According to Grice's maxim of quality we generally work on the assumption that an utterance is true, but here the *unable* may well be a cover for 'unwilling', or even, 'you're not important enough to take up his time'.

Activity 15. Combining clauses into sentences

- The subject of the main clause is *the man*, the main verb *had left* and the object of this main clause *a note*.
- Subordinate clauses are introduced by *when, who, that, which* and *that*.
- The difficulty lies in the way the main subject and verb are buried in the middle of the sentence, rather than being placed at the front, where we usually expect to find them. There is also a pair of subordinate clauses (*who had said* and *that he would be coming to read the meter)* inserted between the main subject (*the man*) and the main verb (*had left*) – making it very easy to lose track of who is doing what to whom!

Activity 17. Morphemes

The basic word at the heart of *impossibilities* is, of course, *possible*. *Im-* is a morpheme which means either 'not' or 'the opposite of', *-ity* turns the adjective (*impossible*) into the noun (*impossibility*), and the final *-s* makes it plural.

In *unthinkable*, *think* is the base (or stem) of the word, *un-* is another morpheme meaning 'not', and *-able* turns the verb into an adjective with the sense of *capable of* (as *in do – doable, drink – drinkable* etc).

Stable is at the heart of *destabilising*, but the word also includes the morphemes *de-* (= to undo something), *-ise* (= a transforming action, as in *liquidise, magnetise* or *homogenise)* and *-ing* (the progressive aspect of a verb*)*.

As well as the basic name *John, John's* contains the morpheme *-'s*, which indicates attribution or possession.

Activity 18. Sounds and spellings

It is worth noting Sophie's understanding that there is a correspondence between graphemes and phonemes, but that it is not a simple matter of equating 1-for-1. Thus, she spells correctly words with a simple letter-to-sound correlation like *but* and *is* but also manages *make*, where the phoneme /eI/ is represented by the addition of the 'magic e' at the end of the word. In the case of *roome* she is over-extending this principle where it is not needed – elsewhere she shows she knows that *oo* usually represents the long /ʊ/ phoneme and writes *too* even when we would prefer *to*.

Some words correctly spelt seem to show visual memory and awareness that phonemically identical words can have distinct spellings and meanings. Thus she spells *woods* correctly and elsewhere writes *wud* for would. In other examples, Sophie seems to be making a guess using the knowledge she already has about graphemic/phonemic correspondences. Thus, *scviral* is a fair stab at *squirrel*, allowing for the easy misformation of *w* as *v*. The ending *-al* is just as likely as *-el* to represent /ə + l/.

Some of Sophie's misspellings also reveal a lot about both her own learning and the English spelling system as a whole. If you figured out that *cipe* = *keep* and *waylb* = *wild*, you may have noticed that *c* can and does represent the phoneme /k/ in words phonemically similar to *keep* like *cup* and *cap*; however, we know as adults that the combination *ci-* is more likely to represent the soft /s/, as in *city, citrus* or *cinema*.

Sophie's text also reveals some apparent confusion between lower- and upper-case forms, and occasional reversals of the letter *b* for *d* (in *granddab* and *waylb*)

The conventions of written punctuation are almost entirely absent.

Activity 19. Which frameworks?

Film previews

It is certainly worth investigating the **text structure** of each one to look for any recurrent patterns; how common, for example, is the structure *Brief* ***summary of key plot elements + evaluation/judgement*** ? What other text structures (if any) are used?

You might also ask what are the common factors in each preview (names of directors, actors, characters?). And how are these presented (e.g. the use of **pre-modifying adjectives** in *weaselly Nick Leeson . . . princely McGregor)*

A common feature seems to be the thumbnail summary of the film compressed into an **extended noun phrase**, as in *Old-rope sequel, expletive-stuffed debut feature* and *daisy-chain of historical vignettes.* You might ask what are the advantages of such structures given the restrictions of space which apply to such texts.

At a lexical level there is much to discuss. The **register** is a mixture of highly literate, abstract language (*Scream school of self-referentiality, historical vignettes, sexual machinations, languid and ruminative*) and colourful colloquialism (*cheesy, a dud, a turkey*). The expression of pejorative judgments often seems to draw on this register (as in *half-arsed rise and fall*). Can the proportions of these contrasting styles be measured and quantified, perhaps? There is also a certain amount of **topic-specific vocabulary** (*sequel, prequel, feature*, etc.).

In the expression of damning judgments there are also some notable uses of **figurative language** like *the last stale crumb in the bucket* and *labouring in third gear* – the latter, interestingly, a colourful equivalent of the *languid and ruminative* used elsewhere.

What can you guess about the intended **audience** for these texts, judging from the cultural references such as *Icarus-like*, *this year's Godzilla*, and the inclusions of names of various films/directors?

There is also a tendency to coin **phonologically striking phrases** such as *monster-mash, battling a bandaged bogeyman*, and *the magic movie mill moulds . . .*

How are these sound-bite phrases constructed, and what is their value?

Advertising slogans

Slogans have to be memorable, and in many cases different kinds of phonological patterning make them so. There are examples of full rhymes (*Go well. Go Shell.*) but more interesting ones of other sorts of phonemic repetition; *goodness/Guinness*, *Switch* to/*Michelin*, or the alliterative *It wouldn't be the weekend without Woodpecker wood it?* One especially common pattern is rhythmical repetition (often, like *Designed by a computer. Silenced by a laser. Built by a robot*, or *A Mars . . . helps you work, rest and play*) structured in the groups of three which often appear in rhetorical language (see *AS English Language for AQA B*, pp.74–75). These triadic groupings can be discussed as a matter of phonology (rhythm) or text-structure. Another variable in terms of textual organisation is the placement of the product name (at the front, back or middle of the slogan). In fact, there are also things to say about **sentences**, as a group of three such as *Call it Wrigley's. Call it Spearmint. Call it Gum*, which works by repeating parallel identical sentence structures.

In terms of **lexis and semantics** there is, as usual, much to discuss. Much use is made of various kinds of **puns and ambiguities** (*Let colour go to your head/The prose without the con*), some of which depend on an audience recognising a well-known phrase, which is being manipulated (*there's no present like the time/no pride in prejudice*). In the case of *Every bubble's passed its fizzical*, the joke depends on the use of non-standard **spelling.** Elsewhere, advertisers coin distinctive **neologisms** (*cookability/guintelligence/schweppervescence*).

Activity 20. Children's stories

Initial observations and suggested frameworks for analysis. This is quite a substantial set of data and it could provoke a wide range of initial observations. Underpinning most of these is likely to be a set of questions relating to the developments in narrative and linguistic skills as the writers get older. It may be possible to measure and quantify some, at least, of these developments.

You may have noted, first, the changing nature of the stories themselves, both in terms of subject matter (the fantasy and imagination of some of the younger children's writing yielding to more realistic and ultimately quite mystical responses of the older authors) and the **text structure** of the narratives. Clare Martin's story, for example, is very deliberately structured in terms of past and future before the climactic reference to Jesus Christ. The relative proportions of description, narration and dialogue also vary interestingly among the stories (this variation could be represented diagrammatically using pie charts) and the different endings of the stories reveal a development in the authors' intentions and sophistication, ranging from *so the dinosaurs took over the world instead of the people* to the understated and partly inexplicit *Beyond the street party he saw the phone box* of Clare Forster's story.

Clearly, it is interesting to observe the extension of the writers' **lexical range** and **grammatical control** as they get older – we see this in the increasing proportion of polysyllabic and abstract language in the work of the older writers (this could be quantified by simple word counts of, say, frequency of abstract nouns), and also in the development of **syntax** from the basic, extended compound sentences of Thomas Heenan's story to increasingly confident use of complex sentences (as in Suzi Keating's *As the village clock chimed midnight on this special eve, I was with this amazing old man*). In some cases, you may also note the deliberate departure from conventional word order for dramatic effect – interestingly, we find some examples of this even in the youngest writer (as in *down the volcano came big eggs* as opposed to *eggs came down the volcano*).

You might also have noted the increasingly skilful manipulation of language (via repetition, metaphor and other **rhetorical** devices) for deliberate effect. In the younger writers this may be a matter of **word-class** selection (using intensifying verbs, adjectives and adverbs), though we also find some early examples of personification in Dan James's and Suzi Keating's stories. In the older writers, you may have noted Clare Forster's extended use of figurative language with *A chance to build bridges over the troubled waters of teenage years. Bridging the rivers of quarrels and pride . . .*, or the air of expectation generated by the parallelism in Gemma MacInnes's *trees whispered . . . Animals everywhere sniffed the air . . .*

We can also observe variations and developments in the presentation of character, point of view and dialogue, and the acquisition of confidence in the handling of the appropriate verb **tense** and **punctuation** conventions.

Additional research. There is a large body of research into various aspects of the development of children's writing skills into which you should delve when pursuing an investigation in this area (see Further Reading, p.244).

Activity 21. Horror books

Initial observations and suggested analytical methods. There is plenty to consider at the level of text structure. The blurbs may begin with a present-tense sentence which describes the situation from which the story is to develop. Within this situation is contained an apparently innocent detail which is to be the seed for this development – the purchase of a game, a routine outing, the 'dark' history of an otherwise ordinary town. Then the blurbs seem to switch to the problems that develop, referred to in fairly general terms – *trapped in a house of horrors, kids become restless and aggressive, Little by little [Delia] starts to become more like the girl . . . .* The final section of each text looks ahead to some vague, unstated threat or crisis, sometimes by using incomplete sentences punctuated by multiple dots *(And the killer is after her again . . .)* and sometimes by an unanswered question *(Or has he?)*. In each case, the brevity of the final sentence achieves its effect by contrast with what has preceded it. In some cases, this underlying structure – starting from a routine, everyday situation and moving into a darker and threateningly vague crisis – is reflected in the semantic fields and register of the texts. More generally, there is a distinct register which is common to all these texts – *terrible, horrifying, terror, mysteriously, killer, vengeance . . . .*

The blurbs all introduce the main characters of the stories, and encourage immediate familiarity by the use of first **names:** Eddie, Delia, Kaitlyn, Nick, etc. The threat to each of these main characters is sometimes unnamed – the someone whom Eddie hit, the author of Delia's diary, the 'they' who are forcing Kaitlyn into the unspecific 'inside', and even when named the Julian of Extract 2 remains a *gorgeous stranger* and *the Shadow Man*. The threat is, by definition, something or somebody in some way unknown.

You might also notice that traditional syntactic rules are being manipulated for dramatic effect in some of these texts, whether it be the final sentence beginning *And* or the sequence of sentences in Extract 3, beginning *Especially Eddie.*

Additional research. A possible extension of the scope of this investigation could be to compare the nature of such blurbs across different genres – do, for example, the back covers of science-fiction or romance books seem equally formulaic, and what do they have in common with those studied here?

MODULE 5 Editorial Writing

This module counts for 15% of the total A Level marks.

ASSESSMENT OBJECTIVES

The skills and knowledge that you develop and demonstrate in this module are defined by the Examination Board's Assessment Objectives. These require that you:

AO1 communicate clearly the knowledge, understanding and insight appropriate to the study of language, using appropriate terminology and accurate and coherent written expression (5%)

AO2 demonstrate expertise and accuracy in writing for specific purposes and audiences, drawing on knowledge of linguistic features to explain and comment on choices made (7½%)

AO4 understand, discuss and explore concepts and issues relating to language in use (2½%)

This module is organised into the following sections:

- What is editorial writing?
- Working with sources
- Producing new texts
- Some editorial experiments
- Preparing for the examination
- Commentaries

What is editorial writing?

You may find it helpful to refer to much of the material covered in Module 3 of your AS course.

In Module 3 of your AS course; you will have built on the writing skills you brought from your GCSE courses by developing a folder of texts of your own composition. In the course of preparing your Module 3 submission, you will have learned that written texts are usually the result of careful planning, drafting and redrafting. Your experience may also have taught you that very few texts are created out of nothing; in producing texts written to inform, instruct or persuade you will almost certainly have drawn on a number of other sources for the raw material you needed, which you then used to create your own text. This may also have been the case for texts whose primary purpose is to entertain. In fact, 'original' writing is less likely to mean creating something *absolutely* original than doing something genuinely new with pre-existing materials.

Editorial writing embraces every aspect of the process by which a writer exploits this raw material and transforms it to create new and original texts. It is the theory and practice of the writer's craft – these are the same skills that are involved in journalism, report writing, and a thousand other applications. What's more, they are also the skills you need to be a successful student in *any* subject, making effective use of research to produce essays, reports, presentations and other outcomes.

So, by working towards the 'Editorial Writing' module of A Level English Language, you are not only developing further some of the skills you worked on in Module 3; you should also be enhancing your wider study skills and preparing yourself for the demands of Higher Education and professional life.

Ultimately, this module is all about you becoming an apprentice professional writer.

There should also be plenty of opportunities in the module to generate the evidence you need to achieve Level 3 of your Key Skills (Communications) qualification.

When you take the final examination for this module, you will be required to demonstrate your language skills by:

- studying and preparing two substantial booklets of source material on different topics released three days before the examination
- using and transforming the material contained in one of these booklets to create a new text for a specific context, purpose and audience in the examination itself
- writing a brief commentary explaining and evaluating the success of your case study.

This book will focus on the skills you need to develop to complete these tasks successfully, using some sample source materials and activities to do so. The materials you have to work with can cover any topic, and the examples here can only reflect a small selection of the possible subject matter. Some source material with a linguistic theme is also included, in the hope that this may be useful as you pursue your preparations for Modules 4 and 6 of the A2 specification.

However, space does not permit the inclusion of a full-sized set of materials similar in bulk to the very substantial booklets you will need to work with in the final examination. Your tutors will almost certainly have access to exemplars of these and will no doubt use them to provide appropriate practice as you approach the examination.

Activity 1. Producing a text

First, have a look at a few basic principles that apply when you sit down to produce a text – *any* text.

The following chart lists under 'Output choices' some of the principal questions which any writer needs to ask him/herself before producing a text. Your task is to list the various factors which will influence your decisions about these choices in the parallel column, 'Input factors'.

Producing a text

Input factors	Output choices
	Content: what should I include or omit? *In other words, what sort of balance do I need between*: • Serious and lighter material? • Emotional and factual material? • Opinion and information? • Body text and headings, images/graphics? How long should my text be? *Text structure*: how should the text be organised and structured? *Format*: what is the most appropriate arrangement of the text on the page, and its graphological presentation? What are the appropriate *style* and *tone* for my text? *In other words*: • What lexical range and register should I adopt? • What sentence types and structures should I use? • What sort of balance do I need between personal and impersonal features? • What sort of balance do I need between a serious and a light-hearted tone?

Compare your completed chart with the commentary on p.132.

Activity 2. Where do texts come from?

When we read a published text it is easy to take it at face value without realising the extent to which it is the result of the kinds of choices you considered in Activity 1. Equally, you would not normally be aware of the many other source texts that stand invisibly behind the finished article and have provided the writer with his/her raw material.

The diagram below illustrates the way a single text may draw on a number of different sources:

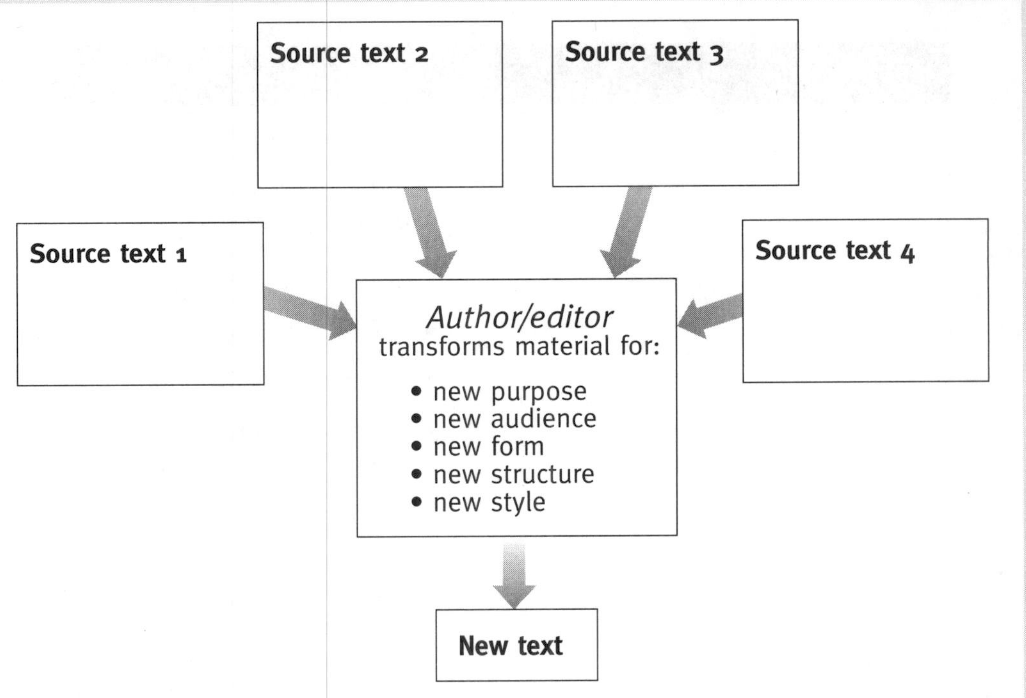

In order to understand how the principles of editorial writing work, you need to apply to some familiar kinds of texts a process which in other spheres is known as **reverse engineering** – deconstructing or working back from the finished products to understand exactly how they have come into being.

To illustrate this with a relatively simple and familiar example, below is a reference produced by a school/college for a student applying for a university place under the UCAS system:

Alison joined this sixth form from a local 11–16 school where she achieved some very sound GCSE results. She was initially uncertain about her career intentions and decided to choose a combination of four AS subjects which reflected her academic strengths and interests, whilst keeping a wide range of options open. She made good progress in three of these, achieving Grade C AS passes in English Language and History, and a D in Sociology, though she narrowly missed achieving an E in Maths. Alison is continuing to make steady progress in her chosen A2 subjects and we expect her to gain Grades C or D in all three (Eng.Lang, History and Sociology). We also expect her to achieve Level 3 on Key Skills Communication, and level 2 in IT and Application of Number.

Alison has developed her analytical skills in all her subject areas; in Sociology she can evaluate research findings and understand their implications, whilst in English Language she has gained a firm grasp of linguistic frameworks and how to apply them. She can also analyse historical problems clearly and make effective use of primary sources. She is able to organise her analysis clearly on paper, though on occasions her work on English has lacked the necessary degree of precision and detail.

Alison's written work is thoughtfully prepared, generally thorough, and clearly presented. She usually maintains a satisfactory level of technical accuracy, though on occasions her subject staff remark that a level of carelessness creeps in. She has however, acquired and uses appropriately the specialist language required, especially in Sociology and English Language. In oral discussions, she is gaining in confidence though is sometimes inhibited from contributing to plenary discussions. Nevertheless, she is certainly capable of clear and articulate speech.

It has been pleasing to note the gradual development in Alison as a student; initially, she was rather hesitant and heavily reliant on her teachers for guidance. However, as she has matured, she has become much more independent, and is now strongly self-motivated. She works well to deadlines and has been very reliable in terms of attendance and commitment. In History, she has taken the opportunity of attending additional lectures as part of the college's History Society. She has worked particularly well on her individual Investigation in English Language, where she has studied and researched aspects of child language.

Alison has worked hard to develop her Key Skills in all areas. Her communication skills are satisfactory, and she has been attending additional IT workshops to extend her skills in this area. Her AS Maths (Statistics) course enabled her to extend somewhat her numerical skills. For her wider Key Skills, as part of the Enrichment programme, she has taken part in a community project assisting old people.

Alison is a pleasant and cooperative student who has made the most of her potential in the sixth form. She can appear a little reserved at first but relates easily to both staff and students, and achieves a sensible balance between college work, her part-time job and her other interests. I am sure she will go on to be a successful student in Higher Education.

(a) What different source texts might the tutor have drawn on to produce this reference?

(b) Look closely at the following extracts from some of these sources. Try to say what the writer has done with this material to create paragraph 2 of the finished text above.

Maths Alison struggled to achieve a basic statistical understanding and found solving problems difficult. Without strong teacher guidance she was seldom able to analyse data effectively.

English Language Alison found the transition to AS work challenging but has now developed an OK grasp of linguistic frameworks and how to apply them. Her written work usually reveals some linguistic insight but is often rather waffly and imprecise as she is slow to make proper use of specialist terminology.

Sociology Alison showed plenty of interest in this subject though at first she trusted to anecdotal rather than properly informed insights. However, now she has shown she has learned how to evaluate research findings and understand their implications.

History Alison's work is usually well organised and clearly expressed, and she has learned to make effective use of primary material to analyse historical problems.

(c) Consider each of the texts in the left-hand column below. In the right-hand column, suggest what sources of raw material a writer might use.

Text	Possible sources
Script for BBC news bulletin	
Prospectus for your school/college	
Feature article about a media celebrity	
An essay you are currently working on in one of your other subjects	

Script for a radio documentary about the sinking of the *Titanic*	
A learning pack for GCSE students about the history of the English language	
This textbook	

Compare your suggestions with those in the commentary on p.133.

Working with sources

Studying your sources

Anyone who has attempted to decorate a room or carry out any other piece of practical DIY will know that the quality of the finished product depends to a large extent on the effectiveness of the preparation. Before painting and wallpapering, you will need to have stripped, cleaned and made good any damaged plasterwork on your walls and ceilings, ensured that you have the appropriate tools and materials to hand, and chosen the right colour schemes etc. in advance.

Similarly, a writer setting out to produce a text must prepare him/herself thoroughly if the text itself is to be successful in achieving its purposes. In editorial writing, this means working very closely indeed with your sources.

In the final examination, you may be confronted with a large collection of apparently chaotic source texts. If you are to make effective use of these, and not be swamped by the material, it is important to approach the task of reading systematically.

It is a good idea to tackle this job by reading/studying the material *three* times:

First reading	Tagging, cataloguing and summarising
Second reading	Detailed evaluation, information extraction and glossing
Third reading	Cross-referencing

First reading: tagging

However many different kinds of source texts you are dealing with, you first need to be clear about exactly what *kind* of material it is. This means that on each source you encounter you need to put a 'tag' noting several key features, as in the panel below:

Know your sources

- where the text has come from
- the medium and genre of the text
- its author
- its date of publication
- its apparent purpose
- its apparent intended audience.

Activity 3. The importance of 'tagging' your sources

Some of this information will usually be obvious – the extracts you find in your pre-release materials, for example, will usually provide the source, author and date of publication – but this may not always be the case in your own researches, and you will certainly have to infer some aspects of a text's purpose and audience.

Before going any further, try to suggest *five* reasons why it is important for any kind of researcher to tag their sources in this way.

Compare your notes with the commentary on p.134.

Activity 4. Black holes

Reproduced below are extracts on the same topic – the cosmological phenomena known as black holes – from four different sources.

(a) Information about the origins of these texts is given at the end of the activity – but not necessarily in the right order. Your first task is to infer from the content and presentation of each text which of these four sources it may have come from.

(b) As you do so, make a note of the textual features that lead you to your conclusions. What differences do you note in the ways each text presents and explains the information, and how might these differences be explained?

Compare your work with the commentary on p.134.

EXTRACT A

Introduction to Black Holes

What is a Black Hole?

A black hole is a region of spacetime from which nothing can escape, even light.

To see why this happens, imagine throwing a tennis ball into the air. The harder you throw the tennis ball, the faster it is travelling when it leaves your hand and the higher the ball will go before turning back. If you throw it hard enough it will never return, the gravitational attraction will not be able to pull it back down. The velocity the ball must have to escape is known as the escape velocity and for the earth is about 7 miles a second.

As a body is crushed into a smaller and smaller volume, the gravitational attraction increases, and hence the escape velocity gets bigger. Things have to be thrown harder and harder to escape. Eventually a point is reached when even light, which travels at 186 thousand miles a second, is not travelling fast enough to escape. At this point, nothing can get out as nothing can travel faster than light. This is a black hole.

EXTRACT B

Black hole, an extremely dense celestial body that has been theorized to exist in the universe. The gravitational field of a black hole is so strong that, if the body is large enough, nothing, including electromagnetic radiation, can escape from its vicinity. The body is surrounded by a spherical boundary, called a horizon, through which light can enter but not escape, it therefore appears totally black.

EXTRACT C

Black Holes

Of all the odd creatures in the astronomical zoo, the 'black hole' is the oddest. To understand it, concentrate on gravity.

Every piece of matter produces a gravitational field. The larger the piece, the larger the field. What's more, the field grows more intense the closer you move to its center. If a large object is squeezed into a smaller volume, its surface is nearer its center and the gravitational pull on that surface is stronger.

Anything on the surface of a large body is in the grip of its gravity, and in order to escape it must move rapidly. If it moves rapidly enough, then even though gravitational pull slows it down continually it can move sufficiently far away from the body so that the gravitational pull, weakened by distance, can never quite slow its motion to zero.

The minimum speed required for this is the 'escape velocity'.

EXTRACT D

Birth of a Black Hole

Black holes are probably the most widely celebrated theoretical prediction of General Relativity. In fact the idea that such objects might exist predates Einstein by over 100 years. Only in this century, however, did the strange behaviour of such objects become fully appreciated. Today they have outgrown mere speculation and become a phenomenon we definitely expect to find in reality, perhaps lurking at the centres of galaxies.

Black holes are the result of a process called gravitational collapse. The atoms of a star are squeezed closer and closer to each other so that the star gets ever more dense – a little like the difference between say, balsa wood and lead. One way in which this could happen is when a giant star explodes violently.

The outer layers of the star are flung off into space. If there is enough material left in the core, it collapses inward to form a small super-dense globe called a neutron star. A single matchbox of it would weigh 100 million tonnes. As a neutron star spins, it beams out rapid bursts of radiation to the universe.

Some neutron stars shrink still further to become black holes. A black hole is an object infinitely small, yet infinitely dense! A black hole bends the fabric of space creating a sort of 'plug-hole' effect. Anything falling inside it is likely, as far as we can tell, to be completely crushed or sucked right out of our universe.

It was originally thought that nothing, not even light, could escape from the gravity of a black hole (hence the word 'black'). Here in Cambridge the physics of black holes was revolutionized when Stephen Hawking, applying quantum mechanics, realized that in fact a black hole must glow gently, slowly radiating its substance away into space at a rate which increases as the black hole shrinks. Hence black holes slowly evaporate. The quantum physics of black holes may also have cosmological implications.

Sources:

- *Faber Book of Science* 1995 (article by Isaac Asimov first printed in the *Daily Telegraph* 1979)
- *The Young Scientist Book of Stars and Planets* (Usborne 1977)
- Microsoft Encarta 98 Encyclopedia
- Cambridge Relativity www.dampt.cam.ac.uk/user/gr/public/bh. Intro.html

First Reading: Cataloguing

As you meet and tag your different source texts you will probably find it useful to keep a record of the key facts about each of them in the form of a text catalogue. Such a catalogue might look something like the one opposite:

Catalogue of source texts

Text	Source/ author	Date	Medium/ genre/form	Images	Subject	Purpose	Audience	Style
1. Give it your own title, if it doesn't have one already			*Is it an article, encyclopedia, etc?*	*Does it include images or diagrams?*	*A one-sentence summary of what it is about*	*Does it seem to be intended to inform, persuade, entertain or instruct – or a mixture of some of these?*	*Can you infer what kind of audience it seems to be designed for?*	*Note the key features of the style of the text – what degree of formality: personal factual/ emotional specialised/ popular*
2. etc								

First reading: summarising

As you read your source material for the first time, you need to be clear about the purpose of this reading. You will certainly return to the material for a much closer look at the detail of its contents, but initially you should be aiming for the **gist** of the piece. You will have to do this in order to give the piece a title, to enter in your Catalogue of Texts – this title should be, in effect, a summary of the contents of the whole piece.

However, you may also find it useful to break down the material into shorter sections and give each one its own short title or summary. This will help reveal the structure of the piece and will also help you to establish a more secure initial grasp of it. In the next activity we suggest an approach to this process.

ACTIVITY 5. *THE TWITTER MACHINE*

In Module 6 one of your main subjects for study will be the development of language in young children. The following article from *The Twitter Machine*, a book about linguistics by Neil Smith, was reproduced in *The Times* newspaper. It considers some of the amusing yet puzzling features of children's early speech, and tries to lead its readers towards an understanding of them.

Read the article for gist and give it your own working title. Apply 'reverse engineering' to the piece:

- suggest what underlying text-structure the writer worked from
- identify no more than half a dozen sections in the piece

- give each section a title, using a table such as the one below. The first one is suggested for you, and the paragraphs have been numbered for ease of reference.

Section	Summary of content (one phrase only)
1	Paras (i) and (ii) raise questions about a child's pronunciation
2	
etc.	

Compare your results with the commentary on p.135.

(i) Amahl was two and, like all very young children, had difficulty pronouncing the words he was learning. Duck came out as 'guck', knife became 'mipe' and his *Magic Roundabout* hero was consistently mangled into 'Gougal'. As a linguist, I was intrigued to work out why my son made these 'mistakes'. Did he have difficulty hearing? Did he need speech therapy? Or were these pronunciations just examples of normal development and open to rational explanation?

(ii) The first task was to discover whether he could hear the differences between the sounds in the adult language. He pronounced many words identically, saying 'mout' instead of both mouth and mouse, for instance. Seeing how hard the French find it to separate such pairs, it seemed likely that he just could not hear the difference. However, when I put pictures of a mouth and a mouse in a different room and asked him to 'bring me the picture of the mouse or mouth' he always fetched the right one.

(iii) So that hypothesis was wrong. At least he could hear perfectly and clearly knew more than his performance indicated. His linguistic 'competence', as the jargon puts it, was only imperfectly reflected in his speech.

(iv) So maybe the reason for his mispronunciation was simply that, like the French, he was unable to get his tongue round some English sounds. This guess turned out to be inadequate, too. There were certainly some sounds he had not learnt to pronounce, but there were some puzzling exceptions. As well as changing Dougal into 'Gougal', Amahl consistency pronounced bottle as 'bockle', pedal as 'pegal' and puddle as 'puggle'.

(v) This was interesting because the change was so regular that his behaviour was clearly rule-governed, not random: knowing that he pronounced zoo as 'doo' and lazy as 'lady' for instance, changing the adult 'z' into 'd' enabled me to predict that he would pronounce puzzle as 'puddle'. As indeed he did. But if he pronounced puzzle as 'puddle' then the reason for pronouncing puddle as 'puggle' clearly could not be that he was simply unable to say puddle.

(vi) And there were other bafflements. I had noticed that he pronounced the 'n' in hand, but left out the 'm' in jump, even though 'm' and 'n' are as close to each other in pronunciation as they are in the alphabet. I asked him to say 'jump; he responded with 'dup'. What did he think he was saying when he told me only I could say 'dup'?

(vii) Moreover, if I presented him with his own pronunciations, he interpreted them as though they were mine. At three, when he was pronouncing both mouth and mouse as 'mout', we had the following exchange:

ME: What does 'mouse' mean?
AMAHL: Like a cat.
ME : Yeah, what else?
AMAHL : Nothing else
ME : It's part of you
AMAHL : (expression of disbelief)
ME : It's part of your head
AMAHL : (expression of fascination)
ME : (touching mouth) What's this?
AMAHL : Mouse.

Only a few seconds later did it dawn on him that they were the same.

(viii) To explain all this we need a theory of the child's linguistic mind. The simplest model would be that in which adult pronunciations are changed into infantile ones by a single set of rules: the adult pronunciation and the child's mental representation are equivalent; this is converted by a set of rules to give the child's pronunciation.

(ix) The rules vary from child to child, but within strict limits. For instance, Amahl's versions of duck and Dougal are examples of 'consonant harmony': 'd' is pronounced in a different part of the mouth to 'ck' and 'g' (try saying them slowly), but the 'g' used instead of 'd' is pronounced in the same part of the mouth. The 'd' harmonises to make things easier.

(x) Consonant harmony is common. The full range of possibilities, what kind of rule can feature in the first model, is largely predicted by linguistic theory.

(xi) Unfortunately, this simplest model does not work. Although Amahl could tell puzzle and puddle apart, there were some adult contrasts between which he simply did not discriminate: puddle and puggle, for example.

(xii) Of course, there is no adult word puggle, so it was hard to tell this at first, but mistakes he made with other words, such as pronouncing pickle as 'pittle', changing 'ck' to 't' rather than vice versa, showed that he had temporary perceptual problems.

(xiii) It was enough, however, to necessitate a change from the first model to a second model, in which perception is accorded an explicit place. In this model, adult pronunciation goes through a perceptual filter to give the child's mental representation, which is then converted by a slightly smaller set of rules to give the child's pronunciation.

(xiv) We can now explain most of Amahl's behaviour. He said 'puggle' for puddle and 'pittle' for pickle as a result of a perceptual difficulty. He said 'guck' for duck and 'mout' for both mouse and mouth not for any perceptual reason but as a result of general (universal) rules which apply in slightly different ways to any child learning any language.

(xv) Finally, to explain what he was thinking when he said 'Only Daddy can say "dup"', we assume that, despite his pronunciation, he could keep the adult pronunciation for jump in mind. As this was the same as his mental representation, it is not surprising. What is surprising is that two-year-olds are so complex and interesting.

Neil Smith, *The Twitter Machine*, Blackwell 1989

We will return to this extract later (see Activity 6, below).

Second reading: understanding and evaluation

Having completed an initial survey of your material, you now need to carry out a more detailed study of the text(s) which are to be your sources. The purposes of this process are:

- to gain a detailed understanding of, and familiarity with the material
- to evaluate the material in terms of its validity and reliability.

Understanding

If you have identified the main sections of a piece of material and summarised it successfully, as in Activity 5 above, you will already have started to gain a fair grasp of the gist of a text. However, to establish the detailed familiarity with the text you will need if you are going to make effective use of its contents, you now need to return to it – and carry out a closer scrutiny, paragraph by paragraph.

ACTIVITY 6. *THE TWITTER MACHINE* – SECOND READING

Go back to the sections into which you broke down the text during your first reading. For each paragraph within each section:

- try to summarise its content with a *three-* or *four-word* label. Note your labels in the margin of the text itself. It is usually best to use your own words for this, though you may find it useful to include a keyword which seems to be central to the paragraph
- use a dictionary to check meanings of unfamiliar words and make an appropriate note on the text. When it comes to your final examination, it is important that you do not neglect this basic task – no writer should ever be in a position of having to use material which s/he does not fully understand.

Compare your work with the commentary on p.136.

Evaluation

As we suggested earlier (see commentary to Activity 3, p.134), any writer needs to be critical in the way they approach a source. How far it can be trusted as a valid source of information may depend on a number of issues. The questions you need to ask about any source are suggested below, along with some of their implications:

When was the text published?	Some information may no longer be accurate; the text may, however, be interesting as an example of how ideas have changed.
Where was it published, and in what form?	A reputable academic source is more reliable; other sources (e.g. anonymously produced Web pages) should be regarded with caution. Extracts may have been selectively edited.
Who wrote it?	Unnamed pieces should be treated carefully; on the other hand, some authors may have a well-known bias on certain issues.
How far does it present judgments and opinions, as opposed to facts?	Remember, bias can be explicit (overt expression of opinion, judgment or persuasion) or implicit (selective use of information, or presenting an interpretation as fact). Other texts may be designed to amuse or entertain, not to be taken literally.
Is it consistent with other sources?	Are any of the facts, interpretations or opinions presented in the text different from those in other texts? What might account for any such discrepancies?

ACTIVITY 7. FACT AND OPINION

The extract below is an account published in 1917 in the British publication, *The War Illustrated.* It tells the story of an engagement that took place at sea during the night of 20–21 April 1917.

As you read the extract:

- suggest any ways in which the context of the piece might make you cautious in approaching the information in the text
- suggest any ways in which you suspect the writer may be over-dramatising, romanticising or sentimentalising the events in this account
- identify those aspects of the text which seem to indicate a degree of bias and subjectivity. You may find it useful to highlight these on the text itself

- suggest any alternative sources you think you would have to consult in order to corroborate the information presented here
- list the most important *facts* you can extract from the text
- use this information to produce a *purely factual* bulletin of no more than 50 words.

ENEMY FLOTILLA SIGHTED & ENGAGED

What was happening out there on the still dark sea? You could make out little from the shore, though some that sailed in ships perceived the lightning-like flashes of the guns and heard a thunder of report. But nothing definite was known, though could the veil have been lifted the play was dramatic enough. For here observe that two British destroyers, the *Swift* and the *Broke*, were at that time – twenty minutes to one o'clock, to be exact – proceeding on a westerly course of their patrol, when lo and behold! out of the darkness there emerged upon the port bow an enemy flotilla of six returning to its 'spiritual home' at the best speed possible. We can imagine the excitement upon our little ships – how every Jack was instantly at his station, how guns were manned, how the quick words of command were uttered. Six hundred yards away there were six German destroyers, their funnels glowing, their engines racing, the line of them magnificent to see. And what a prey was that for a British sailor longing for the adventure – what a splendid hour for the two little ships thus chosen for this surpassing good fortune! Instantly the fray begins. The fire-gongs on board the German destroyers began 'to ripple down the line' while, 'in a blaze of flashes,' the enemy opened fire. As instantaneously, the *Swift* replied; but replying, her commander, Ambrose M. Peck, asked himself a question. Should he ram the leading enemy destroyer, or should he not? He determined to do so, and at his order the wheel was wrenched round and the *Swift*, with every occupant of her bridge temporarily blinded by the flashes, drove straight for the enemy.

Remember, she was plunging forward in the blackest darkness, her speed must have been nearer thirty than twenty knots an hour, and failure might well have sent her to the bottom – since in failing she would have been rammed herself by the second boat in the enemy line. So we can imagine the feelings of her crew when this apparent tragedy overtook her. She did not hit the German destroyer at which she aimed, but by a miracle she herself escaped the threatened fate.

SWIFT TORPEDOES ONE OF THE SIX

Turning like a weathercock, she dashed again at the escaping German – yet not before she had landed a torpedo in her tracks and seen it go home. Unfortunately she missed with her ram for the second time; but while she was mourning her misfortune, her good consort had already launched a torpedo at the second boat in the line, and then had opened fire with every gun. Here began the full fury of these incomparable minutes. Full of flight but not of fight, the German destroyers absolutely glowed with the fires their stokers had fed. Masses of foam swept over their bows as they raced for that pleasant haven of Zeebrugge, which alone seemed able to save them. And to them the *Broke* was clinging always. Holding his course for a moment to gather speed for the blow, Commander E. R. G. R. Evans, C.B., suddenly swung to port at full speed, and rammed the third boat fair and square abreast the after-funnel. Then began that which a commentator has justly said has hardly happened since the days of Nelson. Locked together, the crews of the two destroyers fought with any and every weapon that came to their hands.

Compare your work with the commentary on p.137.

Third reading: cross-referencing

When preparing to produce a text that draws on a number of different sources on a given topic, the final preliminary stage involves tracing the various links between the different pieces of source material. You should find that this process helps you in two key ways:

(i) it will increase your confidence and familiarity with the source texts

(ii) it will enable you to collate related material from different texts rapidly when constructing your new text.

A useful approach to this task is:

Task	Benefits
After the second reading, identify five or six major aspects of the subject which are covered by the various sources you are dealing with. For example, you might break down a set of sources on Formula One Racing into Drivers, Technical developments, Disasters, Venues, and Finance and Sponsorship. Of course, one piece of material can often touch on more than one aspect of the main subject.	• makes the bulk of material more manageable • helps you begin to organise the different possible sub-sections of your eventual piece of writing
Allocate each of these aspects a colour and, as you skim through your sources, use dots/lines of different colours in the margin to indicate which parts of which texts relate to each sub-topic.	• allows you to skim the material quickly when looking for material on a single aspect of the subject
Where two or more texts refer to the same specific piece of information (even if they disagree about it) make a marginal note alongside each referring to the page of the other (e.g. 'see also p.12').	• confirms key facts – or may bring out any discrepancies in the material • can help you make rapid cross-references between two or more texts • can help you organise specific information and avoid possible repetitions

ACTIVITY 8. *TITANIC*

Imagine that you have been commissioned to produce a piece of writing about the sinking of the *Titanic*. There is a lot of material available but you have narrowed down your range of sources to the ones in the table below. Note the brief summary of the contents of each text.

Source material	Contents summary
Letter from passenger posted from on board ship	Account of setting sail; excitement etc.; description of ship
Transcript of interview with survivor (1)	Setting sail; description of conditions on night of wreck; impact of iceberg
Transcript of interview with survivor (2)	Iceberg; getting into lifeboats; rescue by SS *Carpathia*
Extract from official inquiry into disaster (1)	Seeing iceberg; reaction of crew and captain; trying to contact *Californian* by radio
Extract from official inquiry into disaster (2)	Technical explanation/illustrations of design of *Titanic* and why it flooded
British newspaper article published the day before sailing	'Unsinkable' etc.; comparison with sister ship *Olympic*
US newspaper article published the morning after the disaster	Account of rescue of survivors; failure of radio contact with neighbouring ship *Californian*
Two extracts from *The Riddle of the Titanic*, by R. Gardiner & Dan Van Der Vat (published 1995)	• account of design of ship; link to sister ship *Olympic* • was *Titanic* going too fast?
Extract from screenplay of *A Night to Remember* (film about disaster)	Ship's musicians playing on to end; last speech by conductor
Promotional poster for *Titanic* movie	Image of ship used to promote film
Web page from Encyclopedia Titanica	Plans and photographs of ship, exterior and interior

Study the range of content supplied by this material and suggest the five or six categories into which you would group it for cross-referencing purposes.

Compare your suggestions with the commentary on p.138.

You may find that two or more texts conflict with one another – and interpretations of information, opinions and judgments almost certainly will. Take, for example, the two texts in the activity below. They are both offering information on the same subject – the Elizabethan theatre – and on the same aspect of the topic (scenery).

Activity 9. Sources in conflict

As you read the texts, make notes under the following headings:

- In what ways does the factual information contained in the text conflict?
- What differences are there in the interpretation and presentation of the information?
- How might you account for these differences – and how might this affect the way you choose to use these sources when producing a text of your own?

Compare your notes with the commentary on p.138.

Extract A

An absence of scenery, with two doors set symmetrically in the façade, meant that the platform could virtually disappear before the eyes and the scene on stage need not be localized. The absence of scenery also denoted the absence of time, or at least its extreme elasticity, as in the last scene of *Doctor Faustus* where the eleventh hour is made to seem like eternity. Place and time remained unimportant until the one or the other was called for. This might be done by the specific appearance of a character whose location was known, by an indicative prop (a throne, a tomb) set on the stage or by a simple cue line like 'Now, Hal, what time of day is it, lad?'

Even then, some scenes carried a dual location, as in *Richard III* when Richard and Richmond both have their tents on the same stage, and 'simultaneous staging' on the large multi-centered Elizabethan platform could take many forms. An upstage door, or any other solid physical feature of the stage, could unexpectedly be made to seem a realistic item, like the door to Shylock's house in *The Merchant of Venice*, but the neutrality of the empty platform at the same time permitted the unreal make-believe of the folk tale to grow according to a different set of laws, the real and the unreal co-existing. A designated location could also fade into oblivion after it had served its turn, as when Lear's heath dissolves into the symbolic wilderness of his imagination and madness.

The late-Victorian theory of a 'traverse curtain' hung between two pillars and behind which scenery could be changed is now discounted, together with notions of a pattern of 'alternating' scenes devised to make use of it.

None of this means that some *scenic pieces* were not called for on occasion, as they were in the medieval pageant wagon. In Henslowe's *Diary*, the important account books kept by the theatre owner and manager Philip Henslowe for 1592–1602, he kept a note of painted cloths, including a 'city of Rome' for *Doctor Faustus*, scenic props like a mossy bank and 'one cauldron for the Jew' in Marlowe's *The Jew of Malta* and other items of a realistic nature including severed heads and blood in 'bladders' and 'vials' – presumably from a sheep's gather. Even then, these spectacular devices did not necessarily localize a scene or provide scenic illusion: Henslowe's props, touched with residual symbolism though they may be, were the nuts and bolts of practical performance on an empty stage.

The English Stage: A History of Drama and Performance, J. L. Styan, C.U.P. 1996

Extract B

In its employment of scenery, properties and effects the Elizabethan theatre wavered between the plausibly realistic and the naively conventional; wherein it adopted the habit of the theatre at all times. Even the intensely realistic drama of today, so far gone in realism that it pretends that the audience does not exist, rests upon the convention of the 'fourth wall': a convention which the Elizabethans did not contemplate and which is in fact as naïve as any they adopt. In their public theatres the Elizabethans used just so much scenery as the action demanded, and often this was a good deal. It is mistaken to suppose that their stage had its only adornment in a couple of chairs and a table, for at times they went to considerable labour to produce convincingly realistic effects. Ben Jonson, in his lordly way, was contemptuous of these effects. In the Prologue to the revised version of *Every Man In His Humour* he boasted of offering the audience a play

Where neither chorus wafts you o'er the seas,
Nor creaking throne comes down the boys to please;
Nor nimble squib is seen to make afeard
The gentlewomen; nor roll'd bullet heard
To say, it thunders; nor tempestuous drum
Rumbles, to tell you when the storm doth come.

The players not only made ready use of the permanent features of their stage, the posts, and the two doors with their overhanging windows; they had also a large stock of properties and rudimentary scenery. Thus a throne, a table laid for a banquet, the gates of a castle, would be set in the inner stage to give locality to the platform; or a more elaborate effect would be achieved by the use of flats or a painted backcloth, such as Henslowe's 'cloth of the Sun and Moon', or the 'City of Rome' which he had made for *Faustus*. The 'property plot' of some Elizabethan plays must have been remarkably detailed, for an inventory of the properties belonging to the Admiral's Men Henslowe listed, among many others, the following items:

I rock, I cage, I tomb, I hell mouth, I tomb of Guido,
I tomb of Dido, I bedstead, I pair of stairs for Phaeton,
I heifer for the play of Phaeton, the limbs dead.
Phaeton's limbs & Phaeton's chariot, & Argus' head.
Old Mahomet's head.
Kent's wooden leg.
Iris head and rainbow.
I boar's head & Cerberus' iii heads.
I Caduceus; ii moss banks, & I snake.
Bellendon stable; I tree of golden apples; Tantalus' tree.
I chain of dragons.
I lion; ii lion heads; I great horse with his legs.
I wheel and frame in the Siege of London.
I frame for the heading of Black Joan.
I cauldron for the Jew.

This sort of apparatus (much of it costly: for 'poles and workmanship for to hang Absolem' Henslowe paid 'xiii d.') meant that the audience were not expected to piece out all the action in their imaginations.

Shakespeare: his World and his Work, M.M. Reece, Edward Arnold

Producing new texts

In Module 3 of your AS course, you will have researched, drafted and presented some of your own writing. As a result, you should now be able to:

- research your material
- produce a text that is appropriate to its purpose and audience
- research possible style models for the kind of text you aim to produce
- draft and re-draft in the light of editorial advice and testing the text on a sample of its intended audience
- reflect analytically and critically on the writing process in a written commentary.

As you developed your folder of Original Writing the emphasis was on the development of your writing skills in a number of respects, but the choice of subject matter and the type of texts you produced was yours, within the regulations of the specification.

However, in Module 5 of your A2 course, you are placed in the position of having to respond to a commission for a specific type of text designed to do a particular job. This could be a written or spoken text, on any topic, designed for any context and purpose.

The activities in this section are designed to develop the many skills that are involved in the 'production' side of the process. They will often include prompts for a commentary, to encourage you to get into the habit of reflection required to produce the short commentary required in the examination.

a. 'Style Models'

In order to be able to produce a variety of such text types on demand, during your A2 course you need to expose yourself to and investigate a wide range of texts. You need to be aware of the typical forms, conventions, styles and tones of writing that are appropriate in different media and contexts. You will need to build your experience of these 'real world' texts into a mental stock of possible 'style models' upon which you can draw in the final examination.

Activity 10. Surveying style models

This activity should help you begin this process of investigation – but it needs to continue throughout your course.

Below is a list of common genres of text – both spoken and written – which you may be called upon to produce. It is far from comprehensive. For each one, find an example and note its distinctive formal and stylistic features as prompted by the table below.

You could keep adding to this table throughout your course, each time you encounter a new type of text. You may be able to compile a class database of such information, based on the researches of individual students.

	Text	Source/example	Formal features	Key features of tone and style
1	Speech radio documentary programme	Radio 4 is the principal source of such programmes. You will need to understand its conventions. However, other speech radio programmes (e.g. on local radio, schools broadcasts, talk radio, etc.) may use different styles.	What use does it make of: • signature tune and other music? • audio SFX? • 'anchor' in the studio? • other pre-recorded materials?	What level of formality/ Standard English is used? How do the speakers address each other? How do they address their listeners?
2	Popular reference book or encyclopedia	e.g. David Crystal's *Encyclopaedia of the English Language*	How are panels, boxes, graphics and diagrams used to present information, as opposed to continuous text? How does the use of headings/subheadings/bullet points help organise the information? How are technical vocabulary and statistical data introduced?	How does the author convey his fascination for language, and the idea that it is an amusing and interesting subject?
3	Taped commentary (e.g. for visitors to a gallery, exhibition or National Trust property)	Visitors may be offered personal stereos with an audio guide to illuminate their understanding of the exhibits they are viewing.	How do music and SFX enhance the effectiveness? How does the tape incorporate instructions about how to use it at the same time as guiding listeners around the attraction?	What methods are used to make it more interesting than a straight lecture? How many different voices/characters are used?

4	Public Information leaflet	For example, information on aspects of health care, as found in doctors' surgeries.	How do the layout and organisation of the pamphlet allow people to find the information they need? How is it made accessible to a wide range of potential readers?	How does the pamphlet address the readers, if at all? What use is made of illustrations, images? Is the information presented factually, or does it use examples/human case studies?
5	Chapter from a modern school textbook	For example, a chapter on the Romans in a History book aimed at Key Stage 3 pupils.	What use is made of panels, boxes, colours and illustrations?	How is the language tailored to the age of the readers? How, for example, are topic-specific vocabulary and key facts introduced into the text?
6	Script for an illustrated lecture/talk/ presentation	A talk delivered by a teacher to parents on the subject of applying to university.	How does the speaker introduce him/herself and the subject of the talk? How does s/he let the listeners know the structure of the talk – the order in which different parts of the topic are going to be discussed? What use is made of OHT slides/handouts? Is any attempt made to involve the listeners actively in the event? How does it end?	How does the speaker 'break the ice', create humour, and vary the tone and pace of the talk to retain listeners' interest? Does s/he introduce anecdotal stories about individual students?
7	Educational wall chart	A chart displaying the story of the History of English for use in a Key Stage 4 classroom.	What images are used to represent the subject of the chart? How has the information been broken down and organised for visual impact?	How is the language of the text tailored to the age of the readers? How does it avoid seeming too formal?

8	A guidebook to an area or attraction	A guide to your local area and its tourist attractions aimed at visitors to the area.	How is the text structured and organised? (List of contents? Section headings?) How are images used, and how are they captioned?	Does the text address the reader directly ('you . . . ')? Does it tend to 'talk up' the area? How does it offer alternative activities?
9	A 'part work' i.e. a reference work published in weekly or monthly instalments	A monthly magazine devoted to a particular interest or pastime, e.g. angling or computing.	How is the page laid out for visual appeal and effective presentation of information? What use is made of diagrams, images, panels, bullet points etc. to present information and instruction? Does it refer to any previous, or subsequent issues of the part work?	How does the language convey the ideas that (a) the subject is fun and interesting, and (b) developing your skills and knowledge is relatively straightforward?

Some brief notes are included in the commentary on this activity (p.139) – however these are not designed to replace the findings of your own researches.

b. Selecting material

Whatever the overall theme of your source materials, they will include texts relating to different aspects of the topic. As part of your preparation of the material, you will have identified these as five or six sub-sections within the main subject. As an editor or writer, one of your earliest tasks is to decide what kinds of material you are going to use in your new text – and what you are going to omit.

Consider these questions again:

a. What should I include or omit?

b. What sort of balance do I need between:

- serious and lighter material?
- emotional and factual material?
- opinion and information?
- body text and headings, images/graphics?

As with every other editorial consideration, your choices will be driven by these questions:

- what is the major focus or purpose of the new text?

- who are my readers/listeners, and what do they need to know?
- what kinds of material will help me convey this information in an interesting way?

These factors should serve as a kind of editorial filter which will enable you to sift through the different sources.

Activity 11. The history of the English language

The diagram overleaf represents a selection of materials which could be available on the subject of 'The history of the English language.' This topic and some of these source materials will be referred to throughout this section – and also in Module 6 (Language Development).

In studying this topic, you will need to:

- know the main facts about the historical development of English, and the impact of the Roman, Anglo-Saxon, Viking and Norman invasions on its vocabulary, grammar and pronunciation
- know something about the influences of other languages on English, e.g. Latin, Greek, other European languages, and modern US English
- know something about the emergence of Standard English and the concept of Received Pronunciation
- know about more recent twentieth- and twenty-first-century developments in English
- understand the processes whereby changes in the vocabulary, pronunciation and grammar occur
- understand some of the issues involved in linguistic controversies surrounding language variation and change.

Imagine that you have carried out your preparatory readings of the material and sub-classified it by topic. You have also noted the nature of the information (whether it is seriously factual, anecdotally light-hearted, etc.).

Listed below are five different editorial writing outcomes that could be produced from the same set of sources. Your task is to decide which of the materials you would include, and in what proportions.

Sketch your own pie chart for each writing outcome to represent the relative amounts of each type of material you would use.

Commentary: Justify your decision by referring closely to the audience and purpose of each.

Overall subject: The history of the English language

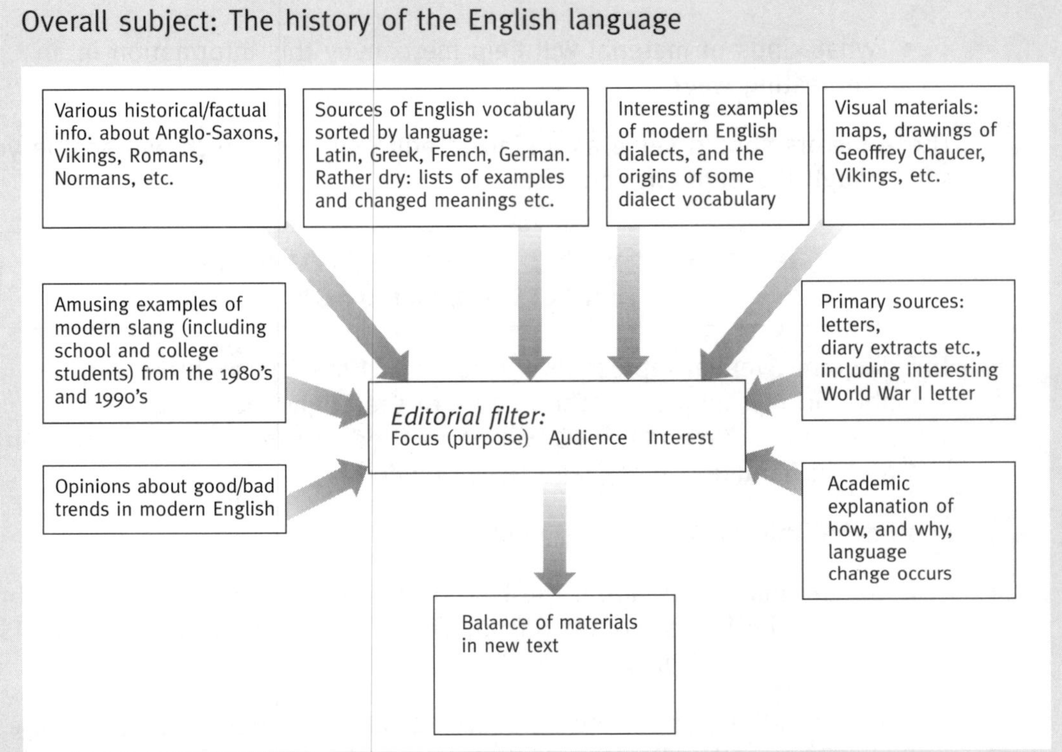

New text (a) An illustrative wall chart for an English classroom in a secondary school.

New text (b) A script for a Radio 4 documentary on the subject of 'our changing language'.

New text (c) A section of a language textbook aimed at A Level students.

New text (d) An article to be included as the introduction to a new edition of a popular dictionary in which you discuss the question of which words to include in the light of the history of English.

New text (e) A website devoted to the study of the English language, aimed at students and anyone with an informed interest in the subject.

Compare your results with the commentary on p.140.

c. Text structure: sequencing and signposting the material

You may find it helpful to refer to the section 'Discourse structure' in *AS Language for AQA B*, pp.13–19.

Once you decide on the 'mix' of contents for your text, the next stage is to decide on an appropriate way of organising and sequencing this material. It is fairly certain that most of your source materials will have been written for a purpose, audience and context very different from the text you are aiming to write. Each individual extract will follow its own structure – whether this is a chronological narrative, a list, a logical series of arguments, a series of questions and answers, or any other kind of discourse structure. The way in which you encounter different pieces of material, whether in your own researches or in the booklet you are given for the Module 5 examination, is likely to be more or less random.

So – your new text has to have a structure of its own – one that you decide is the most appropriate for its purpose, and which you impose throughout the text.

Activity 12. A history of the English language – Which structure?

Think again about the kinds of source material you had in mind for Activity 11. They might lend themselves to a number of different types of structure and sequencing of the material, as listed below.

- for each source, try to suggest some of the advantages and disadvantages of these different structures and sequences
- go back to the four texts proposed in Activity 11. Suggest which structure/sequence you would use for which text, and why.

Structure/sequence	Advantages	Disadvantages	Suitable for texts?
1. Chronological sequence: tell the story of English as a narrative in historical sequence.			
2. Flashback: start with modern English, slang and dialects, then retrace their origins.			
3. Organise the material in terms of the different influences on English, e.g. the influence of Latin, French, US English etc., devoting a section to each one.			

4. Take the ideas from 'Why Language Change occurs' and use each one as a section heading, with appropriate examples from all the material.			
5. Start with a short collection of samples of English from different periods – the primary sources – to raise questions about the language. What changes have there been? How have they taken place? Are they for the better, worse, or neutral? Answer each question in turn.			

Compare your responses with the commentary on p.141.

Signposting your text

Imagine that the reader or listener who receives your text is going on a journey, and you, as the writer, are their driver. When you have chosen your text structure and sequenced your material accordingly, as above, you have, in effect, plotted your route.

However, your passenger has no wish to be blindfolded, or to participate in a 'mystery trip'. On the contrary, they need to know where their journey is leading them, and to be given periodic updates on where they are now and what direction they will shortly be following to order to arrive at their destination. Besides, in some cases, your readers may wish to find their way directly to one part of the text – and without your help, they would be doomed to read through every word before finding the information they require.

We may refer to the ways in which writers flag up the underlying structure and direction of a text as **signposting**. Once you have decided on your structure and sequence you will need to consider what form this signposting is likely to take.

Activity 13. Signposting survey

Carry out a survey of a range of different texts – some suggested examples are given below, but don't limit yourself to these. Remember, you could be called upon to produce a text of any type in the examination. Note the different kinds of signposting devices used in each.

Written texts		Spoken texts	
Text type	*Signposting features*	*Text type*	*Signposting features*
Informative pamphlet		Lecture, talk or presentation	
Feature article in a Sunday supplement		Radio programme	
Chapter from this textbook		Audio-tape guide	
Web page		Charity appeal	

Compare your survey with the suggestions in the commentary on p.142.

d. Text formats

Written texts

In the Module 5 examination you will not be expected to produce your own elaborate art and design work as part of your text, and you should certainly not waste your time drawing fine detailed illustrations in multicoloured splendour. However, you *are* expected to show that you have visualised what the finished product would actually look like, and to have taken this into account as you write your text.

You should be able to indicate your intentions for the major design features of your written text via notes/sketches to the editor (see Preparing for the Examination, p.126 below).

Activity 14. Survey: written text formats

As we suggested earlier (see Activity 10, above) your preparation for the Module 5 examination should involve a good deal of surveying and studying different kinds of texts. Here, you should focus on how such features vary according to the nature of the text, its purpose and its audience:

	Text:	Text:	Text:	Text:	Text:
Page size May vary from poster size down to postcards; may have a landscape or portrait orientation, or be folded into a gatefold format.					

Column width A page may be a single block of text, or be broken down into columns/panels of different widths					
Text : white space ratio An important feature of readability can be the amount of white space on a page. Notice how such space is used – at the margins and in the body of the text					
Text : image ratio Another important ratio. What kinds of text favour a higher proportion of image space?					
Headings : size, type and frequency Note the ways in which these are used to break up and label sections of text					

Spoken texts

If you are producing text which has to be spoken, you should write your script to the following format:

Voice/speaker	Text	Music/SFX
Male or female? Age (approx.)? Accent? Tone of voice?		Specify as far as possible any music or sound effects to be used. Give timings in seconds. Indicate fade up, fade down, etc.

Activity 15. Spoken text survey

Record and listen to some examples of speech texts. Note how the use of voices, text and music/SFX vary according to the nature of the programme, the source and the audience. Some suggestions are offered below.

Feature	Presentation/ lecture	Radio 4 documentary	Audio-tape instructional guide	Radio 5 documentary	Other
How many voices? Gender? Age? Accent?	*(Can you think of an example where more than one presenter was used?)*				

If more than one, how rapid is the interchange between them?					
What kind of music/SFX are used? How frequently?					
Is the spoken text supported by any written products (handouts, illustrations, etc.)?					

e. Your new text: writing and rewriting

This is the nitty-gritty of editorial writing: rewriting and re-presenting the material of your sources in ways that are appropriate to your new text. You know the kinds of information you are going to use, and you have chosen to sequence and organise the information in a particular way. You have imagined and designed the appropriate format. All you have to do now is write the text.

Activity 16. Editing options

Imagine that you have identified a passage from your source material which contains information you have decided to use. What do you do with this material? In general, you have five options, listed below. For each one, consider its possible advantages and problems. Some suggestions are included in the table.

Editing text: your options

Option	Advantages	Problems
1. **Summarise** the extract – compressing its content to the minimum, using your own words.		It takes time and skill to achieve an effective summary without distorting or omitting important/relevant aspects of the text.
2. **Paraphrase** the extract – essentially rewriting it entirely in your own words.		Takes time and skill.

3. **Edit** the extract – using essentially the same text but cutting out what you don't need and/or changing occasional words/phrases as required.	A fairly quick way of using the material.	
4. Include it all, but **present it as a quotation** by identifying its original author and source. (In audio texts, you would be able to make this clear by giving it to a different speaker.)		This may be easier to handle than Option 1, but it may not always be appropriate to quote a text directly. It is only worth quoting if it comes from an interesting source, or says something better than you could yourself. Even a quotation needs to be intelligible to your readers/listeners.
5. **Cut and paste** the entire passage and 'absorb' it into your own text.	May save time.	

Compare your results with the commentary on p.143.

Activity 17. Editing skills in practice

In the course of producing a new text for Editorial Writing, it is likely that you will, at some points, need to exploit all of these possibilities. Each of them requires specific writing skills and the following activities will focus on these.

Now imagine that you are working on the tasks outlined in Activity 11 (above), relating to the history of English. Reprinted below are some extracts from four pieces of your source material.

First, read and prepare the materials as recommended in the 'Working with sources' section of this module (pp.79–93 above).

Then suggest, for the three outcomes ((a)–(c)), whether you would find the material relevant, and if so, which would be the most suitable editorial option.

Record your decisions on the table below, and add a commentary in which you give your reasons.

Text outcome	Extract	Preferred editing options	Comments
An illustrative wall chart for an English classroom in a secondary school	a		
	b		
	c		
	d		
A script for a Radio 4 documentary on the subject of 'Our Changing Language'	a		
	b		
	c		
	d		
A section of a language textbook aimed at A Level students	a		
	b		
	c		
	d		

Compare your results with the commentary on p.243.

EXTRACT A

Is our language sick? You might think so, judging from complaints: 'The standard of speech and pronunciation in England has declined so much . . . that one is almost ashamed to let foreigners hear it', moaned a writer in a daily newspaper. 'The language the world is crying out to learn is diseased in its own country', ranted another. 'We are plagued with idiots on radio and television who speak English like the dregs of humanity, to the detriment of our children', lamented yet another.

But why? At a time when English is a major world language, is it really in need of hospital treatment? A wide web of worries, a cobweb of old ideas, ensnares people as they think about language – any language, and this must be swept away.

Naturally, language changes all the time. This is a fact of life. In the fourteenth century

Geoffrey Chaucer noted that 'in forme of speche is chaunge' – language changes – and the same is true today. But change is one thing. Decay is another. Is British English really changing for the worse, as some people argue?

Of course it isn't. Over a hundred years ago, linguists, those who work on linguistics, the study of language – realised that different styles of language suit different occasions, but that no part of language is ever deformed or bad. People who dispute this are like cranks who argue that the world is flat. Yet flat-earth views about language are still widespread. As the Swiss linguist Ferdinand de Saussure said over seventy-five years ago: 'no other subject has spawned more absurd ideas, more prejudices, more illusions or more myths.' Things haven't changed very much since then.

Jean Aitchison, 'The Language Web' the 1996 Reith Lectures, broadcast on Radio 4 in 1996

EXTRACT B

A language all of its very own

English is a magpie among languages, stealing words from all over the world. But what was once a hotchpotch of local dialects has grown into an internationally understood tongue, Standard English.

Most of us think of language as a product, like something you buy in a supermarket. We use words for our convenience without giving any thought to how they arrived. But nowadays when we buy something from a shop, we all want to look at the list of ingredients. We want to know where things come from and the effect they will have on the world around us. The more you know about a product, the more control you have over your environment. The same is true of language. The more you know about it the more you can control it.

The dawn of English

500 BC–AD 1066

About 2,500 years ago a tribe called the Celts arrived in the British Isles. They came from Europe and spoke a language we now call Celtic. Many places in Britain still have the names that were given to them by the Celts. Look for names ending in *combe* or *comb*, such as Ilfracombe in Devon or Winchcomb in Gloucestershire. A *cumb* was the Celtic word for a deep valley.

By the time the Romans invaded in 55 BC a number of Celtic languages had developed. For the next 500 years the Romans tried hard to take over the country and its language. They did not succeed. Even now Celtic survives in Wales, Ireland, and Scotland and, until quite recently, in Cornwall.

The Romans spoke a language called Latin. They built camps in various parts of Britain. Many of the towns which grew up around those camps still have the Roman word for camp – *castra* – in their names. In many cases this has been changed to *chester* or *cester*.

A great many Latin words found their way into the English language, either at this time or later: words such as *indicate, connect, attract* and *substitute*. The word Englaland, later shortened to England, started to be used in about AD 1000. By now several new groups of people had invaded. The best-known of the invaders were the Angles and the Saxons. We call the language which they spoke Anglo-Saxon or Old English.

If you could go back in time and listen to the Anglo-Saxons speaking you would find it very difficult to understand but you might recognise the odd word here and there, for example: *eat, sleep, drink, son, sister.*

The *Young Guardian* supplement, 13 November 1990

EXTRACT C

Old English

29. The languages in England before English

We are so accustomed to think of English as an inseparable adjunct to the English people that we are likely to forget that it has been the language of England for a comparatively short period in the world's history. Since its introduction into the island about the middle of the 5th century it has had a career extending throughout only about 1500 years.

The first people In England about whose language we have definite knowledge are the Celts. It used to be assumed that the coming of the Celts to England coincided with the introduction of bronze into the island. But the use of bronze probably preceded the Celts by several centuries. We have already described the Celtic languages in England and called attention to the two divisions of them, the Gaelic or Goidelic branch and the Cymric or Britannic branch. Celtic was the first Indo-European tongue to be spoken in England and it is still spoken by a considerable number of people. One other language, Latin, was spoken extensively for a period of about four centuries before the coming of English. Latin was introduced when Britain became a province of the Roman Empire. Since this was an event that has left a certain mark upon later history, it will be well to consider it separately.

A. Baugh & T. Cable, *A History of the English Language*, Routledge 1951

EXTRACT D

Language Change

The phenomenon of language change probably attracts more public notice and criticism than any other linguistic issue. There is a widely held belief that change must mean deterioration and decay. Older people observe the casual speech of the young, and conclude that standards have fallen markedly. They place the blame in various quarters – most often in schools, where patterns of language education have changed a great deal in recent years (see S.44). but also in state broadcasting institutions where any deviations from traditional norms provide an immediate focus of attack by conservative, linguistically sensitive listeners. The concern can even reach national proportions, as in the widespread reaction in Europe against what is thought of as the 'American' English invasion.

The Inevitability of Change

For the most part, language changes because society changes (see S10.) To stop or control the one requires that we stop or control the other – a task which can succeed to only a very limited extent. Language change is inevitable and rarely predictable, and those who try to plan a language's future waste their time if they think otherwise. These days, there is in fact a growing recognition of the need to develop a greater linguistic awareness and tolerance of change, especially in a multi-ethnic society. This requires, among other things, that schools have the knowledge and resources to teach a common standard, while recognising the existence and value of linguistic diversity.

David Crystal, *The Cambridge Encyclopaedia of Language*

ACTIVITY 18. SUMMARY AND PARAPHRASING

Summarising involves compressing the information content of a text into as few words as possible. It is an important skill for editorial writing, and it is one you do need to practise.

Suppose you are working to a very tight word limit at a particular point in your new text, and you need to compress the content of Extract B to just 70 words.

You will need both to be highly selective in your identification of the key facts, and to compose your sentences skilfully to stay within this limit.

Compare your 70 words with the example in the commentary on p.144.

A summary is, of course, a special kind of paraphrase – though a paraphrase need not necessarily be any shorter than the original text. If, for example, the source text is rather dense, and contains a lot of specialist vocabulary, you may need to offer a rather *longer* paraphrase to explain points more explicitly.

When paraphrasing or summarising, however, you are not just extracting the information most relevant to your new text; you are also immediately confronted with these basic questions about your approach to the material you are working with:

- What are the appropriate register, tone and style for my new text?
- What is the best way of presenting information in this text?

You can only answer the first of these questions by referring to your audience, your subject and the context in which your text will be produced and consumed – and your own experience of similar style models in the 'real' world. However, some useful stylistic points to consider are listed below. Use the final column to note examples you find in the four extracts above, or as part of your wider survey of texts.

The right style?

Stylistic feature	Effect	Guidelines	Example
Use of first person singular (*I, me*)	Introduces personality of narrator/speaker/author. Personalises and achieves some informality.	Fairly common in speech texts, though be careful not to overdo this – it can make the speaker, rather than the subject, the focus of attention. Less common in informative written texts, unless the writer wishes to draw attention to him/herself.	
Use of first person plural (*we, us*)	Can either refer to a kind of corporate identity (*We at Ainsley Manor Hotel hope you'll have a pleasant stay*) or to a group to which both writer and audience belong. Also used in more academic texts (*As we have already seen . . .*).	Useful in some spoken and written texts in helping to personalise the tone without going all the way to the exposure of the first person singular. Can feel patronising in large doses (*We don't want to catch cold, do we?*).	
Direct address of readers and listeners as *you*	Helps establish a relationship between writer and audience, and involves audience from the start.	Very useful if giving direct instruction or guidance. Tends to be compatible with texts in an informal and semi-formal register. Some more formal texts may avoid this, along with first-personal pronouns	
Light-hearted/ joking remarks	Can be a good ice-breaker in spoken texts, but getting the tone right is very difficult in writing.	Be cautious here. If you are confident that you have a 'feel' for the audience you are aiming	

		at, go ahead if the text seems to require some informality and lightness of touch. Otherwise, play it straight!	
Colloquial language, slang and other spoken language features	Features such as rhetorical questions, mild slang, and common idiomatic language are often used in spoken texts to create the illusion of spontaneous speech. Even some less formal written texts strive to *feel* as if they are being spoken to the readers, and these features can help do this.	Another area for caution. Spoken texts are likely to feature some of these, but don't overdo it. Achieving a lively, semi-formal style in a written text can be trickier. As with the humour, err on the side of caution.	
Passive voice structures	Tend to create a feeling of formality (e.g. *Laws were passed and people were forbidden to go out at night*). Also contribute to a text's 'difficulty' rating more than their active equivalents (*The government passed curfew laws and stopped people from going out at night*).	They can sometimes be a useful solution to the problem of not wanting to immediately identify the subject of an action (*The chair had been broken. The porridge had been eaten. The bed was being slept in. And Goldilocks was in it.*) However, they can also lead to some clumsy writing. If aiming for a lighter, more accessible style, perhaps avoid passives unless used for a particular reason.	

The right register: glossing

In trying to gauge the appropriate register for your new text, you will be aiming to control your sentence length and structures and your lexical range. One particular challenge is knowing what kinds of specialised vocabulary and other specific references you can introduce into your text – and the kinds of introduction you need to accompany them with.

ACTIVITY 19. NAMES AND REFERENCES

(i) To explore this problem, first take a couple of names with which most people will be familiar. Imagine that you are writing a text in which the names Shakespeare, Paris and Eminem are used. How do you refer to these in the text? The answer will depend on how much prior knowledge your intended audience has. Consider each of the glossing options listed below, and suggest in the 'Comment' column what kind of prior knowledge each one implies for its readers/listeners.

Technique	Shakespeare	Paris	Eminem	Comment
Common name only	Shakespeare	Paris	Eminem	
Full name	William Shakespeare	Paris, France	Eminem	
Familiar/nickname only	Will	Gay Paris		
Full name preceded by definite article and explanation	The playwright William Shakespeare	The capital of France/ home of fashion/ etc. Paris	The rap artist Eminem/ the pop singer Eminem	
Full name preceded or followed by indefinite article + explanation	A playwright called William Shakespeare	A city in France called Paris	A singer called Eminem	
Full name preceded by indefinite article + less specific explanation	A man called William Shakespeare	A place called Paris	A man who calls himself Eminem	

(ii) Now consider the wider question of using specialist and advanced vocabulary. Extract B, for example, has the word 'dialect', and Extract C has the phrase 'an inseparable adjunct'.

If you intend to paraphrase or summarise either of these extracts, you will need to decide what to do with these items. Your options are summarised below. For each of them, suggest in the 'Comment' column the circumstances in which each option might be appropriate. Which would be appropriate for each of the writing tasks you have been considering?

Glossing lexical items: options

Method	Dialect	Inseparable adjunct	Comment
Use 'straight'	A hotchpotch of local dialects	. . . as an inseparable adjunct to the English people	
Use with some contextual explanation	A hotchpotch of regional varieties, or dialects	. . . as part and parcel, an inseparable adjunct we might say, ...	
Use with explicit definition/explanation	A hotchpotch of regional varieties of vocabulary and grammar, which we call **dialects**.	. . . as part and parcel of the English people. This is what is meant by 'inseparable adjunct'	
Avoid the term and paraphrase more simply	A hotchpotch of different regional speech	. . . as part and parcel of the English people	

(iii) Listed below are some more examples from the four extracts of (a) the introduction to the text of names/places/titles, and (b) the use of topic-specific and other advanced vocabulary.

For each of them, identify which, if any, glossing technique has been used, and suggest how this has helped create a register appropriate for the audience of each text.

Text/audience	Reference	Vocabulary
Extract A Radio 4 listeners	Geoffrey Chaucer. The Swiss linguist Ferdinand de Saussure	Linguists, those who work on linguistics, the study of language.
Extract B *Young Guardian* readers (13–18?)	A tribe called the Celts. A language we now call Celtic. The Romans spoke a language called Latin.	Dialects.
Extract C University students of English and other students of academic subjects.	The Celts. Celtic was the first Indo-European tongue to be spoken in England.	It used to be assumed that the coming of the Celts to England coincided with the

		introduction of bronze into the island.
Extract D General; educated readers with an interest in language.		The phenomenon of language change. The focus of attack by conservative linguistically sensitive listeners. The existence and value of linguistic diversity.

A note on presenting information: analogies, statistics and graphics

Sometimes you will find factual information in source material which could be presented more accessibly. In the case of the four extracts above, for example, we are given a number of dates. Elsewhere, you may encounter various kinds of statistical information.

When re-presenting such material you should consider some alternatives to continuous prose. Some of these are suggested below.

Analogies introduce or explain new ideas by making an interesting comparison to something your readers/listeners will recognise. In Extract B, for example, the notion of English 'borrowing' words from other languages is conveyed by comparing it to a magpie. The next section of this textbook will try to explain the notion of textual cohesion by comparing a text to a piece of fabric.

Statistics in their raw state are not always particularly meaningful. Instead, consider presenting statistics as charts – **pie charts, bar charts** – or by using other **graphic symbols**. Where your material has a chronological emphasis on a sequence of events, a **time line** can be useful. Even if using continuous prose, translating raw data into small numbers ('three out of every four people admit to drinking too much') or into 'real' images ('if the spaghetti we eat each month was put end to end it would go round the world three times') can be more effective than just saying '100,000 tons of spaghetti are consumed every year'.

ACTIVITY 20. REWRITING EXERCISES

Now try out all of these ideas (summarising, paraphrasing, glossing and presenting information) by rewriting any, or all, of Extracts A–D for one or more of the tasks originally set out in Activity 11 above.

Editing, quoting and cut and paste

You may find it useful to refer to the section on cohesion and coherence in Module 4, pp.20–23. That section focused on how a text achieves fluency, consistency, direction and structure – in other words, **cohesion** – and established that a cohesive and coherent text has:

- an underlying plan and structure
- logical connectors and other signposts that make the structure apparent
- stylistic consistency
- grammatical connectors that form links within and between sentences
- lexical and semantic connectors that form chains of meaning throughout a text.

One of the biggest challenges of editorial writing is to ensure that the new text you create has all these characteristics.

To use a commonly cited analogy, if you think of the new text as a new garment made from a number of different materials, the result should not appear to be a patchwork of different colours and fabrics roughly sewn together, but a smooth, seamless cloth betraying nothing of the different raw materials from which it has been fashioned.

You should bear this in mind constantly as you compose and 'sew together' the different sections of your text, but when you opt to edit, quote or cut and paste sections of source material, it is particularly important to focus on the need to achieve cohesion.

Editing can be a useful way of cutting out those parts of an extract which are less relevant to your needs – for example, to remove references such as 'see page 36' which do not apply to your new text. However, you do need to make sure the passage still coheres *after* your cuts!

Quoting can be a useful way of dealing with texts that are obviously subjective, opinionative or out of date. It enables you to present the ideas and information in an extract whilst keeping it at a distance. However, make sure you introduce the quotation in such a way that it is clear what it is referring to. For example, if you wished to quote from Extract A: 'Is our language sick?', you would usually need to add:

'asked Jean Aitchison in her 1996 Reith Lectures, when referring to the many popular complaints about declining standards in English'

Cut and paste can sometimes seem an attractive option when you find a significant chunk of source material that you feel can be used more or less as it comes. However, it is fraught with dangers and should only be used if you are absolutely confident that it can be assimilated smoothly into the flow and style of your new text.

ACTIVITY 21. SPOT THE JOIN!

Some of the problems associated with editing and cut and paste are illustrated below in an extract from a student's draft of a proposed article entitled 'Recent Developments in Modern English'.

The writer has been editing material from a number of different sources – but how successful has s/he been in stitching them together to create a truly seamless text?

(i) Read the extract and decide:

- how many separate pieces of text have been stitched together here
- what the problems are with the text's cohesion as it stands.

The key aspects of cohesion on which you should focus are:

- stylistic consistency
- logical connectors
- lexical/semantic cohesion
- grammatical cohesion.

Recent Developments in English (draft)

If the English language could have its own emblem, it ought to be the magpie. The magpie is a bird that steals any bright thing that takes its fancy and brings it back to its nest.

Of course not all these new items will be widely intelligible. In the late 1980s, alongside intifada, perestroika and glasnost we find prhyzhok (Russian, 'leap'), visagiste (French, 'beautician'), and zaitech (Japanese 'large-scale company financial speculation') all found in English newspapers and periodicals. Several of the items in the world map are of this recondite character, requiring an up-to-date dictionary before one can be sure what they mean. (see Chapter 3, above)

So how did he see this argument being resolved? As we have seen, every new stage in the development of English has provoked the same questions: does change mean revitalisation, or does it mean corruption and deterioration? English is in a constant state of renewal.

So, all of you out there take a look around and keep your ears wagging for some cool new words – they may just be the language of the future!

Compare your suggestions with the commentary on pp.144.

(ii) Rewrite the text in a style appropriate for A Level students, ironing out the creases – to return to our textile analogy – in the text. Some of the problems have been highlighted to help you make a start.

f. Headings and captions

When you produce your new text you are also responsible for creating your own headings/headlines and sub-headings and captions for any images or diagrams you use.

We have already considered the importance of headings and sub-headings as textual signposts in many kinds of written texts; however, their style and type will vary according to the general style of the text you are aiming to produce.

All images or diagrams in a text should usually have a caption attached. Once again, it is extremely unlikely that the original caption you find attached to an image in a piece of source material will be suitable for your text.

Headings

Headings and sub-headings may be designed to:

- **signpost** the text by giving a simple summary of the text to which they refer
- **attract** readers by making the subject of the text sound dramatic
- **amuse** readers by clever word-play
- **make the text memorable** by using recognizable catchphrases.

Activity 22. Headings

Consider the following sets of headings, each of which was used in a different text about the history of English. Suggest what kinds of text/audience they would, or would not, be appropriate for, and how effective they are.

Section of text	Set 1	Set 2	Set 3
The history of English – text as a whole	Our changing language	The History of English	Whose English?
Recent developments in English	All Change!	Current developments	Is English changing right now?
The impact of the Norman invasion of 1066	One in the Eye	The coming of the Normans	Who were the Normans? How did they change English?
The variety of English dialects and where they come from	Ecky thump! Tha's talkin' Viking, tha' knows!	Dialects and their origins	Why do people in different regions talk differently?

Compare your suggestions with the commentary on p.145.

Extension activity

Survey and analyse a range of headings/headlines from different kinds of texts. Look at the way word-play, figurative language, and quotations from popular catchphrases, song/film titles and other sources are used.

This could also provide the material for a language investigation for Module 4.

Captions

An image by itself may be seen in different ways, or may have several potential meanings. As the writer of the text, you wish the image to be read or understood in a particular way. For this reason, captions are sometimes referred to as 'anchoring' the images to which they refer. Any images in your source materials are likely to have captions already – but these are, of course, unlikely to be suitable for your new text.

ACTIVITY 23. CAPTIONS

Examine the image reproduced opposite, one of the most famous of the twentieth century. It shows American astronaut Buzz Aldrin photographed on the surface of the moon in 1969 by his commander, Neil Armstrong, who had earlier been the first man to step onto the surface.

Look at the table overleaf. On the left are five kinds of text in which this image might appear – on the right are five captions to accompany the image.

- match up the text with the appropriate caption
- suggest alternative captions for additional texts 6–9 in which the photo could appear.

Texts	Captions
1. A modern encyclopedia of the twentieth century for young readers	(a) Neil Armstrong snapped fellow astronaut Buzz Aldrin in this famous shot. Neil's reflection can just be made out in Aldrin's visor.
2. A book on the subject of modern English aimed at school/college students	(b) One giant step . . . This photograph, snapped by Neil Armstrong on the moon in 1969, was to became one of the defining images of the century.
3. A biography of Neil Armstrong	(c) Smile please . . . but this snap cost billions. Was it worth it?
4. An exhibition of memorable photographs called *The Twentieth Century in Pictures*	(d) American astronaut Buzz Aldrin photographed by Neil Armstrong during their historic moon landing of 1969.
5. An article critical of the resources spent on space exploration	(e) The first man on the moon was American and the first language heard in outer space was English. Buzz Aldrin is photographed by mission skipper Neil Armstrong.

Additional texts

6. A chapter in a book entitled *Famous Conspiracies* which suggests that the moon landings were faked in an American film studio.

7. Buzz Aldrin's autobiography.

8. A preview in TV listings of a programme about space exploration to be broadcast this evening.

9. An article in a young men's magazine about the possibility of space flights soon becoming available to members of the public.

Compare your suggestions with the commentary on p.146.

g. Opening and closing

Getting a text started – and finished – can often seem the trickiest part of all. It is too easy when planning a text simply to write down 'introduction' and 'conclusion' as a substitute for careful thinking about the best ways of leading your readers/listeners into and out of the text.

Activity 24. Openings

Examine the three examples of text openings below. Identify those features that make each one effective, in its own way, as an opening.

Extract A. Pamphlet, 'Exploring Pennine Countryside by Train', published by Northern Spirit Train Company

Take the train and discover the delights of the Pennine Countryside and Lancashire's Hill Country

The train journey from Leeds and Bradford through Lancashire's Hill Country to Blackpool and Manchester has become known as 'The Pennine Leisure Link'.

Passing through the stunning scenery of the Calder Valley, stopping at fascinating towns such as Hebden Bridge, Halifax, Mytholmroyd, Littleborough, Sowerby Bridge and Todmorden, the train offers easy access to the surrounding hills valleys and moors.

Extract B. Opening of Chapter 1 of *Words and Rules* by Stephen Pinker, a popular science book about language and the human brain

The Infinite Library

Language comes so naturally to us that it is easy to forget what a strange and miraculous gift it is. All over the world members of our species fashion their breath into hisses and hums and squeaks and pops and listen to others do the same. We do this, of course, not only because we like the sounds but also because details of the sounds contain information about the intentions of the persona making them. We humans are fitted with a means of sharing our ideas, in all their unfathomable vastness. When we listen to speech, we can be led to think thoughts that have never been thought before and that never would have occurred to us on our own. Behold, the bush burned with fire, and the bush was not consumed. Man is born free, and everywhere he is in chains. Emma Woodhouse, handsome, clever, and rich, with a comfortable home and happy disposition, seemed to unite some of the best blessings of existence. Energy equals mass times the speed of light squared. I have found it impossible to carry the heavy burden of responsibility and to discharge my duties as King without the help and support of the woman I love.

Extract C. The script for the opening of an audio-guide tape for people visiting the ruins of Blackstone Abbey

Voice/speaker	Text	Music/SFX
		Medieval choral music – monks singing plainsong
Brother Francis (male, middle-aged, slight west-country accent)	Hello, and welcome to Blackstone Abbey. My name is Brother Francis, and I was a member of the brotherhood of Franciscan monks here when the Abbey was in its	5 seconds, then fading and continuing under voice

heyday. Yes, life was very different then. I hope you'll enjoy your visit today – and as you look around the ruins of what used to be our community, let me be your guide. I'll show you round, and perhaps you'll be able to imagine the glories of the Abbey, as they were when I was alive.

Compare your analysis with the commentary on p.146.

Extension activities

You may like to extend this survey to include a wider variety of texts. Such a study could even become the material for your language investigation (see Module 4).

Carry out a similar survey of the way different kinds of text are closed. Look out for final sentences which ask questions, sum up using a list of three, or use a balanced antithesis (see *AS Language for AQA Spec. B*, pp.74–75.)

Some editorial experiments

In this section, we include some material and suggested activities to develop your editorial writing skills on a manageable scale before attempting the full-size tasks required by the examination.

Activity 25. Black holes

Turn back to the extracts on this topic on pp.81–82 above, and refamiliarise yourself with the contents.

Channel 4 is to run a programme about black holes. You have been asked to produce the script for a 30-second trailer for the programme. Using the extracts as the sole source of your information, *in no more than 100 words*, produce a script that will persuade the audience to tune in and watch the programme.

Commentary:

- Justify your selection (and omission) of material.
- Say how and why you have changed the written language of the originals to the scripted speech of the new text?
- Say how you have tried to interest and persuade the audience?

Activity 26. Biographical blurbs

The text below is a 'blurb' for a biography of the poet and engraver, William Blake. It appeared on the back cover or inside the fly-sheet of a book:

Four years after his innovative masterpiece, *Dickens,* Peter Ackroyd presents us with his imaginative and eagerly awaited biography of William Blake.

Born in 1757, the son of a London hosier, Blake was one of England's most fascinating and original sons. Poet, painter, engraver and visionary, his was a radical spirit fired by genius. Yet his life has remained an enigma, with much of his poetry unknown to the general reader and his art only properly studied by scholars and art historians.

Now, Peter Ackroyd discloses the true nature of Blake's life and art. He traces his progression from early childhood in a Dissenting household, through his apprenticeship as an engraver and his studies at the newly formed Royal Academy Schools, to his full maturity when he produced the masterpieces upon which his reputation rests – works such as *Jerusalem*, *Milton* and *Songs of Innocence and of Experience*, works that were as neglected during his lifetime as they are celebrated today.

But we also see Blake in the context of his period; caught up in the Gordon Riots, excited by the French Revolution, being tried for sedition during the Napoleonic wars, attracted to various forms of spiritual radicalism and sexual magic. He was a man whose faith in the eternal world of the spirit was fiercely mocked and attacked by those who were attracted to the prevailing belief in scientific rationalism. Yet he remained true to his own vision of the world, a vision that is wonderfully confirmed in all of his work.

This is the first biography to reveal the true affinities between Blake's art and his poetry; in the magnificent biographical narrative we see Blake as a Cockney visionary and a London tradesman, as a prophet and an artisan. In the course of Blake's history, Peter Ackroyd brilliantly recreates eighteenth-century London in a manner of which only he is capable. *Blake* is the work of a major writer at the height of his powers.

(i) Define the characteristic features of such a 'blurb' in terms of its purposes, its structure and its stylistic features.

(ii) Now study the following extracts about the soul singer James Brown. After carrying out the appropriate study of the materials, produce the 'blurb' for an unofficial biography of James Brown. An unofficial biography might use information which the subject would prefer not to see in print. It might also express opinion about that or other information available. The publisher has allowed you up to 200 words.

EXTRACT A

Quite possibly the only man in history (certainly in soul music) to have a number one single in 4 different decades. James Brown has numerous world-famous titles, including Soul Brother Number One. The hardest working man in show business, Mr. Dynamite, The Godfather of Soul, Soul Brother Number One, Minister of new Super Heavy Funk, and the Original Disco Man. No other single African American has been so influential on the course of popular music for the last 45 years.

Living a childhood of poverty, he formed his group the Famous Flames. He established himself in 1958 with 'Try Me' on King. He had several hits after this and truly became a living legend after his performance 'Live At the Apollo' in 1963. After squabbles between the King and Smash labels over recording rights, he cut 'Out of Sight' and 'Papa's got a Brand New Bag' which could arguably be the first funk cuts ever created.

He was a determined and controlling bandleader, leading to brilliant music but disgruntled employees. This caused a band walkout in 1969, and he recruited his new act from a Cincinnati band called 'The Blackenizers'. Enter Bootsy and Catfish Collins, and enter the Sex Machine-Super Bad era from 1969 to 1972. Some of James Brown's meanest funk cuts were produced during this era.

Despite the commercial decline of his works after The Payback in 1974, there are many funk gems to be heard from the Godfather through 1978. Musically some of James Brown's most sophisticated work was made in this period. Well-rounded albums like 'Hell' and 'Get up Offa That Thing' were recorded during this period.

In 1980 he cracked the charts again with a duet with Afrika Bambaata entitled 'Unity'. He hit number one again in 1986 with 'Living in America', which was used in a soundtrack for a Rocky film. In 1988 he was charged with assault and battery of his wife. During this period he had also been arrested for drug possession and use, and was hounded by the IRS. James Brown toured recently, performing his hits, and doing a fine job of it. Here's to the Godfather!

Extract B

James Brown
American soul singer
Born 1928

James Brown had a hard childhood. When he was only 16 he was jailed for armed robbery. Turning to music kept him out of trouble, and in 1958 he had his first million-selling record, 'Try Me', a song in the gospel and rhythm 'n' blues styles. He gradually added hard, rhythmic guitars and frantic, punchy horns, creating a style which became known as funk.

His exciting live shows earned him the title Godfather of Soul. Hits like 'Papa's Got a Brand New Bag' (1965) and 'Living in America' (1986) confirmed his star status over a period of 20 years.

Extract C

Brown, James [1928–], American gospel-soul singer, songwriter, and bandleader, born in Macon, Georgia. Beginning as a gospel singer in the late 1940s, Brown learned to play the drums, organ, and piano. By the mid-1950s he was leading his own group, the Famous Flames, and had signed a contract with King Records.

Although Brown was virtually ignored by the American mass market throughout much of his career, he recorded more than 40 gold records. 'Please, Please, Please' [1956] was a success in England and was his first top-selling single in the United States. 'Try Me' [1958] also became a gold record. By the mid-1960s the James Brown Revue, a rigorously disciplined and choreographed stage show, was filling concert halls and auditoriums and commanding top fees. Brown dominated the rhythm-and-blues market with 'Prisoner of love' [1963], 'I Got You' [1965], 'Papa's Got A Brand New Bag' [1965], and 'It's a Man's World' [1966]. 'Cold Sweat' was a top single in 1967, followed by 'Say it Loud, I'm Black and I'm Proud' [1968].

In the 1970s his recordings did well on both rhythm-and-blues and popular charts.

Brown used his popularity to address the importance of education, self-improvement, and the need for minority-owned businesses (he owned his own recording studios, three radio stations, and a real-estate company). He appeared in the film *The Blues Brothers* (1980). Brown toured and recorded in the 1980s, publicly encouraging a rivalry between Prince and Michael Jackson, whom he viewed as his successors. He wrote his autobiography, *James Brown, The Godfather of Soul* (1986), and was one of the first ten inductees to the Rock and Roll Hall of Fame and Museum (1986). In 1988 Brown was sentenced to six years in prison for assault and for eluding police during a car chase. He was paroled in 1992 and resumed his music career, recording *Love Over-Due* the same year. In 1992 he received a Grammy Lifetime Achievement Award.
Commentary:

- Suggest how the material you have selected will help to sell the book.
- Point out any material you have included that might not have featured in an official biography.
- Explain how far you have modelled the structure of your text on your style model.
- Explain how far, and for what reasons, you have departed from the rather formal, academic style of the blurb for Ackroyd's *Blake*.

ACTIVITY 27. DINOSAURS

Study and prepare the following series of extracts about dinosaurs. We suggest two possible tasks: you may like to attempt both, and reflect in your commentary on how the difference between them has affected the selection and presentation of material.

Task (a) The organisers of an exhibition on dinosaurs at a local museum have asked you to write the text for the display exhibiting some fossil remains of *Tyrannosaurus rex*. The text will appear on a plaque fronting the exhibit and should be about 150 words long. Visitors will include members of the general public and school parties.

Task (b) For the same exhibition, produce the script for the relevant section of an audio-tape guide which will be issued to visitors.

Extract A

A long time ago, before men lived on earth, dinosaurs roamed the world.

Some lived on land, others in the water. Some were very big, others were very small.

What were the dinosaurs?

The name means 'terrible reptiles'. Some of them were very terrible. Flesh-eating dinosaurs had big teeth and ate other animals.

Tyrannosaurus, the 'king reptile', was sixteen metres long.

This terrible flesh-eater ran on its powerful hind legs, but like all reptiles, had to stop often to cool off.

Extract B

The Age of Dinosaurs

Dinosaurs were a group of reptiles which lived from 200 million years to 65 million years ago. Palaeontologists have found thousands of fossils which show what dinosaurs looked like and how they lived. There are fossils of bones and teeth, footprints and skin and even fossil eggs with baby dinosaurs inside.

The name dinosaur means 'terrible lizard'. There were dinosaurs on the earth for about 135 million years, which is 70 times longer than people have existed.

A fierce carnivore

Tyrannosaurus rex was the largest carnivore. Its name means 'king of the tyrant reptiles'. It weighed over eight tonnes and was nearly 15m long. Most carnivores moved on their hind legs and could run fast to catch their prey.

Tyrannosaurus rex had very short arms. Here, it is attacking a sauropod dinosaur called *Alamosaurus*.

Extract C

Dinosaur, one of a group of extinct reptiles that lived from about 230 million to about 65 million years ago. The word *dinosaur* was coined in 1842 by the British anatomist Sir Richard Owen, derived from the Greek words *deinos,* meaning 'marvelous' or 'terrible', and *sauros,* meaning 'lizard'. For more than 140 million years, dinosaurs reigned as the dominant animals on land.

Owen distinguished dinosaurs from other prehistoric reptiles by their upright rather than sprawling legs and by the presence of three or more vertebrae supporting the pelvis, or hipbone. Dinosaurs are classified into two orders, according to differences in pelvic structure: Saurischia, or lizard-hipped dinosaurs, and Ornithischia, or bird-hipped dinosaurs. Dinosaur bones occur in sediments that were deposited during the

Mesozoic Era, the so-called era of middle animals, also known as the age of reptiles. This era is divided into three periods: the Triassic (dating from 245 million to 208 million years ago), the Jurassic (208 million to 144 million years ago), and the Cretaceous (144 million to 65 million years ago).

Tyrannosaurus Rex (Latin, 'tyrant –lizard king'), large, bipedal, carnivorous dinosaur of the family Tyrannosauridae, of the latter part of the Mesozoic era. Up to 12m (39ft) long, about 6m (20ft) tall, and weighing more than 5 metric tons, Tyrannosaurus was well equipped for preying on the large herbivorous dinosaurs of the time, about 70 million years ago. Its long skull was equipped with powerful jaws in which were set sharp, doubly serrated teeth, some of which were 15cm (6in) long. The tiny forelimbs, seemingly out of proportion to the rest of the animal's massive body, each bore two sharp claws; the powerful hind limbs each were armed with three forward-pointing claws, well suited for tearing flesh, and a fourth backward-pointing claw. Fossils that were found in North America (Montana and South Dakota) and Mongolia in strata of Upper Cretaceous age indicate that the species came into being and became extinct in the relatively short space of a few million years.

EXTRACT D

Tyrannosaurus with its huge muscular jaws, its teeth like saw-edged scimitars, its strong flexible neck and its powerful hind legs, was the mightiest killer that ever walked. Crashing out of the jungle it could have thundered down on the biggest animals alive at the time and killed them quickly and savagely with great tearing bites and slashes. What a monster!

But was it such a monster? Doubts arose in the 1960s when studies seemed to show that the hips of *Tyrannosaurus* would only have allowed the animal to take small, mincing steps and move at only about 5 kilometres per hour (3 mph). The huge teeth were definitely for tearing up meat, but what kind of meat? Probably just the rotting carcasses of dead animals. Mighty *Tyrannosaurus* was just a scavenger!

Since the 1960s, however, scientific opinion has turned the other way. The eyes of *Tyrannosaurus* could be directed forward to give a three-dimensional view past its narrow nose. Only active hunters can do this. The teeth were strong enough to grip struggling prey. The feet had small claws and few heavy muscles – these are adaptations for speed. The skull and the powerful jaw muscles were designed to withstand the impact of the 6-tonne body crashing into the flank of an unsuspecting hadrosaur at a speed of 30 kilometres per hour (20 mph). So, *Tyrannosaurus* could really have been a swift and deadly hunter, rather than a placid scavenger, after all.

Scientists have reached a compromise: it was both a fast hunter *and* a scavenger.

EXTRACT E

Sharp-Toothed Terror

Charging through the Cretaceous landscape, eight-ton, 42-foot-long *Giganotosaurus,* one of the largest of all carnivores, dwarfs a herd of human-size herbivores, larger cousins of *Gasparinisaura.* Based partly upon *Giganotosaurus's* remains, paleontologists propose a later-than-supposed link between the continents of South America and Africa, where a related beast lived 25 million years before North America's *Tyrannosaurus rex. Giganotosaurus*'s dagger-like teeth suggest that the creature preyed on plant-eaters many times its weight. Unlike the longer, wider, bone-crushing teeth of *T. rex* , the teeth of *Giganotosaurus* were best suited to cutting flesh. 'This was an animal that would run in, take a very large bite, then back off and watch,' says Canadian dinosaur expert Phillip Currie. 'Basically, the prey would bleed to death.'

Preparing for the examination

The examination tasks

This module is assessed by one written paper of $2^1/_2$ hours. The examination will be based upon the two sets of pre-released material which you will receive approximately three days before the examination. In the examination you will you will be offered the choice of two tasks on each set of material. You do ONE task only on one set of material. You will also be asked to produce a brief commentary (250 words) explaining and evaluating your work.

The material can be on any subject and can include many different kinds of sources – articles, extracts, letters, fiction and non-fiction, poems, songs, transcripts, photographs, maps, diagrams and more.

Some examples of the diverse range of subjects covered in the past include the crime writer Raymond Chandler and films based on his work, guidance on caring for babies and young children, the history of recorded sound, the history and design of castles, the science of volcanoes, choosing and caring for guinea pigs, the story of slavery, the history of emigration to the United States and many more. The subjects may embrace history, language, science and technology, social issues, recent current affairs – or anything else!

The tasks will require you to make a selection of material from the sources and to use it to construct a completely new text. This must fulfil a stated purpose and suit the needs of a specified audience.

The task will test the full range of editorial skills on which this module has been focusing. We can sum these up as:

- reading, understanding and assimilating a significant corpus of diverse materials
- making appropriate selection of material relevant to a particular purpose and audience
- creating an appropriate structure for your new text in the way you choose to sequence the material
- ensuring the text is cohesive and coherent

- summarising and paraphrasing material where appropriate
- using the appropriate conventions of the form/genre within which you are writing
- sustaining an appropriate style of writing/presentation throughout
- reflecting on and evaluating your choices in a short commentary.

In the examination, your assignment 'brief' will prescribe:

The **form/genre** of the new text: for instance, you could be asked to produce a guide book, a taped commentary, a handbook, a pamphlet, a feature article for a local newspaper, a script for a radio programme, a magazine article, a study pack, a talk script etc.

The **audience** may be defined as visitors to a particular exhibition, parents of young children, listeners to local radio, students of your own age group, primary-school children etc.

The **purpose** will be clearly defined – it is usually possible to identify a primary purpose (to entertain, inform, persuade or instruct), though the brief may also indicate secondary purposes (e.g. the script for a lecture may be primarily informative but will also need to stimulate and involve an audience).

The **extent** (length) may be defined in terms of a word limit, physical size (e.g. an A1-size wall chart) or, for spoken texts, the time allocated.

Preparing the material – both sets!

You will have roughly 48 hours to prepare your material. You should aim to prepare both sets of material adequately; although you may find one subject more interesting than the other, it would be foolish to depend on being able to follow this preference in the exam. It is impossible to predict the nature of the task you may be set on a particular set of material – and if you were to find the assignment asking you to produce a text in a form/genre with which you were largely unfamiliar, you would be in considerable difficulty. You should therefore plan to work through the three readings and the associated activities outlined on pp.79–89 above for both sets of material.

In the examination

Examinations are stressful – and to help control this stress, you need to go into the exam room with a clear strategy for the next $2^1/_2$ hours. So, you need to have plenty of practice on exam-length assignments, keeping the following guidelines beside you so that they become second nature when you come to the real thing.

The adrenaline rush of the first few minutes of the examination is not necessarily very conducive to cool, calm thinking and writing, so allow yourself time to think through the various stages of the task carefully. As we have suggested before, the success and quality of a piece of writing is, no less than a more practical task, likely to reflect the degree of planning and preparation beforehand. If you look around you in the first few minutes of the examination and notice fellow-candidates apparently plunging straight into the writing of their final texts – instead of rushing to follow their example, console yourself that they cannot possibly be in a position to produce a good text so quickly.

Suggested below is an approximate timescale for the $2^1/_2$ hours. You will notice that the actual writing of the final text may not begin until nearly an hour has passed!

Time	Task	Comments
0–5 mins	Deconstruct each assignment brief and make choice of assignment	Don't jump in! An assignment that appears at first sight to be attractive can sometimes turn out to be less manageable once you've started work on it – but there won't be time to change track once you've started. So, ask yourself and note down for each of the two assignments: • the *form/genre*: What kind of text is required? Can you visualise/hear it? Can you think of an example/style model of a similar text that you have come across? • the *purpose*: primary and secondary • the *audience*: is this an audience you feel confident you can address? Have you experienced texts aimed at such an audience? How successfully do you think you can achieve the right tone/register for them? If the answer to any of these questions is 'no' for one of the assignments, choose the other one, irrespective of the subject matter!
5–15 mins	Make initial broad selection of material	Check the terms of the assignment. Which of the sub-headings that you used to classify the materials are likely to be most/least relevant to the purpose and audience? Use your colour-coding to help you identify this material. Start by crossing out materials you decide *not* to include. (This may include up to a quarter of the source material!)
15–20 mins	Decide on format and possible layout	Although in the examination itself you will not be expected to actually *produce* the final text in its completed form, your task is to submit to an editor (the examiner!) the kind of finished manuscript which s/he would then be able to publish. This means that you do need to have considered the format and layout of the final text in your writing.

		So – if your brief is for a *written* text: • sketch out a rough 'mock-up' of what the pages will look like • What size/format? • How will the text/images be arranged on the pages? You can include this sketch with your script and indicate where you would imagine headings, images, page-breaks and other text features appearing in the final product. • Will the text be continuous, or broken up by headings/sub-headings? • Will some information be presented in panels? For a *spoken* text: Use an appropriate format for your script that allows you to indicate instructions to speakers about (where appropriate) style of delivery, timing and emphasis. If, at any point, you require a speaker with a particular regional accent, say so. Include instructions about any music or sound effects (SFX) you wish to include, and for how long.
20–35 mins	Decide on the structure of your new text and the sequence of your material	Now go back to the materials you have decided are likely to be relevant and want to include in some form. Sketch out – perhaps as a flow chart – the sequence of the major sections of your material. It should be possible to envisage five or six sections/stages in the text. Skim the materials and use your annotations to help you assemble the more detailed materials you intend to use in each of the sections. This may mean physically tearing/cutting up the materials and sorting the pieces into piles (use paper clips to keep these together).
35–40 mins	Decide on appropriate tone and register	Consider the style models you have in mind, and the nature of the relationship the brief implies between you and your audience. For example, will you be writing as an 'expert', or as 'one of them'? When weighing up the most appropriate levels of formality, personality and seriousness, consider these key issues: • How appropriate is it to use 'I', 'we', or 'you'? • How appropriate will it be to include light-hearted material designed to amuse? • What level of specialist language would the audience be comfortable with?

		• What knowledge of/familiarity with the subject matter can you assume the audience has? • How can you make the writing lively and interesting? This does not mean making everything sound like breakfast TV or a tabloid newspaper; it *does* demand that you use your ingenuity and writing skills to produce a document that serves its purpose for the specified audience, in a way that will interest them.
40 mins–2 hrs	(a) Write the text	The remaining 1 hour 20 mins should be sufficient – if you've prepared the materials properly and carried out all the stages above. Only physically cut and paste extracts to save time either when you are sure the language in which they are written is appropriate and can be invisibly absorbed within the text you are writing, or when you are actually presenting an extract as a piece of quoted material. As you write the text, you may wish to include the occasional short 'note to editor' to convey your intentions regarding page layout, type of text font, or some other graphological feature which you are unable to achieve within the limitations of the examination conditions. You should present these as: *'(Note to Ed: . . .)'* Don't worry about crossings-out as long as your final intentions are clear. If you need to make corrections as you go along – e.g. you wish to insert a passage into a page you have already written – do so by using an asterisk (*) and footnote *(*Ed: please insert this passage here)*.
	(b) Ongoing 15-minute checks	As you are writing it is easy to lose sight of the big picture and be diverted from the main thrust of the text, or lapse into stylistic inconsistencies. So, every 15 minutes or so, when you complete a paragraph or section, run briskly through this check-list: • Keep looking back at the assignment brief. Are you doing exactly what is required? • Are you constructing a 'seamless' document? Make sure that you are consistent in terms of style and register throughout. When rewriting, summarising and paraphrasing the original, make sure that you keep this in mind. Have you made sure that tense, for instance, is consistent? • Are you guiding the audience through the text? Does it link to what has gone before, and to what is to follow?

		• Have you ensured that your audience can follow the text? Have any specialist terms been glossed? Have you ensured that you do not assume too much, or too little, knowledge, on the part of your readers/listeners? • Does what you have said make sense? Are you sure that you have not contradicted something you said earlier? • Have you inadvertently changed register? Moved from one viewpoint to another when not appropriate? Started persuading when you should be informing?
2hrs–2hrs 10 mins	Proof read and correct your text	Rather than doing a general read-through, it is often more productive to look for specific, correctible snags in the writing such as: • sudden jumps or failures in cohesion. Look closely at the seams between one part of your text and the next, particularly if you have cut and pasted any extracts • where you have used source material directly, ensure that you have linked smoothly, changing speaker, tense, pronouns etc. • lapses in style/tone/register • poorly punctuated or ungrammatical sentences • spelling.
2 hrs 10 mins–end	Write your commentary	This is your opportunity to meet the Assessment Objective 'discuss and explore concepts and issues relating to language in use'. As with the commentary you produced for your Original Writing in Module 3, you should use this to explain some of the major choices you had to make as a writer. In the limited time and space available (200 words), you should not attempt to describe every aspect of the process above. Rather, answer the questions listed here using brief illustrations from your finished text: • Why did you select and arrange the material the way you did? (Refer to the audience, genre and purpose of the new text here. You may wish to discuss briefly why you *omitted* some of the material.) • How did the purpose, audience and context for the new text affect your selection of lexis and control of register and tone? (Show how you have changed the style/tone/register of the source material by quoting examples.) Identify and illustrate the stylistic features of the mental style model you have tried to maintain throughout the piece.

		• How did you ensure that the text coheres? (Give examples to illustrate how you achieved syntactic, lexical and stylistic cohesion.) • How successful do you think your final text is? How well does it meet the requirements of the brief? Would you do anything differently if you had the chance to re-draft?

A sample commentary

The following commentary illustrates the kind of brisk, selective but revealing account which is required. It refers to a writing task in which the students were asked to produce an audio-tape guide for visitors to an exhibition of objects/cuttings related to the sinking of the *Titanic*.

I realised that as my audience was a very wide and general one a lot of the technical language in the source material relating to marine engineering etc, would need to be simplified or glossed. For example, I needed to explain what watertight bulkheads were. Also, the statistical information — numbers of people of different classes on board, numbers of lifeboats, etc — needed presenting vividly as people can only take in so much through the spoken mode.

To entertain my audience as well as to inform them, I decided to use a survivor of the ship's crew as fictional narrator. I gave him a southern accent as many of the ordinary sailors might have come from around Southampton, and I tried to make his language fairly colloquial and sailor-like. I thought this would help younger visitors, especially, identify with him as a character and get more involved in the story. The use of SFX and music of the time also helped to create the right mood and atmosphere. I used other voices to bring the eye-witness material in the sources to life.

- As this was an audio-guide, I also had to remember to give directions and refer the listeners to particular things to look out for in the exhibition.

Commentaries

Activity 1. Producing a text

The factors you listed in the 'Input Factors' column should have included:

- the purpose of the text
- the audience/readership for whom it is designed and the nature of your relationship with them
- the genre to which the text will belong
- the medium in which it will appear

- any restrictions on length implied by any of these, or externally imposed (e.g. by an editor).

Activity 2. Where do texts come from?

(a) UCAS reference. Usually, the person who writes this sort of reference will draw their information from three or four sources. Each subject teacher will have written an academic reference, possibly following an agreed common format, and there may be a more personal reference from a tutor. Other material may be contained in Profiles/Records of Achievement.

(b) First there has been a process of **selection** (and **omission**). Anxious to be positive about the student's skills, the writer has made no mention of her difficulties in Maths, for instance. Her initial difficulties in Sociology are also omitted.

Then, the writer has brought together, or **synthesised,** all the relevant information from the four reports into a single paragraph focusing on analytical skills. Note how the paragraph starts with an overall **summary** of these skills. Simple connections (*whilst*, *and*, *also*, *though*) have been used to create a fluent paragraph and to achieve textual cohesion.

Finally, the writer has eliminated one or two **stylistic inconsistencies** (e.g. the English teacher's rather casual use of terms like *OK* and *waffly*) to ensure that the reference is consistently formal in tone.

(c) Sources of raw material:

Script for BBC news bulletin	News reports are gathered from news agencies such as Reuters or News International as well as the BBC's own reporters, but these reports will themselves draw on other sources such as interviews, statements, press conferences and archive materials.
Prospectus for your school/ college	Subject departments will all submit the relevant copy for their own course and facilities, and different areas of the school/college may submit pieces of text about resources, recruitment, Inspection Reports etc., which will be edited together by the publicity team.
Feature article about a media celebrity	This may draw heavily on a transcript of a specially arranged interview, but will also refer to previous interviews, other statements attributed to the star and archive research about their background.
An essay you are currently working on in one of your other subjects	It is likely that you will be encouraged to use more than one source for your researches – whatever subjects you are studying. After all, no one source can be guaranteed as comprehensive, contemporary, unbiased or even accurate. Sources may include different textbooks, websites, audio-visual material and news/magazine articles.
Script for a radio documentary about the sinking of the *Titanic*	The writer of this script may draw on a variety of eyewitness accounts, letters and contemporary news articles, the report of the official enquiry into the accident and more technical archive materials relating to the ship's design and the cause of the disaster.

Learning pack for GCSE students about the history of the English language	There are several very scholarly textbooks on this subject as well as entries in reference books and encyclopedias, though a writer would obviously need to be very selective in their choice of material and imaginative in its re-presentation to suit a young readership.
This textbook	The authors of this textbook have drawn on a variety of different language/linguistics research materials and textbooks, data from a number of sources, (including transcripts of interviews and other spoken language), newspaper and magazine articles, the Examination Board's specifications, web pages, and many more.

Activity 3. Tagging your sources

Five of the key points are:

- You need to know how trustworthy your source is. Is it from a reliable publication, and attributed to a named author? If not, you may need to question its veracity.
- The author/publication may also raise the issue of bias and objectivity. Is the author (or publication) known for his/her/its opinions and point of view?
- If the text seems to have a distinctly opinionative, judgemental or persuasive flavour, you need to be especially alert for distortions or inaccuracies in the content, and to separate the information from the opinionative/emotional content.
- The date of the source can also be vital, depending on the nature of the material. The information and views it contains may no longer be accurate, though the source may still be valuable as evidence of how knowledge and understanding have developed since its publication.
- It is highly unlikely that the texts that you are eventually going to write will have the same audience, purpose and form as your source texts – so it's useful to be clear, right from the start, about the extent to which you will need to transform any material in your sources which you wish to use.

Activity 4. Black Holes

- Text A is from *The Young Scientist Book of Stars and Planets*
- Text B is from Microsoft *Encarta 98 Encyclopedia*
- Text C is from the Isaac Asimov article in the *Faber Book of Science*

- Text D is from the Cambridge Relativity group website www.dampt.cam.asc.uk/user/gr/pulbic/bh.Intro.html

Although text A seems to begin with a piece of scientific language which might baffle even some older readers (*spacetime*), the use of a highly practical everyday analogy (the throwing of a tennis ball) and the second-person address to the reader (*the harder you throw the ball . . .*) indicates that it may be aimed at younger readers. The technical term *escape velocity* is introduced carefully by stating the concept (*the velocity the ball must have to escape*) and then the phrase *is known as*. Although the language is still fairly formal and scientific – note the shift from the active structures of the first paragraph to the passives of the second – the step-by-step explanation in terms of the analogy is characteristic of an educational text for younger readers.

Text B follows the recognised format of an encyclopedia entry, with the **headword** followed by a succinct definition (*an extremely dense body,* etc.) which takes the form of a minor sentence. The explanation is couched in more abstract, scientific terms – no analogies here – and assumes the readers are comfortable with quite an advanced lexical register, though the specialised use of the term *horizon* is introduced with the phrase *called a* . . . ..

Text C bears some resemblance to B, exploiting as it does a figurative comparison of black holes to *odd creatures* and addressing the reader directly (*concentrate on gravity*). This is nevertheless fairly dense, technical language, presumably assuming an adult audience, and it prefers non-specific generalities (*anything on the surface of a large body*) to concrete analogy (the tennis ball), though the opening *creatures* metaphor and the occurrence of quasi-colloquial phrases such as *what's more* reveals the journalistic origins of this piece. There is some evidence of the author's American origins in the spelling of the word *center* – if re-presenting this text for a British audience a correction would need to be made.

Text D reveals its origin most explicitly with the phrase *here in Cambridge,* which refers the reader directly to its source, and its language is fairly technical, though like text A it exploits analogy (*balsa wood/lead* and *sort of 'plug-hole' effect*) to explain complex concepts and even uses a dramatic exclamation mark (*infinitely dense!*) to capture something of the extraordinariness of the concepts being explored. We might infer that the intended audience for this web page is fairly wide, and that the aim is to speak to younger or less-expert browsers.

Activity 5. The Twitter Machine

- When the article appeared in *The Times* it was headlined 'A child's crossed words puddle'. You are unlikely to have come up with something similar, as the journalist or sub-editor responsible was clearly using typical journalistic word-play to achieve a 'catchy' headline rather than just summarising the article. For our purposes, a title such as 'Reasons why children mispronounce words' would do just as well.

- There is not necessarily a single 'correct' analysis of the underlying structure of the piece. The one offered below is merely a suggestion:

Section	Summary of content (one phrase only)
1	Para. (i) raises questions about a child's pronunciation
2	Paras. (ii) and (iii) theory 1: can he hear the difference?
3	Paras. (iv) and (v) theory 2: just a physical pronunciation problem?
4	Paras. (vi) and (vii) more puzzling examples of child's speech
5	Paras. (viii)–(xiii) working out an explanation
6	Paras. (xiv)–(xv) solution: final answers to question

Activity 6. The Twitter Machine – *second reading*

Text section/title	Suggested paragraph summaries	Possible items for glossing
Para. (i) raises questions about a child's pronunciation	(i) puzzling e.g.'s and possible explanations	(i) Who was the *Magic Roundabout* hero?
Paras (ii) and (iii) theory 1: can he hear the difference?	(ii) experimental evidence: mouth/mouse (iii) conclusion: yes he can!	
Paras (iv) and (v) theory 2: just a physical pronunciation problem?	(iv) partly true – but puzzling exceptions (e.g's?) (v) conclusion: *not* just a physical pronunciation problem!	
Paras (vi) and (vii) more puzzling examples of child's speech	(vi) more puzzling e.g.'s (vii) transcript of mouse/mouth dialogue	
Paras (viii)–(xiii) working out an explanation	(viii) first explanation: set of rules (ix) examples – rules in action (consonant harmony) (x) consonant harmony (xi) not this simple! (xii) perceptual problems also (xiii) 'perceptual filter'	(iii) adult pronunciation and child's mental representation are equivalent = child recognises and understands adult sounds (ix) and (x) consonant harmony = tends to use sounds which are similar within a word (xiii*)* perceptual problems = couldn't tell the sounds apart (xiv) *perceptual filter* = a child's recognition of the sounds in an adult's speech is limited by his/her inability to fully distinguish every sound
Paras (xiv)–(xv) solution: final answers to question	(xiv) explanation (xv) concluded	

Activity 7. Fact and opinion

Any piece of popular journalism produced in wartime may include elements of distortion or even propaganda. We should therefore be cautious about the accuracy or, at least, the comprehensiveness of this account without corroboration from an alternative, more independent source.

A number of features of the text suggest that an element of dramatisation is involved, inviting the reader to respond imaginatively and emotionally to the narrative rather than simply registering the facts of the situation:

- the opening rhetorical question
- the interjection *when lo and behold!* and other direct authorial commentary such as *what a splendid hour for the two little ships thus chosen*
- invitations to empathise emotionally such as *we can imagine the excitement upon our little ships* and *remember she was plunging forward in the blackest darkness*
- the figurative, almost literary quality of descriptions such as *lightning-like flashing of the guns, their funnels glowing, their engines racing, turning like a weathercock*, and dramatic verbs like *plunging, dashed, raced* etc.
- the focus on the (imagined) emotional states of individuals (*how every Jack was instantly at his station, Ambrose M Peck asked himself a question . . . .*

The text consistently attributes heroic characteristics to the actions of the British ships (it was an *adventure*, for which they have been *longing,* whereas the Germans are also the enemy whose cowardliness is implied by the emphasis on their desire for escape (*full of flight but not of fight*).

An account of the same incident from the point of view of the German flotilla might offer an interestingly conflicting perspective; eyewitness accounts would not, individually, be any more reliable but taken as a whole might allow a fair picture of events to be pieced together. We may get closer to the objective 'truth' – if this is to be had at all – from an 'official' report as recorded in a confidential memo.

The key facts would seem to be:

- the *Swift* and the *Broke* were proceeding westwards at 12.40 a.m. on 21 April 1917
- they encountered a German flotilla of six vessels 600 yards to port
- the Germans opened fire first
- the *Swift* replied before the commander, Ambrose Peck, attempted to ram the leading German vessel

- the *Swift* failed to ram the ship but scored a direct hit with a torpedo and was saved thanks to the torpedo attack by the *Broke* on the second German vessel
- the *Broke* (commanded by E. R. G. R. Evans) pursued the Germans as they fled and rammed the third German boat
- hand-to-hand fighting broke out between the two crews.

So, an appropriate summary could be:

Two British destroyers engaged a six-vessel German flotilla at 12.40am on 21 April. Responding to enemy fire, the *Swift* tried unsuccessfully to ram the leading vessel as fire was exchanged but both destroyers scored direct torpedo hits before the *Broke* rammed the third German vessel. Hand-to-hand fighting then broke out.

Activity 8. Titanic

The obvious categories here might include:

- design and technical aspects of the ship itself
- setting sail
- the circumstances of the impact with the iceberg
- the reactions on board up to the evacuation
- the sinking and the rescue of survivors
- explanations for the sinking.

Activity 9. Sources in conflict

The fact that both writers refer to Henslowe's list is interesting – it suggests that both had access to the same source material but chose to select and interpret the information differently. Text A refers to some examples of props and *scenic pieces* but B includes a long inventory of such items. The basic premise of A is *an absence of scenery* and *the scene on stage need not be localised.* Text B on the other hand starts from the *employment of scenery, properties and effects* and stresses that various items were used *to give locality to the platform.*

However, when we look more closely, the conflict between these texts is more a matter of interpretation and presentation than fact. Both agree that the theatre consisted of a platform augmented on occasions by various props and bits of scenery. They differ in the importance they attach to these items – Text A presents them almost as the exception to the rule, and certainly does not disprove the basic idea of an 'unlocalised' stage; Text B suggests that the amount of scenery, and realism created on the stage, was greater than is sometimes supposed.

When producing a new text, one way of dealing with this difference of emphasis is simply to acknowledge it. You could make use of the factual elements – the examples of actual props used – but your interpretation might be to say something like 'Although it is clear that a range of stage properties was certainly used in the Elizabethan theatre, there is some dispute about the importance of these devices in creating a realistic sense of a particular place and time on stage . . . '

Activity 10. Surveying style models

Some common features to note in each of these text types:

1. Most speech radio programmes have a signature tune, and are introduced by either one or two 'anchors' in the studio; they will usually present information directly and introduce pieces of pre-recorded material from other contributors. These will be edited from previous interviews. Where two presenters are involved, they will often carry out a kind of conversation, with one asking the questions which the other answers. Sometimes short bursts of thematically relevant popular music may be used to underline the theme of a story, or cover a link to the next item. Other types of incidental music and SFX may be used to enhance mood or create a particular atmosphere.

   The language is predominantly Standard English, though accents other than RP are to be heard these days, and the style is not as stuffily formal as some people might think. One common radio convention is that all speakers are frequently addressed by their full names for listener identification (e.g. 'Bill Brown, what did you think of that speech?').

2. In many encyclopedias – and Crystal's is an excellent example of lively, effective presentation of complex and varied information – panels, bullet lists and graphics are often used to separate dense information or key facts from the continuous text and present it in a visually striking way. Amongst the serious information and discussion, Crystal amuses his readers by including some surprising or quirky examples of language in use.

3. These commentaries may be either a straightforward lecture guide, or (at historical sites) may be more creative in using fictional historical characters to recreate life as it used to be. Atmospheric and appropriate music will often be used. So a tape for visitors to a ruined abbey may purport to be the narrative of Brother Francis, spoken over a background of medieval plainsong. The listeners are usually guided round with instructions such as 'stop the tape and walk towards the gate. When you reach it, switch the tape on again'.

4. Public information leaflets need to be easily accessible to all without seeming patronising. Hard facts will be 'chunked down' into short paragraphs/sections and itemised using bullet points. Language will be clear and non-technical, but will avoid any hint of condescension.

5. Textbooks may use a similar range of resources to encyclopedias, but they usually include suggestions for activities of various sorts: discussions, writing tasks or suggested research. New vocabulary may be highlighted in bold and is usually carefully introduced and explained. General information may be presented via individual case studies, since younger students may respond with more interest to stories about people.

6. Speakers will generally introduce themselves and outline the different aspects of the subject they are planning to discuss. Some initial small talk and a joke or two may help to establish a relationship with the audience. OHT slides may provide the key words, or reinforce the different sections of the talk. A creative speaker may ask his/her audience to carry out short discussions in pairs, respond to 'how many people here . . . ' questions by raising their hands or even fill in worksheets or questionnaires. S/he is also likely to lubricate the talk by introducing some amusing, or human anecdotes and introduce and explain complex abstract subjects by using everyday analogies – just like this textbook's comparison of the production of a text to a piece of DIY.

7. Wall charts use a range of appropriate images and symbols, so the development of English could, for example, be shown as a straightforward timeline, or more imaginatively as a journey along a road with various milestones and junctions. A variety of different text fonts and sizes will be used to present the information, usually boxed in panels of different shapes and sizes.

8. Guidebooks are usually colourful and fully illustrated, and are laid out in a clear and attractive style. Section headings such as 'Eating out', 'Sport and Recreation', 'History and Traditions' may be used, and readers may be addressed directly as 'you' when activities are being suggested. The tone is likely to be fairly lively and friendly, with some attempt to simulate the language of speech. The aim? To create the impression of a warm personal welcome.

9. These have many of the characteristics of a popular encyclopedia. The visual material may include numbered step-by-step instructional guides to particular skills/techniques. A lively style (punctuated, perhaps, with occasional exclamation marks!) can help convey a sense of fun and enjoyment along with the information.

Activity 11. The history of the English language

Of course there is no 'correct' choice, but the following suggestions seem sensible.

For Text (a) you will be looking to include as much interesting visual material as possible (the maps and other illustrations) and given the audience, may pick out the more amusing details to balance the serious factual information. The examples of modern school/college slang would seem to have a place here. Lists of other words may be effectively presented in boxes or panels. It is unlikely that there will be room for the opinionative material, but anything personal and real is likely to appeal.

Text (b) of course, being for a spoken medium, rules out the visual materials, and seems to demand a fairly high information load. Be careful, though, not to overdo this; there is a limit to the quantity of sheer facts that can be absorbed from spoken language, and you may decide to lighten some of the historical material with the more anecdotal content. Radio would allow different voices, for example, to read the letter and diary entries. This is also a good medium to present the arguments about whether dialect, slang, etc. are 'a bad thing'.

With Text (c) it is important to strike a happy medium. You will need to include some of the obviously appealing material such as the amusing examples of dialect vocabulary, perhaps to 'hook' the readers in – but also include sufficient historical information to provide the knowledge the students need. There needs to be some material relating to the academic explanation of the process of language change, and as debate and discussion are important ingredients in any language course, you should indicate some of the opinions and arguments about the subject.

Text (d) may turn out to be the densest in terms of the quantity of hard information to include. Even so, the examples of modern slang and dialect (and the history and different opinions surrounding them) may be cited to illustrate the dictionary writer's dilemma of which – if any – of these words to include.

The same may be true for Text (e) as for Text (c), but here there may well be room to be more inclusive – the issue is more likely to be one of textual organisation, and how you sort the material into different pages for linking from the home page.

Activity 12. Which structure?

Structure 1 would appear to be the most obvious and straightforward way of presenting chronological material. It enables you to present the factual material about the main developments in English as a straightforward narrative, and would certainly be suitable for the wall chart. You might also consider this as a useful structure for the A Level textbook, but there are a couple of drawbacks with this. First, it starts from the most distant and unfamiliar mists of history, which may or may not be intrinsically interesting to students. Second, in a straightforward narrative it is not obvious how, or where, the theoretical and controversial aspects of the topic (how and why the processes occur; are they for better or worse?) would fit into the sequence.

Structure 2 is really a variation on (1) but has the advantage of grabbing readers'/listeners' interest immediately by focusing on modern and accessible material, looking at current slang rather than plunging straight into the obscurities of ninth-century Anglo-Saxon! It may be a useful structure for texts (b) or (c).

Structure 3 would not have the clear chronology of the first two – indeed, it could be confusing for anyone wishing simply to trace the line of development of English – but would be useful as a reference source if readers were particularly interested in tracing the influence on English of separate languages. This could be one focus of Text (c), and may well be an approach that would also suit the introduction to the dictionary (Text (d)).

Structure 4 goes straight into the theoretical, analytical aspects of the topic. Again, it would not have the chronological clarity that might be useful as an introduction to the subject, but could help focus on the issues (as opposed to the story) more directly. It is worth considering for texts (b), (c) or (d), therefore.

Structure 5 is a variation on (4), but uses the more immediately interesting materials to 'hook' the readers/listeners into the analytical issues, much as Structure 2 does with its chronological approach. It could have the edge on Structure 4, therefore, for text (c).

Activity 13. Signposting survey

Written texts	Spoken texts
In textbooks, **contents pages** provide the overall 'map' of the whole text, and individual chapters/sections may also have bullet-pointed or numbered summaries of their content. The home page of a website fulfils a similar function. **Introductions/forewords** may outline the overall scope of a text and in most written texts, the opening paragraph or so will outline the scope of what is to follow and hint at the direction the text will follow. **Titles, headlines, headings** and **subheadings** are important signposts to help readers navigate their way through most written texts. They also help to break up the text into manageable sections. In more formal texts, **headers** and **footers** may repeat chapter/section headings at the top/bottom of each page. Textbooks may include explicit **cross-references** (*see p.xx/above/below*) anaphoric previews (*in the next chapter we will consider . . .*) and cataphoric references (*as we have seen earlier . . .).*	An **introduction** may fulfil similar functions in a talk, radio programme or audio-guide. It is likely to outline the scope of what is to follow and may indicate the sequence of points/topics. A live talk may reinforce this via bullet points on a whiteboard or by OHT slides. Different stages of the text may be introduced explicitly by the equivalent of section/chapter headings (*and now, let's think about . . .*) or by a series of **questions** (*we're all worried about the environment, but what can we do about it? Jenny Smith of the Green Party thinks she has some of the answers. Hello, Jenny . . . .*) Even **music** can act as a signpost; a radio programme may use a short piece of thematically related popular music as a recurrent motif which punctuates the text and acts as an audio equivalent of the breaks between different sections. Audio texts may also include **cross-references** such as 'we said earlier' or 'coming up later there is . . . '.

Conclusions/endings may offer a brief summary of what has gone before – and remind the reader of where they started from, telling them, in effect, that the 'journey;' through the text is complete.	The **conclusion** may similarly remind the listener of the journey they have been on. A lecture may go back to the 'list of contents' itemised at the start and remind listeners how the talk has answered any questions raised. One piece of advice to lecturers might be 'Tell 'em what you're going to do, do it, then tell 'em you've done it.'

Activity 16. Editing options

There are many benefits to Option 1. You can use the information you need, but re-present and re-sequence it in a style appropriate to your new text.

Option 2 is similarly useful and enables you simultaneously to be selective with the material, and to ensure that it fits in with the rest of your new text.

With Option 3, some skill is needed when carrying out the editing – see Activity 18 on p.108 – to ensure the text still coheres and is in the appropriate style and register.

On the benefit side, Option 4, like Option 5, may sometimes offer some time-saving, and it can be interesting to introduce quotations/different voices into a text. Presenting material as a quotation avoids the risk of plagiarism.

The problems with Option 5 are (a) that even if the content is appropriate for your new text, the style and register may well not be, (b) you may be including material you don't really need, (c) you may be infringing copyright by presenting someone else's text as your own, and (d) it may be difficult to lead into and away from the passage smoothly.

Activity 17. Editing skills in practice

Text outcome	Extract	Preferred editing options	Comments
An illustrative wall chart for an English classroom in a secondary school	(a)	nil	Probably not really relevant to this task.
	(b)	1 or 2	Dates and basic facts useful, but will need completely re-presenting, in a visual form. Style of writing quite suitable, though.
	(c)	1 or 2?	Probably doesn't give us anything not contained in (b). Very academic style would need completely rewriting.

	(d)	nil	As for Extract (a).
A script for a Radio 4 documentary on the subject of 'Our Changing Language'	(a)	3 or 4	Ideal material – same medium, direct style and sounds controversial. May need some editing. Good to quote rather than cut and paste, as it is clearly presenting a subjective point of view, and the author needs to be acknowledged.
	(b)	1 or 2	Useful factual material but style a little young for a Radio 4 audience.
	(c)	1 or 2	More useful facts, but style rather too academic. Besides, we need to remember that this is a written text: speech, even relatively formal educated Radio 4 speech – cannot carry as much information.
	(d)	4 or 5	Could probably be assimilated into the new text quite easily. Option 4 may be necessary to acknowledge this famous author!
A section of a language textbook aimed at A Level students	(a)	3 or 4	Taken whole or edited down, would be a useful quote to introduce the controversy surrounding the subject of language change.
	(b)	1 or 2	The facts are useful but the style inappropriate for older students.
	(c)	1 or 2	As above, but the style this time it may be too dense.
	(d)	4 or 5	Useful and very readable for the new audience.

Activity 18. Summary and paraphrasing

2,500 years ago, Celtic was the original language of the British Isles and many Celtic place names remain today. Although the Latin-speaking Romans lived here for 500 years from 55BC, some Celtic languages survived. However, many Latin words did eventually come into English. It was the invading Anglo-Saxons who brought what was to be called 'Old English', some words of which are recognisable today.

Activity 21. Spot the join!

In fact the writer has tried to stitch together four fragments here, and although they are very loosely connected by the subject matter, the text is barely coherent – and certainly not cohesive.

For a start, there are striking **stylistic inconsistencies**. The piece runs the gamut from the rather simple *the magpie is a bird that . . .* (edited from a text aimed at younger readers) via the scholarly *of this recondite character* (extracted from an academic textbook) through to the cringingly colloquial and upbeat *all of you out there . . . keep your ears wagging*.

Then there are problems with the **logical connectors**. Does the first *so* really follow from what has gone before, or does it actually refer to something in the text from which this fragment has been edited? Similarly, the second *so*, having been cut off from the 'arguments' which we guess must once have preceded it, now makes no sense.

Pronouns and other **deictic references** are also faulty. In the text as written, the pronoun *these* appears to refer to the bright items stolen by the magpie – in the text from which this sentence was taken it actually referred to a list of new English words recently collected. We guess that the pronoun *he* referred to a named individual in the source text, but the way in which the passage has been edited and pasted leaves us confused.

There is also an inconsistency in **verb tense** at this point, as we switch to the past tense *did*. The writer has retained a confusing reference to a *world map* which was part of the source material but is not included here and the phrase *as we have seen* clearly refers to something found in the source text, not the new text!

Activity 22. Headings

Set 1 is designed to be entertaining as much as informative. The headings only really make sense after you have read the text to which they refer – but then we can enjoy the joke and see their relevance. *All Change* is a familiar enough catchphrase (from rail travel), and *One in the Eye* refers cunningly both to an idiomatic expression and the literal fate of the Saxon King Harold at the hands of the invading Normans at the Battle of Hastings. The third headline incorporates dialect in an amusing, if rather stereotypical fashion. These headlines are fairly close to popular journalism and would work well in texts which need to amuse and entertain as well as inform.

Set 2 is a more straightforward and functional set of summaries which does not attempt to be humorous or even particularly 'catchy'. They function perfectly adequately and are what we might expect to find in standard reference texts. They summarise accurately and succinctly the contents of the text sections to which they refer.

Set 3 illustrates a technique commonly used in instructional and educational texts: a series of questions and answers which structures and signposts the text by creating a pseudo-dialogue on the page to reflect the imagined questions which the reader/learner would be asking of the text.

Activity 23. Captions

- The texts and captions were matched as follows:

  Text 1 and caption (d), text 2 and caption (e), text 3 and caption (a), text 4 and caption (b), text 5 and caption (c)

- Some suggestions:

  Text 6: Man on the Moon? The world stopped to watch in 1969. But was this famous shot taken on an American film set?

  Text 7: The author on the moon. The Lunar Module can be seen reflected in my helmet.

  Text 8: One small step . . . man on the moon in 1969. But what next in space? Tonight's BBC 1 documentary offers some answers.

  Text 9: Wish you were here? Soon holiday flight into space could be a reality . . . .

Activity 24. Openings

Extract A: The opening heading, or slogan, works well on a number of levels. *Take the train* is a memorable phrase – the alliteration and assonance help – and the alliterative *discover the delights* invites the reader both into the countryside and into the main body of the text. The paragraph that opens the text enacts the very journey it wishes you to take – *passing through the stunning scenery* etc. – and lists the stations the train may stop at. The adjectives *stunning* and *fascinating* engage the reader's interest, and the variety of the landscape is caught with the summary of *hills, valleys and moors*. We should not be surprised to find lists of three being used to construct an effective sentence (see *AS English Language for AQA B*, pp.74–75). This also indicates that the remainder of the text will provide us with details of how we can enjoy such pleasures – the answer, of course, will be – by train!

The writer of Extract B sets out to make his readers marvel anew at something they may well take for granted – language. He does this by reducing to absurdity the appearance of the mechanics of language (the alien's eye view of humans exchanging hums and squeaks and pops etc.) and then contrasting this with the *unfathomable vastness* of human ideas which language is used to exchange. He assumes he is writing for reasonably educated and mature readers, as he assumes they will be able to recognise the quotations which he includes as examples of these ideas – quotations from the Bible, Karl Marx, Jane Austen, Albert Einstein and Edward VIII's abdication speech respectively.

Extract C: In an effort to make history 'real', this text uses a fictional character to talk directly to the listeners about the abbey rather than a traditional academic historian. The music is used to establish to historical setting and the character introduces himself and talks directly to the listeners. The text simulates spoken language (with comments like *Yes, life was different then*) and invites the listeners to recreate in their imaginations the Abbey in its *heyday*.

MODULE 6 Language Development

The final module of your A2 course consists of *two* distinct areas of study – the development of language in children – **language acquisition** – and the developments in the English language which have taken place over time – **language change.** The whole of the module counts for 20% of the total A Level marks.

This final part of your A2 course is also what the Examination Board calls a **synoptic** module – this means that it is designed to enable you to demonstrate and apply *all* the knowledge and skills about language that you have developed throughout the whole of your AS/A2 English Language course. In this module, therefore, there are frequent signposts referring you back to previous modules both in this book and in the AS volume. You should follow these links and apply to the linguistic data you explore here the knowledge and understanding you developed earlier.

A word of caution

The A2 examination requires you to have investigated the two areas of language development in much greater depth than there is space to include here. The intention of this module is to get you started by outlining the main areas for study, and to stimulate your further research and investigations. As a candidate for an A2 examination, you are expected to undertake research of your own, consulting appropriate sources in libraries and on the Internet. Each major section, therefore, includes some suggestions directing you to appropriate reference materials for further study.

Many of the possible investigative tasks suggested here could also be the basis of a language investigation appropriate for Module 4, as many teachers and students are likely to be studying for these modules in parallel.

ASSESSMENT OBJECTIVES

The skills and knowledge that you develop and demonstrate in this module are defined by the Examination Board's Assessment Objectives. These require that you:

AO1 communicate clearly the knowledge, understanding and insight appropriate to the study of language, using appropriate terminology and accurate and coherent written expression (2½%)

AO3ii apply and explore frameworks for the systematic study of language at different levels, commenting on the usefulness of the approaches taken (5%)

AO4 understand, discuss and explore concepts and issues relating to language in use (5%)

AO5ii analyse and evaluate variation in meanings and forms of spoken and/or written language from different times according to context (7½%)

In effect, this means bringing to bear on your study of language development all the analytical skills and knowledge about language that you have acquired in your A Level English course to date.

In particular, you will need to be confident about applying different analytical frameworks to linguistic data. This means organising your analysis of language into discussions at the levels of:

- discourse
- pragmatics
- syntax
- lexis
- semantics
- phonology/graphology.

This module is organised into the following sections:

a. Children's Language Acquisition

- Introduction: why study child language?
- The need for language
- The process of language acquisition
- Caught or taught? The language-acquisition debate
- Early literacy
- Preparing for the examination
- Commentaries

b. Changing English

- Getting started: a) perpetual change
- b) the changing lexicon
- A brief history: how language has changed
- The nature of language change: some linguistic issues and controversies
- Data for analysis
- Preparing for the examination
- Commentaries

a. Children's Language Acquisition

Introduction: Why study child language?

Most students and adults find learning a language difficult. You have only to compare your own level of fluency in a foreign language that you have been studying for several years at school with the speech of a native speaker for whom the language is their mother tongue to feel humble about your language-learning accomplishments.

Compared to the average 17-year-old, a newborn infant might seem to be less well equipped to tackle the challenging business of language-learning. It will, after all, be several years before s/he can master tasks as simple as tying a pair of shoelaces; the pleasures and challenges of learning even the basics of most school subjects lie some distance into the future. What chance does a helpless infant have of learning something as complicated as a *language*?

Yet the remarkable thing is that they – or rather, *you* – do just that. By the time you started formal schooling, you had managed to become more proficient in your mother tongue than many people ever become in any second language that they attempt to learn. As older students and adults, you may become experts in nuclear physics or brain surgery, but the merest infant will put most people's language-learning skills to shame. Toddlers may take their time getting to grips with toilet training and such niceties as using a knife and fork, but the phonology, lexis and grammar of language seem to be a matter of child's play.

This remarkable achievement – the development of language skills in the first seven years of a child's life – is the subject of this first section of this module.

Activity 1. First discussions

In groups, consider each of the following questions about language acquisition – you may never have thought about some of these before. Note down your first instinctive responses to these and compare them with the commentary on p.188.

A fuller investigation of these questions underlines our approach to this subject.

A: what are a child's basic needs and how does s/he communicate them?

B: if you have visited a country where you know nothing of the language (and the natives don't speak English!) you will know something of what it feels like to be confronted by an unintelligible stream of sounds.

- What difficulties do you face in trying to decipher a foreign language?
- Are these difficulties greater, or less, for an infant who finds him/herself surrounded by adults speaking what will become his/her mother tongue?

C: do you think some languages are more difficult than others? If so, do you think it takes children longer to learn these?

D: consider how important you think each of the following factors may be in helping children learn their native tongue:

- imitating what they hear
- being carefully taught by parents
- having lots of opportunity to interact with adults
- being clever enough to work out the rules of grammar.

E: what similarities and differences are there between learning to understand and speak your mother tongue, and learning to read and write it?

Activity 2. A language taxonomy

You might start your investigations by placing yourself in the position of an alien visitor to an English-speaking world. This is, after all, not very different from the position in which a newborn infant finds him/herself.

Under each of the headings below, suggest the different skills and knowledge such a creature would need to acquire in order to understand, speak, read and write English like a native.

This should serve as a useful revision exercise, as it asks you to think about everything you've learned about language over the whole of your A Level course.

Phonology	Lexis and semantics	Grammar: morphology and syntax	Pragmatics	Orthography and graphology

Compare your suggestions with the commentary on p.189.

This list, or **taxonomy**, of language might seem to present a daunting challenge to our alien/infant visitor – but in fact it is simply a description of the remarkable achievement of human language acquisition, and it is one which, by and large, all human children achieve. This module will start to explore the ways in which children do so, and will review some of the most popular explanations for their achievement.

Activity 3. Starting your own investigations

The most effective and interesting way of investigating how children actually acquire their own language is to carry out some field research of your own, watching and listening to children, and recording their speech on (preferably) video or audio tape.

Later, you may wish to investigate the development of literacy skills by collecting examples of children's early writing, taping them reading aloud, or even studying some examples of literature written for very young children.

You could, of course, choose to carry out such an investigation for your Module 4 coursework submission. The subjects for your investigation could be:

- younger brothers and/or sisters
- yourself, if recordings have been preserved
- other children for whom you baby-sit.

There are several ways of carrying out such a study, for example:

- a **longitudinal study** of one child: make recordings of or collect writing samples from a single child at regular intervals over a significant period of time i.e. over a period of at least six months
- a **comparative study** of two or more children at different ages/stages of development (this could include a child experiencing some learning difficulties).

You may choose to make any set of language skills the focus for these investigations (pragmatic, grammatical, lexical, phonetic, literate).

Methodology: young children may be less problematic subjects because they are less self-conscious, but they cannot always be guaranteed to 'perform' when you are taping – so some patience may be needed. **Do make sure you obtain the permission of parents before commencing any recording.**

Depending on the focus for your investigation, you should consider setting up a specific situation to collect your data – for spoken language, this may be a game or other activity in which you engage the children. For writing, it could be a specific task or stimulus you provide (for example, asking the children to write a fairy story they already know, or write an account of what they did at the weekend, or continue and finish a story for which you have provided the beginning).

As was stressed in Module 4 (see p.9 above), if you are carrying out a comparative study, it is important to ensure that the situations you set up, and the data you collect, are truly comparable.

Frameworks for studying language acquisition and a cautionary note

In the study of language acquisition, the headings in the table above should provide you with your basic analytical frameworks.

Please note: It is often convenient to generalise about what children do with language at different ages, but of course, all children are different and rarely conform entirely to the textbook stereotypes of infant language behaviour. This can be a source of some anxiety (and pride!) to their parents, and should not unduly surprise you when you start examining the language of the subjects of your investigations. In many textbooks, it is common to discuss language acquisition in terms of 'stages'. This has become a rather controversial concept, for reasons which will be discussed below (see the discussion of the process of acquisition, pp.157–169).

So, whatever the age of your subjects, approach their language with a completely open mind.

The need for language

It is often suggested that the most important feature that sets human beings apart from other species is **language**. Controversial research has been carried out with chimpanzees and other primates in an attempt to verify the apparently unique nature of language, (see, for example, Stephen Pinker's account of this in *The Language Instinct*, pp.334–349), and although there is a debate about some aspects of these experiments, it seems clear that human infants are distinguished by their predisposition to learn language. As you try to understand what prompts them to do so, it may be tempting to suggest that the principal function of language is to enable them to satisfy the basic requirements of existence: communicating to obtain food, warmth and comfort. Certainly, the very early utterances of children give this impression.

However, even a brief consideration of the many ways in which adults use language reveals that its functions eventually become much more varied and complex than this. (This should also warn you against taking too simplistic a view of the uses to which children put language.)

ACTIVITY 4.

Consider the adult uses of language listed in the table below. Your task is to define what **purpose** or **function** the speaker of each utterance is using language to fulfil.

(The final column will be used later.)

Utterance	Context	Function	(Halliday)
'A Big Mac and regular fries, please'	Placing an order in a fast-food restaurant		
'Hello. How are you today?'	Doctor to patient in surgery		
'Hi! How are you?'	Two business acquaintances greeting each other at the start of a meeting		
'Would you close the window please, Michael?'	Teacher to student in classroom		
'Have you heard the latest Westlife CD? It's brill.'	Friend to friend in conversation		

Compare the outcome of your discussions with the commentary on p.190.

There have been various attempts to produce a definitive list of the functions of language which can be applied to the study of child language (see below for Michael Halliday's). However, it is important to understand that most human utterances – including those produced by small children – may, in practice, serve several of these purposes simultaneously.

As you learned in Module 2 of the AS course, 'Language and Social Contexts', and as the commentary to Activity 4 above makes clear, it is vital not to underestimate the *social* function of language. Even the most functional of linguistic interactions may carry with it a social sub-text that sends out signals about attitudes, relationships and status. Indeed, some evolutionary biologists believe that language has been fundamental to the survival and development of human beings as *social* beings; individually weak but collectively strong, human social groups have been cemented and maintained through our apparently trivial linguistic interactions. Passing the time of day, discussing the weather, gossip – these, it seems, may have played an important role in our evolution. It could be that these *interactional* functions of language have contributed as much to this process as the purely *transactional* ones (i.e. those used for achieving practical exchanges of materials and information). Such **phatic** talk may be the human equivalent of the elaborate grooming rituals that seem to contribute to the management of social groups in chimpanzee society (see Robin Dunbar, *Grooming, Gossip and the Evolution of Language*).

Some psychologists have also viewed language as an important vehicle for the internal psychological development of children (see pp.168–9 below), but you should always be alert to the social dimension of even the most basic communication.

Language functions

Several attempts have been made to catalogue the different functions of language, and to chart child language development in terms of the increasing range of these functions to be found in the growing child's repertoire. An often-quoted one is Michael Halliday's, listed below:

Michael Halliday's taxonomy

Instrumental	Language used to fulfil a need on the part of the speaker	Directly concerned with obtaining food, drink, comfort
Regulatory	Language used to influence the behaviour of others	Initially an extension of this, persuading/commanding/requesting other people to do things you want
Interactional	Language used to develop social relationships and ease the process of interaction	The phatic dimension of talk
Personal	Language used to express the personal preferences and identity of the speaker	Sometimes referred to as the 'Here I am!' function – announcing oneself to the world

Representational	Language used to exchange information	Relaying or requesting information
Heuristic	Language used to learn and explore the environment	Using language to learn – this may be questions and answers, or the kind of running commentary that frequently accompanies children's play
Imaginative	Language used to explore the imagination	May also accompany play as children create imaginary worlds, or may arise from storytelling

ACTIVITY 5.

Look again at the table you were working with in Activity 4. Consider how Halliday's functions might apply to each *adult* utterance, and enter these in the fourth column. Remember – even a relatively simple utterance may be achieving more than one of these.

Compare your observations with the commentary on p.190.

Starting to function: the first 12 months

If you have had any experience of very young children, you will already understand that they begin to communicate using sounds long before anything approximating to a word emerges from their mouths. The table below (based on David Crystal, 1996) summarises some of the ways in which this happens:

Cries, burps and burbles	In the first two or three months of life an infant makes lots of noises of pain, hunger and discomfort, to which parents learn to respond, but it is difficult to attribute specific meanings to these sounds.
Cooing and going gaga	Most children add a new variety of sounds to their repertoire before they are six months old – the 'cooing' which may begin to resemble some of the first sounds of speech.
Babbling on	This evolves into babbling – the first extended repetitions by children of some basic phonemic combinations such as 'babababa' etc.
First words	From out of these streams of sounds eventually emerge a small repertoire of utterances that sound something like a word. However, these single words may appear to serve a multitude of functions and to have more than one meaning!

Most of a child's early utterances seem to be direct expressions of physical needs – hunger, pain, etc., but even so, there is a strong suggestion that in the interactions of non-verbal sounds that typically occur between parent and child in this period, there is a rehearsal for the sophisticated social interactions that start to occur with the arrival of 'real' language.

Once the first 'words' begin to emerge (usually at around 12 months), you can usefully begin to consider a child's language, and the ways in which it is used to serve an increasing range of functions.

ACTIVITY 6. DEVELOPING LANGUAGE FUNCTIONS

Below is a selection of utterances from children of various ages. For the sake of clarity, no attempt has been made to represent features of pronunciation; phonological development will be considered later (see p.158 below). For each one:

- try to suggest the possible primary function it may be serving
- suggest the ways in which the language seems to have developed as a means of serving these functions.

It will be helpful to think in terms of developments:

- in the *precision* with which they can express their needs
- in the use of the *phonology, lexis* and *grammar* of English.

As an alternative to Halliday's taxonomy, you may find it helpful to consider a list of specifically infantile language functions such as John Dore's infant language functions cited in Frank Myszor, *Language Acquisition,* listed below:

Child language functions

labelling: simply naming or identifying a person, object or experience
repeating: echoing something a spoken by an adult speaker
answering: giving a direct response to an utterance from another speaker
requesting action: demanding food, drink, a toy, assistance, etc.
calling: attracting attention by shouting
greeting: self evident
protesting: objecting to requests, etc.
practising: using and repeating language when no adult is present

Compare your observations with the commentary on p.191.

Child/age	Context	Utterance	Function/ development
Harry aged 15 months	Hears front door opening	Dada	
	Sees father coming into room	Dada	
	Watching a cartoon video of Laurel and Hardy	Hardy!	
Hannah aged 20 months	Points at father's hat on chair, speaking to mother	Daddy hat	
	Points towards fridge when sitting in high chair, speaks to mother	Juice!	
	Hugs teddy bear in bed	Nice Teddy	
	Television has just been switched off by mother	All gone	
Harry aged $2^1/_2$ years	Looking in room for toy pedal car, spoken to mother	Where red car?	
	Playing with father – long-running joke	Daddy stink!	
	Spoken to friend of father	Ron play Harry car	
	Spoken to mother, getting ready for bed	Mummy got nice hair	
Hannah aged $3^1/_2$ years	Trying on one of mother's hats	Look at me mummy! Wearing Mummy hat!	
	At dinner table, spoken to mother	Can I have some more ice cream?	
	To father, looking at toy	I don't want play that game	
	Playing a game with father	I'm Power Ranger! (*runs around making screeching noise*)	
	Alone, playing with toys	That doesn't go there . . . it doesn't fit . . .	

Functions, grammar and pragmatics

So, as a child develops, you would expect to see both an extension in the range and sophistication of personal and social functions being served by his/her language, and a corresponding development in the precision of the developing vocabulary and grammar of his/her language. S/he has also to learn the sophisticated business of social interaction, and the way that language can be used to convey implicit meanings and get things done (i.e. **pragmatics**).

ACTIVITY 7. LANGUAGE FUNCTIONS: GETTING WHAT YOU WANT

Consider the following ways of making a request (or using the **regulatory** function of language to achieve a result) that a child may acquire as s/he develops. Grammatical and pragmatic development go hand-in-hand as the child learns to request things in increasingly subtle ways.

Identify the advances in both areas represented by each successive utterance.

dada
daddy car
daddy drive car
I want daddy drive car
daddy please will you play with me?
would you like to play cars, daddy?

Compare your notes with the commentary on p.191.

Investigating the process of language acquisition

You should refer to one or more of the following texts as you pursue this subject:

D. Crystal, *Listen to Your Child*
M. Donaldson, *Children's Minds*
Fromkin and Rodman, *An Introduction to Language*
Frank Myszor, *Language Acquisition*
Jean Peccei, *Child Language*
De Villiers and de Villiers, *Early Language*

The previous activity should have highlighted some of the ways in which children can be observed acquiring language skills. This section will consider more precisely just what these skills are.

'Stages' of acquisition

It is common to find child acquisition discussed in terms of stages of development, starting with the so-called **one-word**, **two-word** and **telegraphic** stages. However, while this can be a helpful notion in understanding some aspects of language development, it can also be very limiting for the following reasons:

- these 'stages' refer only to the *grammatical* developments in child language. This can lead you to overlook other elements of language acquisition (such as phonological or pragmatic development) which are of equal importance
- the idea that children of a certain age suddenly jump to the next stage and stay there for a while is a very wide generalisation about the process of acquisition. This can be too blunt an instrument for analysing real utterances made by real children, with all their individuality and variation. At any point in their development, their language may exhibit characteristics of more than one of these 'stages'.

ACTIVITY 8. INVESTIGATING ACQUISITION

The following investigations could also be used as the basis for a language investigation for Module 4. They each suggest a specific focus for an investigation of one or more children's speech – you could, of course, combine them all into a single study of a particular child, or of two or three children at different stages of development.

Use the *Milestones in language acquisition* table on pp.162–65 as a starting point or framework for your study, and make critical use of some of the sources listed above. In your investigation, you should compare the findings of your own analysis with the research and explanations of authors in the field.

Phonology

For a successful investigation of phonological development, you do need to be able to handle the IPA with some confidence (see p.17). You will also need to develop an appropriate notational system to allow you to record prosodic features such as intonation patterns (see Module 4, p.15).

Look again at *The Twitter Machine* on p.83. Carry out a similar investigation of mispronunciations in the language of young children you are able to record. Look for patterns and explanations for deviations from adult speech by asking questions such as:

- Can the child distinguish, but not pronounce, particular phonemes?
- Does the length of the word, or the position of particular phonemes within it, seem to influence the pronunciation?

Lexis and semantics

- Collect a list of the words used by a child at a particular point of development. For example, a 16-month old child called Jake had the following productive vocabulary (variations from adult pronunciation have not been transcribed):

Jake's early vocabulary

Mummy	*daddy*	*Matt (father)*	*Paddy*	*grandad*
dog	*duck*	*elephant*	*lolly*	*banana*
apple	*allgone*	*Barney*	*ball*	*car*
goodboy	*goodgirl (of the dog)*	*yoghurt*	*up*	*balloon*
helicopter	*ta (= thanks)*	*bird*	*plane*	*bye-bye*
quack-quack	*hiya (=greeting)*	*cat*		

- Consider what kinds of semantic fields are most commonly represented.
- Consider the relative proportions of common nouns, proper nouns, verbs and social exchanges. These may vary considerably between different children of a similar age.
- Examine carefully the meanings and functions for which the child is using these words in the contexts in which you have observed or recorded them. These may vary considerably from adult usage! For example, Jake used the word *bird* not only for birds but also for kites and paper aeroplanes, and the word *lolly* to include fruit-juice drinks – a feature known as **overextension.** On the other hand, you may find examples of its opposite (**underextension**), where a child assumes that a word such as *ball* only applies to a specific object (e.g. *his* ball). A **mismatch** occurs when a child has somehow completely mismatched word and meaning.

  In exploring such examples it is useful to think of the meanings of words in terms of **semantic features.** The linguist Eve Clark has suggested that the meanings attributed to words can be broken down into different elements; the word *horse*, for instance, may contain the ideas 'four-legged', 'living', 'domesticated' etc. Other words, such as *cow*, may share some of these features, but will be distinguished from it in some way. A child may overextend (e.g. call a horse a cow) by recognising the semantic features in common, but not recognising those which distinguish the two meanings. Similarly, underextension (e.g. only applying the word *horse* to an individual animal) doesn't take account of the semantic features shared between this horse and all horses.

Grammar

In this complex area, it can be useful to focus on some very specific areas for study, for example:

Study the different ways in which children ask questions or make requests at different stages of development. The 'textbook' sequence is:

1. Intonation is used at pre-verbal and early verbal stages.
2. From about 18 months onwards, *wh-* question words begin to appear and are attached as part of two- or three-word utterances.
3. From the age of two, a child starts to carry out the necessary inversion, switching *you are going* to *where you going* – but usually omitting the *are* (the **auxiliary verb**)

4. From the age of three, the auxiliary verb appears more regularly, producing the complete *Where are you going?* The child may also start to use the short tag questions which we attach to the ends of utterances such as *It's my turn isn't it?*

Just as overextension is a key feature of semantic development, a similar tendency can usually be found as a child extends his/her grammatical competence. Take, for example, the following example in which $3^1/_2$-year-old Harry talks about a recent accident:

ADULT: Have you hurt yourself, Harry? What have you done?

HARRY: I falled.

ADULT: Did you? Did you fall down? Where did you fall?

HARRY: I falled off the chair

Harry has never heard anyone else say 'falled'; he clearly understands the general grammatical principle that to express past tense we usually add a /d/ sound, but is applying this rule to a word that is an irregular exception. This is known as **overgeneralisation**. Far from being worrying mistakes, overgeneralisations are of course very healthy signs that the child is in the process of deducing and constructing his/her own mental model of the grammar of English.

In your investigations, look particularly closely for examples of this at different stages of development, and try to deduce from it what you can about the stage of your child's grammatical development.

Pragmatics

One possible focus is to consider the ways in which children of different ages learn different strategies for directing adults. What, for example, have the children in the extracts below learned about conversational pragmatics?

1) CHILD: I/I think I might need the door closed/

   ADULT: right/

   CHILD: Agh/somebody close the door I'm freezing/

2) CHILD: and you got to watch me/do you want to watch me/do you want to watch me daddy/

3) CHILD: you pick yours up/you pick yours up granddad/

   ADULT: I've picked mine up/

   CHILD: right/let's/let's/I want to play with something else now/

   CHILD: do you want to play with something different/

   CHILD: let's/right/come round here a minute/that's a/good idea we can play with/

   CHILD: well/there's something round here we can play with/look these/what's this/

   CHILD: gran/I need a bit of sugar/

Another important aspect of children's language development is their increasing imaginative and heuristic use of language, often through storytelling and play. Consider for example, the following transcripts of four-year-old Patrick. In the first, he is recounting a holiday tale, and in the second, he is playing with toy soldiers with his grandfather.

With these, and other data which you might gather, some questions to pursue include:

- How do children's storytelling skills develop? (Compare their oral narratives with the written narratives in Module 4, pp.47–49, for example.)
- How do they begin to use language not just to convey the facts of the story but also to create effects in their listeners?
- How do lexical and grammatical developments contribute to their growing skills as storytellers?
- How is language being used to explore new ideas and experiences?

(a) PATRICK: there was a big shark/but we found a big whale in the sea/Cieran found a big whale in the sea

ADULT: oh/

PATRICK: and he said [inaudible] you big whale/'cos he could see/he saw a big thing coming up and it looked just like a whale jumping up/it was/[inaudible] it was trying to/it was going right/and it had its mouth open like that/[5] it was real scary at first when it had its/

ADULT: real scary/

PATRICK: it was a bit scary because it looked a bit like a shark/

ADULT: did you see sharks as well/

PATRICK: yeah/but/sharks have more sharper teeth/

(b) ADULT: what's this man/

PATRICK: he's a missile detector/

ADULT: is he/

PATRICK: he detects the metal/

ADULT: is that in the mines/right/[4] he's fallen down/

PATRICK: he's hiding/

ADULT: why is he hiding/

PATRICK: 'cos he wants to get 'em/he wants to get [3] he's hiding/him/he can destroy them/

ADULT: he can what/destroy them/

PATRICK: [inaudible]

ADULT: I'm on the radio/can you hear me over there please/

PATRICK: yes/I can/you're [] and you're gonna kill/

ADULT: I'm what/

PATRICK: you're gonna kill/aren't you/

ADULT: I'm [3] I don't understand what you mean/I'm not killin' anybody/

PATRICK: you're gonna get 'em aren't you/you're gonna [inaudible]/

ADULT: no/I'm not/

PATRICK: [inaudible] we're in the army and we're gonna kill/

Milestones in language acquisition

The table below summarises some of the principal elements in the development of child language. It charts the key developments in *productive* language acquisition under the familiar linguistic headings. Of course, the *receptive* powers of the child (their powers of understanding) are always likely to be in advance of this.

Such a chart is to be used with caution: it can offer a starting point for your investigations, and prompt you to ask the appropriate questions. But remember: such a chart is never likely to describe accurately the pattern of development in any one child!

Approx. age	Function/ pragmatics	Phonology	Syntax/ morphology	Lexis and semantics
0–9 months	Mainly instrumental and regulatory; attention-seeking; basic statements and requests.	Babbling (see p.154). Basic exchanges of pre-verbal sounds between parent and child rehearse basic patterns of conversational turn-taking. Basic intonation patterns emerge even pre-verbally. These will allow holophrases to be used to		

		express different functions and meanings. Some consonant and vowel sounds appear, often very inconsistently (e.g. /b/, /d/, /m/, /i/, /a/, /u/). Repetition of groups of similar sounds, or **reduplication** (e.g. *baba* = baby, or *nana* = grandma) may be common.		
9–18 months	Interactional, instrumental and regulatory functions start to be served by verbal as well as non-verbal utterances. Early language includes basic statements, labelling and requests.		The **'one-word'** stage. Most utterances consist of a single item e.g. *mamma, juice, teddy*, though they may carry more pragmatic meanings (e.g. *dada = I want daddy to play with me*). Such one-word utterances are known as **holophrases**.	Much naming of people and objects in immediate environment. Semantic fields include food, the body, clothes, family members and toys. Meanings are context- and phonology-dependent.
18 months–2 years	Speech may start to include exchanges of information (representational language).	Some use of stress to distinguish meanings (e.g. ***my*** *car* = not anyone else's). More phonemes appear, though words may be quite different	The **'2-word'** stage. Speech includes many such combinations (e.g. *teddy gone, mammy hat*) including basic questions (*where teddy?*).	Much classification. Spatial location (*up, down, in, out*, etc.). Attributes of objects (*hot, cold, big, small*, etc.).

		from adult speech.	Some grammatical suffixes (inflections) e.g. *-ing, -s* (plurals) *-ed.*	
2–2½ years	More complex requests.	Vowel sounds becoming more consistent; pronunciation generally closer to adult speech as most phonemes appear and reduplication disappears. Intonation/stress/ other prosodic features continue to develop.	Sentences expand to three or more elements – the beginnings of the so-called **telegraphic stage** e.g. *daddy drive car, Harry fall down.* Some grammatical endings (*-s, -ing* etc.) begin to appear.	Lots of actions – sometimes in the past, less often in the future. Words like *the, is, a* begin to appear more frequently.
2½–3 years	Requests for explanations (*why?!*) may mark increasingly heuristic and imaginative functions. Indirect requests such as *Can I have . . . ?*	Continuing stabilisation and development of phonemic and prosodic aspects of speech – though some consonants (such as *l, r, th*) still not acquired, especially in combinations e.g. ***thr**ee*, in which /f/ is likely to be substituted for/θ/	Sentences expand to four or more elements. Simple sentences complete. Inflections on verbs and nouns becoming more consistent. Use of **auxiliary verbs**.	More abstract ideas and relationships.
3–3½ years	A full range of functions now, including representing feelings and attitudes.		More complex sentences emerge, including confident use of pronouns e.g. *I want the car daddy bought me.*	Conditional or hypothetical meanings (*what if . . .*). Specific references to time past, present and future.
3½–4 years	Continuing development in sophisticated	Acquisition of complete phonemic system	More consistent use of irregular verb and noun	Continuing development in ability to use

	uses of interactional, heuristic and imaginative language functions.	completed; some subtleties of intonation/stress patterns continue to be acquired with further development and experience.	endings, and auxiliary verbs (e.g. in questions and negatives). Over-generalised forms (like *I falled*) corrected.	more precise, abstract and varied vocabulary and meanings.
4½ years onwards			Basic grammatical structures in place. Later development will show increasing stylistic versatility and adaptability.	

Caught or taught? The language-acquisition debate

You are strongly urged to consult one or more of the following texts as you explore this topic:

Steven Pinker, *The Language Instinct*

Jean Aitchison, *The Articulate Mammal*

The process of language acquisition has exercised considerable fascination for many observers and students. Psychologists, sociologists, linguists, philosophers and biologists have been intrigued by the many questions it raises. Some of the questions are summarised below:

- Do humans learn language in the same way as they learn other kinds of social behaviour?
- Is language unique to humans?
- Are we programmed to learn language by something unique in the human genetic make-up?
- Which comes first – our ability to have an idea, or our learning how to express it in words?
- What is the role of language in the general psychological and intellectual development of children?
- How important is the role of parents and other adults in the development of children's language?

These are big questions, and what follows is only the briefest outline of the kinds of answers proposed by different thinkers.

As with the rest of your A2 course, you need to follow up the suggestions offered here for further reading, discussion and research.

The Behaviourist model of social learning

Psychologists have always been interested in how humans learn to behave in particular ways. From observations and experiments, it is clear that many different kinds of behaviour are learned in similar ways. Think of how you may have house-trained a dog or cat, or taught it to do tricks; such training will usually involve repetition of an activity, with a reward (or **positive reinforcement**) given for the desired behaviour (either a tangible reward such as a biscuit or a cuddle and a 'good girl!') and possibly a punishment (or **negative reinforcement**), physical or otherwise, for inappropriate behaviour. By these repetitions, animals learn the desired behaviour.

Similarly, some kinds of human behaviour seem to be 'conditioned' in this way. At school, for example, 'good' behaviour is rewarded with praise, merit points, and so on; 'bad' behaviour' is punished by tellings-off, detentions, and more serious sanctions for more serious offences. In this way, it is suggested, children learn to behave in the ways adults consider desirable.

So, one way of looking at language acquisition is to see it as a particular kind of social behaviour that follows this model: according to this, a child is encouraged to imitate the language of its parents/carers and receives positive reinforcements in the form of gratification of needs and attention/praise. 'Punishments' may simply be failure to achieve the desired purpose of the communication or explicit correction.

This view of language-learning was proposed for a period during the 1950s and 60s and is most associated with the psychologist B. F. Skinner. For reasons we shall see, few people now seriously claim that this explains the whole process of acquisition adequately. However, some aspects of language-learning do owe something to the Behaviourist model:

- children usually acquire the pronunciations of their parents and carers – imitation clearly plays a part in the acquisition of phonology
- some social and pragmatic aspects of language seem to be learned this way – the use of politeness strategies, for example.

However, closer observation shows that many aspects of language acquisition defy this explanation:

- children often gain positive reinforcement even for utterances which are 'wrong'. Few parents would deny their child food on the grounds of bad grammar!
- some evidence shows that children do not actually respond to correction of their speech
- some observers claim that children are not exposed to *enough* language to provide them with appropriate models to imitate in the relatively short time involved in first-language acquisition

- children do a lot more than merely imitate, as the examples of overgeneralization and overextension (see p.159 above) illustrate.

(You should refer back to *The Twitter Machine* on p.83 for an example of how this also applies to the acquisition of phonology.)

The genetic argument: Noam Chomsky

In the light of these objections to conventional Behaviourist theories of learning, what alternative explanation might there be for the speed and apparent creativity of the process of language acquisition?

In trying to answer this question, the linguist Noam Chomsky (and many of his followers) took note of the following features of language acquisition:

- children everywhere seem to learn language at a more or less similar pace, moving through similar stages of development at similar ages irrespective of their culture and mother tongue
- there seems to be a critical period in language development between the ages of about two and seven. For many of us, language-learning becomes a less instinctive and more laborious business after that
- far from being driven by the rewards that their behaviour produces, children actually use language far more than they need to, and seem resistant to correction
- children consistently create forms of language that they have never heard (like Harry's overgeneralisation *I falled*)
- experiments with chimpanzees and gorillas to train them to use language using Behaviourist methods seem to suggest that language is a uniquely human characteristic*
- all human languages, as different as they appear on the surface, share some fundamental similarities which Chomsky described as a 'Universal Grammar'.

So, Chomsky came to the conclusion that although some appropriate environmental input – linguistic interaction with parents/carers – was necessary, there was a *genetic* element innate in the human brain that prepared infants for language and accelerated the acquisition process. This element has come to be known as the **Language Acquisition Device**. If Behaviourism stresses the similarities between humans and other animals in their learning mechanisms, Chomsky's genetic explanation stresses the *differences*, and the uniqueness of human language.

The human brain, suggested Chomsky, seems to expect to find certain kinds of structures and patterning in the linguistic sounds it hears, and moves through a

* This is an area of some controversy, with some animal researchers claiming more success than this. See Jean Aitchison, *The Articulate Mammal*, or Stephen Pinker's *The Language Instinct* for accounts of this controversy.

series of provisional hypotheses as to what that structure (or grammar) is. Thus, Harry ignores the adult's attempt to correct his *I falled* because his own provisional grammar is telling him to override the adult's *I fell* as an error, since it contradicts his own rule that past-tense verbs end in /d/**.

According to Chomsky, language acquisition is a largely biological inevitability: learning to talk is as much a part of a child's genetically programmed development as is the more physically obvious process of learning to walk.

Language and child development: Piaget

Another approach to the development of child language is to see it as closely connected to other aspects of a child's psychological and intellectual (or **cognitive**) development. In this model, a child acquires increasingly complex forms of language only when his/her intellectual development is ready for it. This view is most commonly associated with the psychologist Jean Piaget. At first, for example, in what Piaget termed the 'sensori-motor' phase of development, children learn to classify their experiences of the physical world. We should not be surprised, therefore, to find few abstract concepts being represented in their language.

As they grow, they develop an awareness of concepts from their physical experiences such as comparisons of size, or tactile sensations like heat and cold, and they subsequently acquire the linguistic means to express these concepts. It is therefore futile to try and teach children complex forms before they are ready – not necessarily because of any innate linguistic programming, but because they cannot grasp the ideas involved. Forming a complex sentence depends not just on mastery of grammatical rules, but also on understanding the kinds of logical relationships involved, and this understanding must come first.

Piaget's ideas raise the interesting question of the role of language in child development. In trying to answer this, he suggests that child language has two sets of functions: first, as with Halliday's taxonomy (see pp.153–154) there are *social* functions which are all about communicating with and influencing the world in which we live. Secondly, however, Piaget also observed that children seem to use language in other ways, often talking when playing and when no one else is nearby. With this so-called **egocentric speech,** children seem to be using language to help themselves make sense of the world they are experiencing, and to order and classify their environment.

Language and thinking: Vygotski

Lurking beneath the surface of Piaget's work is the problematic question of the relationship between the language we learn to speak and the kinds of thoughts we have. The nature of this relationship has often intrigued philosophers and thinkers; in his novel *1984*, for example, George Orwell envisaged a future society in which the State tried to control the thoughts of the people by changing the language they spoke. This idea that people can only think what

** A. Cruttenden proposed that children commonly learn the irregular forms of verbs such as *fall* first; then, when they figure out the regular pattern, they can appear to be regressing as they start producing overgeneralised forms.

their language allows them to is rooted in the work of two linguists, Sapir and Whorf, in the 1930s. Subsequent research has somewhat discredited this notion, but even so, the debate over the need for 'political correctness' is partly founded on the notion that our way of thinking about things is influenced by the words that are used for them. Why else would an American president have named a new generation of nuclear missiles, each capable of obliterating several cities and millions of people, the Peacekeeper?

Piaget's model is the very opposite of this; he insisted that cognition (the ability to form ideas and concepts in our minds) precedes and is largely indepependent of language. However, another psychologist, Lev Vygotski, challenged certain aspects of this model. Whereas Piaget saw egocentric speech as a phase that children in time outgrew, Vygotski suggested that when children learn that talking out loud is considered anti-social or eccentric, this egocentric speech 'goes underground', and becomes the 'silent speech' that adults use, in effect, to think with. In this model, language and thinking become more closely interconnected, as language is not just the expression, but also the means of cognitive development.

Language as a social process

The wide influence of Chomsky's 'innateness' theory from the 1960s onwards tended to play down the social dimension of language acquisition. As we have seen, he tended to characterise the 'language input' children received in their interactions with adults as imperfect and an inadequate model for language-learning according to the Behaviourist model. He also tended to stress the development of grammar as the key aspect of acquisition.

However, later research has sometimes contradicted these assertions, and there is considerable evidence that the ways in which adults speak to children is much more structured and 'perfect' than Chomsky allowed. In some cases, researchers have found that a child's language development is enriched and accelerated according to the quantity and quality of its social interactions with adults (whose child-directed language has been variously referred to as 'caretaker speech', 'parentese', or 'motherese'). It is only through their interactions with adults that children learn the social *pragmatics* of language use.

ACTIVITY 9. THE EVIDENCE

There is a continuing debate about the role and relative importance of these various theoretical models in language acquisition. Listed overleaf are a number of commonly cited pieces of evidence in this debate.

For each one, suggest which of the principal models of acquisition outlined above seem to offer the best explanation of the linguistic behaviour they illustrate. You may find that the same piece of evidence could be explained using more than one model – and that different pieces of evidence invite apparently contradictory explanations!

Evidence	Which model(s)?
(a) Children produce overgeneralisations like *Harry falled* and *Harry felled.*	
(b) However, in time, children learn to remove these overegeneralisations from their speech and produce irregular forms correctly.	
(c) The case of Genie: the tragic case of a 13-year-old Los Angeles girl discovered in 1961 to have been locked away from all social interaction. Inevitably, she was profoundly disturbed – subsequent attempts to teach her English only ever produced partial success, and she never achieved full grammatical competence.	
(d) Pidgins/creoles: adult speakers from different language communities that come into close contact often create a simplified language called pidgin for practical purposes of trading, etc. However, if children grow up speaking this pidgin as their first language, they develop it into a more grammatically complex and sophisticated language called a creole. (A classic example of this process is the Neo-Melanesian Creole of New Guinea.)	
(e) Parents will typically repeat and amplify one- or two-word utterances, e.g. *Eat chips . . . Yes, Mummy's eating her chips.*	
(f) Medical scientists have identified distinct areas of the brain (known as Broca's and Wernick's areas) which seem to be critical for language-processing and production.	
(g) How do children respond to adult correction? Consider this example: Child: My teacher holded the rabbits and we patted them. Adult: Did you say your teacher held the baby rabbits? Child: Yes – she holded the baby rabbits. (Curtney Cazden *Child Language and Education*)	
(h) Some reseach suggests that children whose language is corrected make faster progress than those whose language is uncorrected.	
(i) Between the ages of five and seven, children from diverse backgrounds reach the same stage of	

grammar acquisition irrespective of whether their parents talk to them constantly or whether they are brought up to be seen and not heard. (V. Fromkin and R. Rodman, *An Introduction to Language*)	
(j) Some research indicates that simple exposure to language (e.g. from television) is not an effective stimulus to language-learning; children make better progress if they have regular one-to-one linguistic interactions.	

Compare your discussions with the commentary on p.192.

From speech to writing: early literacy

In this section, you will find it useful to review the section 'Speaking and writing' (*AS English Language for AQA B*, pp.30–33, and to the International Phonetic Alphabet as discussed on pp.16–18 above.

You should also extend your study of this topic by referring to:

D. Crystal, *The Cambridge Encyclopaedia of Language*, Chapter 34, 'The process of reading and writing'
Ruth Beard, *Children's Writing in the Primary School*
Margaret Donaldson, *Children's Minds*
A. Garton and C. Pratt, *Learning to be Literate*
N. Hall, *The Emergence of Literacy*
Katharine Perrera, *Children's Writing and Reading*
Language in the National Curriculum: Materials for Professional Development (not commercially available but your school/college may have a copy)

By the time a child starts to learn to read and write, s/he will already have gained an impressive command of the spoken language. Unlike the acquisition of speech, however, becoming literate does not come 'naturally'. This is to say that a process of formal learning is required – though there is some dispute about the degree to which children naturally exhibit a predisposition to write and read if sufficiently exposed to appropriate materials and experiences.

You might at first assume that written language is just a matter of 'speech written down', but as you have seen in your AS studies, this is not the case; writing is a distinct and different system from speech, and learning to read and write is all about discovering and applying the rather complex relationship that exists between these two forms of English.

Books written for children, like the early writing of children themselves, are likely to show many speech-like characteristics, as they are designed to help children achieve this transition from speech to writing. Storybooks for very young children may be intended to be read aloud, with parent and child focusing on the page – the child looking at the accompanying pictures as the adult establishes the basic discipline of reading, following a line of marks on a page and 'decoding' them into sounds and meaning.

Learning to read

Rather like learning to drive a car, or learning to play a musical instrument, reading involves the coordination and integration of several different physical and mental processes. As a learner driver, you have to become familiar with the controls of the car and their function, learn to coordinate several different physical actions (steering and changing gear with the hands, using the clutch, accelerator and brake with the feet, monitoring other traffic with the eyes, etc.), understand and apply the rules of the highway code, and make judgements about the spatial movements and speed of your car and other vehicles. At first, there seem to be a great many different things to remember and types of information to process as you consciously juggle with questions of when to change gear, which lane you need to be in as you approach a roundabout, what the road sign ahead means, what the vehicle in the lane next to you is going to do, etc.

However, with practice and experience, these various separate processes become unconscious ones, and are all integrated into the activity known as 'driving'. Practised drivers may hardly be conscious of what they are doing, and will certainly not be aware of the multiple processes their brains are effortlessly coordinating. This section will briefly explore the ways in which the acquisition of reading may be compared to this process.

ACTIVITY 10. LEARNING TO READ

Consider the situation of a child faced for the first time with a page of written language. Try to break down the business of 'reading' into the various separate processes that the child needs to learn and to integrate in order to become a skilled reader. Then compare your suggestions with those in the commentary on p.192.

Eventually, a reader learns both to integrate and to increase the speed and efficiency of these various processes. However, there is considerable debate about precisely how this is done, and consequently, about the most effective methods of teaching reading. What seems clear is that reading is not simply a matter of attending closely to the letters in one word after another. Rather, a number of different strategies are used simultaneously to decode any text:

Reading strategies

Strategy	Examples/notes
We use our knowledge of the **phonemic/graphemic correspondences** not only to match written letters/words to words we know from the spoken language, but also to guess the pronunciation of previously unknown items.	We can predict the pronunciation of a word like *shoomable* or *baddlinge*.

We use our ability to recognise and distinguish visually the **shapes of whole words.**	So much so that we do not need to see the *whole* word; we will probably recognise the shop sign with a missing letter (like Burt ns) or a word imperfectly printed (like **happily**).
We use our knowledge of **syntactic structures** to predict the kinds of word that can fit into a particular 'slot' in a sentence.	In *The car in front of me xxxxx suddenly* we predict that *xxxx* = a dynamic verb of some kind. So if we cannot easily distinguish visually, or phonically between *tops* and *stops*, or even if the text has misprinted the word *tops* for *stops*, we are likely to read it as *stops*.
We use our **semantic understanding** of the meanings in a text to predict what kinds of meanings are possible in a given 'slot'.	Similarly, even if we think the printed symbol looks more like *shops* than *stops*, our 'real world' understanding that cars cannot, in themselves, go shopping, may overrule our faulty visual recognition.
We use our understanding of **text structures** and genres to predict the kinds of meanings we are likely to find.	When we reach the end of a fairy story and the final sentence begins *And th* . . . . we do not usually need to deconstruct each word phonemically to guess the rest of the sentence!

The very complicated nature of the reading process and an anxiety about standards of literacy have combined to produce a long-running and sometimes heated debate about the best way of teaching reading. This has sometimes been reduced (and oversimplified) to a conflict between the 'phonics'-based and 'look-and-say'-based approaches. Most recently, a strong emphasis on the importance of phonics-based learning has been enshrined in the Literacy Hour introduced into English primary schools.

The main points in this debate are outlined below:

Teaching reading: phonics or whole-word (look-and-say)?

Phonics	Whole-word ('look-and-say')
The child is systematically taught the letters of the alphabet and how these correspond to the phonemes of the spoken word (= phoneme/grapheme correspondences). This teaching will gradually move from the straightforward e.g. *d* =/d/ *o* =/ɒ *g* =/g/ so *dog* =/dɒg/ – to more complex variations such as: *gh* =/f/ in *rough, tough, enough, laugh* *ph* =/f/ in *Philip, graph*	The child is exposed to written texts (at first with heavy pictorial support) and gradually learns to identify the shapes of words as a whole without always breaking them down into the phonemes/graphemes they contain.

Advantage: children learn to understand how written words are built and spelt; it can help to decipher new unknown words.	*Advantage:* mature readers do not depend solely on phonemic decoding. 'Look-and-say' allows children to develop their experience of using all textual and contextual clues to assist reading.
Disadvantage: early written vocabulary may be limited to words that illustrate basic sound:spelling correspondences. What is more, the complexities of the English spelling system are such that in a typical selection of 6,000 words occurring in the speech of six–nine-year-olds there may be over 211 different sound:spelling correspondences – too many for confident understanding!*	*Disadvantage:* no real system to the learning process. Spelling 'caught not taught'.
Summary: it is generally agreed that children do need to acquire an understanding of phonics to achieve literacy, and a phonics-based approach offers a systematic way of giving children this knowledge explicitly. Some research evidence points to impressive improvements in the reading of children taught a phonics-based approach (e.g. an early reading project carried out in Essex schools from 1996 resulted in children achieving reading ages six or seven months ahead of children not in the scheme (as reported in the *Times Educational Supplement* (30/3/01).	*Summary:* some research suggests that children acquire phonic understanding in the same way they acquire speech (see above), less by formal instruction than by appropriate exposure to guided reading experiences (e.g. Smith and Elley, *Learning to read in New Zealand*). Phonic awareness need not necessarily be achieved by intensive and systematic drilling: 'there is little evidence that one form of phonics instruction is strongly superior to another', (Stahl, McKenna and Pagnucco, 'The effects of whole language instruction', *Educational Psychologist* 29, 1994) and some research may even point in the opposite direction (Tunnell and Jacobs).

* Reported in Frank Smith, *Reading*.

A **phonics-based** approach to the acquisition of reading may be characterised by the use of carefully graded flash-cards and readers that gradually expose children to lexical structures; children will be systematically taught the phonemic values of the different letter combinations and shown how individual words are made up of a series of these.

A **whole-word-based** (or 'look-and-say') approach would expose children to texts that might include a wider variety of structures. Children are encouraged to become familiar with the shapes of words by frequent exposure rather than by dissecting words into graphemes and phonemes. However, rhymes, tongue-twisters, alphabet books and other similar materials aim to enable children to acquire phonic awareness as they read.

Activity 11. The phonics controversy

Try to find out more about the whole-word/phonics issue and the wider debate about the teaching of reading to very young children. Try to visit a primary school to observe the process in action, or at least talk to a primary-school teacher. You can also visit the *Times Educational Supplement* website (www.tes.co.uk) and search its archive for articles on the subject.

Readability and textual difficulty

The writer of *any* text written to be read by or to young or inexperienced readers will need to carefully control those aspects of written language that make a text seem 'difficult'. It is useful to consider these textual features as they can reveal much about the process of reading itself.

Activity 12. What makes a text difficult?

Listed below are some the factors that may contribute to the perceived difficulty of a written text. Extend the discussion offered in the *Notes* column by carrying out your own investigations as suggested under *Extension activities*.

Linguistic level	Variable	Notes	Extension activities
Graphology	Page layout; font type and size; white space:page ratio; pictures: print ratio	The same text presented with graphological variation can be perceived as having different degrees of difficulty. Undifferentiated blocks of small print in a formal font can be very forbidding; at the other extreme, pages with a low text:white space or picture ratio place fewer demands on a reader.	Survey a range of children's books to chart the gradual change in these features, as the target audience become more confident readers.
Lexis/ morphology	Length of words	For early readers, longer words may prove difficult both to deconstruct phonically and to recognise visually. Simpler texts are likely to have a lower average word length. One common way of measuring the length of words is to count **syllables** – but some words of equal syllabic length may be of different lengths in other ways. For example, the following words all consist of just one syllable, but the numbers of phonemes and letters vary considerably, which may make some words easier to read than others: • *but*: 3 phonemes, 3 letters • *rough*: 3 phonemes, 5 letters • *knead*: 3 phonemes, 5 letters • *creamed*: 5 phonemes, 7 letters • *queens*: 5 phonemes, 6 letters • *searched*: 5 phonemes, 8 letters	Collect a sample of two- and three-syllable words, and carry out a similar examination of the variation in length when measured in terms of letters, graphemes and phonemes.

	Ease of recognition: phonetic/non-phonetic spelling of words	Words in which there is a close relationship between spelling and sounds are easier to process phonically. As the examples above illustrate, words containing 'silent' letters (***k**nead*), digraphs (*sear**ch**ed*) or unusual grapheme:phoneme correspondences (*qu* =/kw/, *gh* =/f/) may present more difficulties than words in which these correspondences are more predictable, like *dog* or *bat*; texts written for very young readers may have a high proportion of these easier words.	Examine some sample passages from texts produced for young readers at different stages and carry out a statistical survey of the proportions of words that contain silent letters.
	Frequency of usage	Words that are likely to be encountered by a child in everyday usage are clearly more likely to be recognised than more adult, obscure or specialist terms.	
Semantics	Concrete or abstract?	Nouns and adjectives that refer to actual objects and attributes (= **concrete**) may present fewer difficulties than **abstract** concepts. In some ways this is less a purely linguistic consideration than a conceptual one; the development of our ability to deal with abstract ideas and concepts is linked to our general cognitive progress (see Piaget and Vygotski, pp.168–169).	Survey a selection of graded texts to test the hypothesis that a higher proportion of abstractions may occur in texts for older readers.
	Context	Even unfamiliar words may be guessed if the context provides enough clues. In the sentence *My cat has a smooth black vgth,* we cannot 'read' *vgth* but may guess that it means *coat*. Children's books provide additional clues in their illustrations. The fewer the clues, and the higher the proportion of potentially unfamiliar words, the more difficult the text may seem to be.	Examine the way in which textual illustrations and contexts provide clues for potentially difficult words in a children's book.
Sentences and syntax	Length	As with lexis, sheer length can in itself be daunting; the longer the sentence, the longer the reader is asked to retain in the memory how the sentence began.	Measuring average sentence lengths can be one of the indicators of textual readability. Test this with some sample passages from some graded readers.
	Type: simple, compound, complex	The structure of the sentence is perhaps a more crucial feature than length alone. **Simple sentences** (*the*	Again, test out these principles by examining

		dog ran home quickly) are easiest to read as they present a single action. **Compound sentences** come next, as they present two or more actions in a straightforward relationship (*the dog ran home quickly and buried its bone*). Complex sentences are hardest, as they may not present the information in a predictable sequence, or describe complex sets of logical relationships (*The dog ran home quickly and buried its bone, having made its escape from the butcher's shop*).	sample texts, or constructing trial texts of your own to test a child's understanding.
	Subject/verb position	One specific aspect of syntactic structure which may cause difficulty is the separation of the subject from the main verb (***The dog** which the butcher had chased from his shop for stealing Mrs Jones's sausages **ran** home*) or the delay of the subject and main verb to the end of the sentence (*Having escaped from the butcher's shop and run all the way from the town, **the dog arrived** home*).	
	Active/passive voice	Similarly, active structures (*the dog chased the cat*) are easier to process than passive ones (*the cat was chased by the dog*), because they present the **agent** and the **action** in the sequence most commonly found in spoken English. In the passive sentence, we have to wait until the end to discover who was doing the chasing; tests show that younger readers sometimes misread passive structures such as this and believe that the cat was chasing the dog because it occurs first in the sentence.	
	Verb tense constructions	The simplest and most common verb constructions in English are the basic forms of the so-called simple and progressive forms (*walk/walked/will walk* and *am walking/was walking/going to walk*). Only as we become more experienced readers can we confidently deal with such modal and complex forms as *might have been going to walk* or *will have been intending to walk.*	

Activity 13. Writing for children

Printed below are some extracts from a series of texts written for young readers.

Carry out a detailed study of the way in which the linguistic content of these texts has been controlled and graded. Show how the texts gradually increase their degree of challenge, using the headings in the table above to structure your investigation. Look out for ways in which these written texts embody characteristics of spoken language.

1. *The Toys' Party* (from the Oxford Reading Tree, Stage 2)

Page	Text	Picture
1	Kipper wanted a party.	Little boy, alone, sitting at table, looking sad, wearing paper hat
2/3	Nobody wanted to come.	We now see boy is at table in kitchen, dog sleeping, and boy's thought bubbles show two adults washing a car, two children playing football outside
4/5	He got his toys.	Boy coming downstairs carrying soft toys; teddy bear now at table, dog awake
6/7	He wanted a cake.	Boy at table with soft toys and large bowl. Thought bubble shows large cake with 'Happy Birthday' written on it
8/9	He put in cornflakes. He put in tomato sauce.	Boy at table with soft toys and cornflakes/tomato sauce. Some in bowl; some on table and floor
10/11	He put in milk. He put in jam.	Similar – increasing mess, boy looking excited, toys looking alarmed
12/13	He put in sugar. He put in baked beans.	Kitchen, boy, toys all now awash with food
14/15	Mum was cross.	Mum appears in doorway looking angry, boy and toys look sheepish
16	Kipper was sorry.	Boy sitting in underwear by washing machine, looking sad as toys revolve inside

2. *Pirate Adventure* (from the Oxford Reading Tree, Stage 5)

1	Biff was looking at a book. The book was about pirates. 'I don't like pirates,' she said.	Little girl looking at illustrated book containing a picture of typical fierce-looking pirate-figure
2	Wilf and Wilma came to play. They went to Biff's room.	Two children going upstairs
3	They looked at the little house. 'It's a magic house,' said Biff. 'Don't be silly,' said Wilma.	Four children kneeling around toy house
4/5	They looked at the key. 'It's a magic key,' said Chip. 'Don't be silly,' said Wilf. The key began to glow. The magic was working. 'Oh help!' said Wilma.	Girl holds key which is glowing bright yellow. Chip is smiling; Wilma and Wilf look vaguely worried
6/7	The magic was working. The children got smaller and smaller. 'Oh no!' said Wilf. 'Oh help!' said Wilma. 'We don't like this,' they said.	Four children now small in comparison to the toy house
8	They looked at the house. The windows were glowing. Biff went to the door.	Wilma and Wilf looking worried; Chip smiling
9	She put the key in the lock. She opened the door.	Biff placing key in lock
10/11	The children went inside the house. 'It's a magic house,' they said. 'Look at the sand,' said Biff. 'Look at the sea,' said Chip. 'Come on,' they said.	Four children emerge from doorway onto deserted golden beach with palm trees and blue sea

The children went inside the house.
'It's a magic house,' they said.
10

'Look at the sand,' said Biff.
'Look at the sea,' said Chip.
'Come on,' they said.
11

3. *Pol and Pax in the Salty Red Sea*, Nelson 'New Way' series, 'Orange' level.

1	Pol and Pax live on a faraway planet with three moons and a ring around it. The children on this planet never have to go to school. They eat a slice of brain food every day and this makes them as clever as they need to be. Pol and Pax had lots of time to play. One day they were fishing in the underground river near their house. They wanted to see which of them could catch the strangest fish.	Two green-haired children in boiler suits fishing on the bank of a red river coming out of a blue tunnel. They have a small fish tank with several fish
2/3	(2) At the end of the day Pol had only caught a few very ordinary fish. He had caught a small shark and two shills. Pax hadn't done much better. He had caught three straps and one stock. Neither of them had seen a scrum or a stink, let alone a skimp. 'I would love to see a real live skimp,' said Pax. 'They don't come this far inland,' said Pol. 'You needn't hope to find one.' (3) 'But one has found you,' said a watery voice. Pol and Pax looked around. They could see no-one. 'Here, right in front of your noses,' said the watery voice. Pol and Pax looked down and saw a nose with four white whiskers sticking out of the water. Soon the rest of the skimp followed. 'A skimp,' shouted Pol and Pax together. 'A real live skimp.' 'You needn't shout so,' said the skimp. 'I'm not deaf'.	Two children looking in some amazement and pointing at a walrus-like creature emerging from the river and smiling
4/5	(4) The skimp wriggled onto the bank of the river and shook the water off its whiskers. Skimps can live in water and on land. They usually stay in the sea, and this skimp was far from home. 'I'm lost,' said the skimp, 'totally lost. I left home three days ago. I was on my way to my cousin in the salty red seas and took a short cut.' 'Never take short cuts,' said Pol. 'They're always long cuts,' said Pax. (5) 'Thanks for your advice,' said the skimp, 'but it's too late. Can you please tell me how I can get to the salty red seas?' 'We'll have to look in our sea and river atlas,' said Pax, 'and that's at home.' 'Please go and get it,' said the skimp.' 'I'll wait here for you to keep an eye on your dinner.' 'That's not our dinner,' said Pol. 'We only eat brain food,' said Pax.	The 'skimp' is looking into the fish tank with apparent excitement. The children are looking on

Compare your study with the commentary on p.193.

ACTIVITY 14. POSSIBLE LANGUAGE INVESTIGATIONS

These suggestions could be used either to extend your study for the Module 6 examination or as the basis for a Module 4 language investigation.

- Gather some examples of your own of texts produced for very young readers. These may be part of a structured reading scheme used in a primary school, or storybooks aimed at children. Carry out your own analysis of some sample passages from these texts, assessing their linguistic difficulty in terms of the features noted in the table above. Where the texts are part of a reading scheme, compare texts at different stages in the scheme.

- The kinds of texts used in primary schools have changed considerably over the years, reflecting not only changing ideas about how children learn to read, but also developments in society as a whole. Try to obtain some examples of readers used in the past, and compare these with modern texts. You could consider, for example, how boy and girl characters are represented through language in these readers, and relate this to some of the ideas about language and gender we considered in AS Module 2.

- If at all possible, arrange either to work with a six/seven-year-old in your family or visit a primary school. With the advice of a teacher/parent, choose a passage from a text at an appropriate level and of some potential interest and record a child reading the text aloud. Follow this up by testing the child's understanding of what they have read by discussing the text with them, and transcribe the child's reading, including any errors, hesitations and self-corrections.

  Use the evidence of this transcription to analyse the child's reading process, and explain what this reveals about the process of reading acquisition.

  The errors and hesitations that a child may make in reading aloud are known as **miscues** and a study like this one is called a **miscue analysis.** One suggested way of transcribing the different types of miscue you may find is adapted here from the *The Primary Language Record Handbook* (Barrs, Ellis, Hester and Thomas). It is important to consider which of these miscues are *positive* indicators which show the reader searching constructively for meaning in the text, and which are more negative indicators of a lack of basic comprehension.

Carrying out a miscue analysis

Type of miscue	Suggested symbol on transcript	Indication
Substitution	The word substituted is written above the corresponding word in the text: *When* Then Mother Tortoise began to look into the picnic basket . . .	If plausible, positively indicates reading for meaning.

Self-correction	Show initial miscue above text with 'c' to indicate correction *C the* They picked up the sandwiches, but just as they were going to eat . . .	Can positively indicate reading for meaning, anticipation and prediction of structures and meanings, and monitoring of understanding against the actual details of the text.
Repetition	Underline any repeated words 'It's six years now,' said Mother Tortoise. 'He ought to be back by now.'	Can almost be a form of self-correction if it offers a second 'run-up' to the next section of the sentence.
Omission	Circle the omitted word	Can be positive and show understanding and anticipation if it is an incidental word – however, if important words are omitted, and no subsequent self-correction occurs, it suggests a failure of monitoring for understanding.
Insertion	Indicate any word spoken not actually present in the text with insertion mark *the* And in /\ three years they reached their picnic place.	Can indicate constructive anticipation, as the child is literally creating the meaning of the text. In this example, some visual confusion of *the/three* is possible: both are semantically plausible.
Reversal	Show reversed words as shown: 'Yes, I suppose he ought,' said Father.	May show anticipation of more common syntactic patterns.
Hesitation/pause	Show hesitation with oblique stroke. Longer pauses can be indicated using (3) for number of seconds 'Well, do/you swear . . . '	May indicate difficulty in recognising next word or phrase, or could indicate monitoring in progress.
Teacher gives help or correction	Use T to indicate, as in: *ravens* they got ravenous *T*	

See: H. Arnold, *Listening to Children Reading*

Learning to write

It was noted earlier that the challenge of literacy involves an understanding and application of the codes and conventions of writing as a distinct system – it is not simply a straightforward recording of spoken language. As you observe the writing of a five-, six-, or seven-year-old, you will see at close quarters the ways in which a child gradually has to negotiate this complicated relationship. Module 4 began to explore this kind of data (see pp.35–38.).

At first, you are likely to find that children's early writing exhibits many of the characteristics of spoken language, as the sequence of children's narratives in Module 4, above (see pp.44–47) showed. The development of advanced writing skills is a long process; just as a child's ability to understand speech will always be in advance of their speech competence, so at any given point in a child's development, reading ability will always exceed the ability to produce written texts.

Activity 15. The writing process

In addition to the various elements of the reading process which you have just considered, now consider the extra skills required by the process of writing. As you did for reading, list the different skills elements involved – physical and mental – in the business of writing.

Compare your suggestions with the commentary on p.195.

As with reading, skilled writers have learned to integrate these various processes and many of them – especially the physical and mechanical challenges – will in time become second nature. However, when you examine the writing that young children produce at different ages, you can usually see fascinating evidence of this learning process in action.

There is some debate about how similar this process is to the acquisition of speech; as you start to examine the writing of young children in the following activity, you can start to answer this question for yourself.

Activity 16. Children's writing

Reproduced on p.185 are two examples of work produced by children in the first year of primary school. Carry out a detailed study of these texts, and try to explain what they reveal about the process of learning to write. Identify positively what the writer already knows and is applying, and also, try to explain what lies behind the errors.

Look out for evidence that the authors of these texts are creating and applying provisional theories about different aspects of writing similar to the overgeneralising and overextension characteristic of spoken language acquisition.

A commentary is provided on p.195 for the first of these; compare your analysis with it before moving on to the second text.

You might find it useful to use the framework below to structure your investigation.

Investigating children's writing: a framework for investigation

Linguistic level	Questions to investigate through analysis	Refer to
Text structure and cohesion	What kind of pattern or structure does the text follow? How cohesive/coherent is the text? Has the writer made use of connecting/ cohesive features?	Module 1 pp. 13–18, 'Discourse structure'; Module 4, pp.20–23.

	Have pronouns been used to avoid undue repetition? Has the writer employed any common conventions of a particular genre (such as *Once upon a time . . .* or *Dear . . .*)?	
Mechanical and spatial control	How far does the writing reveal physical control of the direction and spacing of text?	
Letter formation	How consistently are letter-shapes correctly produced? Are letters being confused, reversed or inverted?	
Spelling	What phonemic:graphemic correspondences are being used correctly? Do the 'mistakes' show evidence of creative guessing or overgeneralization? Do they suggest evidence of *phonic* (if they attempt phonetic spelling) or *visual* (if they include non-phonetic reversals, juxtapositions, etc.) awareness of the words? What patterns can you find in the child's spelling? Make sure you look at what the child is doing correctly as well as the mistakes. One approach is to investigate the ways in which a writer has represented a single phoneme throughout the text (look at the sound /k/ in the first text, for example).	See pp.176 above.
Word selection	Examine the range, register and appropriateness of the words used.	See 'Using the stylistics framework: levels of description', AS book, pp.13–31.
Semantics	What sorts of concrete or abstract meanings are being conveyed? Actions? Descriptions of objects, places and people? Feelings? Reflections? Ideas?	
Syntactic structures	How far is the writing being constructed into distinct sentences? How much is the writer using extended compound sentences to convey ideas?	
Punctuation	Which punctuation forms are being used, and how closely does the writer's 'system' correspond with adult punctuation conventions?	
Narrative and rhetorical methods	How far is the writer beginning to *craft* the text by: • using vivid or dramatic language for effect • making comparisons or other figurative uses of language • showing an awareness that the reader may not share the same context as the writer?	

Monday 21-5-01
The Wich
One a Pon tim ter wer a Wich Live
in a ckasl. She had a Liyn.
ONE littl Boy ckam For a wak.
The liyn Bit the Boy the Boy wet
home. The gel ckam for a work She
met a lemn. The woman wer ckolo
wich. The wich lickt [illegible] the gel.
The ger wer sirh. Sirh wet home.
The wich ckrid the liyn and the wich
wer frends. The wich wer ckolde it
stil rane the liyn wet two the gels
home. The gel giva appl to the liyn.
He et the appl But the liyn ckvdnt
et the appl the the liyn wet to the
Boys home. The boy gev a org to
the liyn Bet the liyn et the orgug.
But the wich wer a loon Bicks the st atid.
to liv wid the Buy.

Witch

Monday 12=5==10 [illegible]
onec a pon tin
w was a witch.
She lev in cas.
The witch wen a wc.
she went shop. The witch
Went sgo. The witch play.
The witch was note. The wetch
had beg trobl. The witch
tec the casl.
In the casl she way
ong. Som chosl cay to
casl. Thegy were Happy.
Theay cam to casl.

Adult transcriptions:

(a) The witch

Once upon a time there were a witch living in a castle. She had a lion. One little boy came for a walk. The lion bit the boy. The boy went home. The girl came for a walk. She met a woman. The woman were called witch. The witch liked the girl. The girl were Sarah. Sarah went home. The witch cried. The lion and the witch were friends. The lion were (*deleted*) cold(?) it started to rain (?) the lion went to the girl's home. The girl gave an apple to the lion. He ate the apple but the lion couldn't eat the apple but the lion went to the boy's home. The boy gave an orange to the lion but the lion ate the orange. But the witch were alone because the (lion) started to live with the boy.

(b) Once upon a time there was a witch. She lived in a castle. The witch went for a walk. She went shopping. The witch went to school. The witch played. The witch was naughty. The witch had big trouble. The witch (went) (?) to the castle. In the castle she was lonely (?) Some ghost (?) (came) to (the) castle. They were happy. They came to (the) castle.

Activity 17. Investigating children's writing

You are now ready to carry out your own investigation possibly by visiting a primary school and asking permission to collect a sample of writing by children between the ages of five and seven.

Note: The Specification for Module 6 does not require you to go beyond the age of seven but you could, of course, extend your investigation into older children's writing as part of a language investigation for Module 4.

This investigation could take several forms:

- take a sample of the same assignment produced by a range of children within a class to investigate the different stages of development within a year group
- take several pieces of writing produced by a single child over a period of time to chart the developments in writing skills (= a **longitudinal** study)
- take similar pieces of writing produced by children of similar ability in different year groups for a comparative study
- compare the writing of an 'average' child with one with unusual circumstances (such as one for whom English is a second language, or who has learning difficulties)
- if your own workbooks from infant/primary school have survived, you could trace your own development as a writer.

Remember:

- always seek the permission of the class teacher before collecting and using data
- do everything you can to ensure your data is valid and truly comparable (see Module 4, 'Language Investigation').

Preparing for the examination

The specification says . . .	This means you must . . .	Tip for success
AO1 communicate clearly the knowledge, understanding and insight appropriate to the study of language, using appropriate terminology and accurate and coherent written expression ($2^1/_2$%)	Write your analysis and essays clearly and accurately. Make sure you use the proper linguistic terminology to define the features of language you are discussing.	Revise by reviewing your own personal glossary as well as referring to the one on p.242. Refer back to clarify your understanding of any terms you have forgotten. In the examination, as you scrutinise the material on the question paper, spend a few minutes brainstorming and organising your thoughts into sections, before sequencing them logically.
AO3ii understand, discuss and explore concepts and issues relating to language in use ($2^1/_2$%)	Show you can apply your understanding of linguistic ideas and theories of acquisition to your analysis and discussions of child language data.	As this is a synoptic module, you should revise the *whole* of your AS and A2 courses. For example, from Module 1 you will need the frameworks for analysing both speech and writing and a clear understanding of the relationship between them; from Module 2 issues relating to conversational analysis and especially language and gender, from Module 4 you will need to bring an understanding of the nature of textual cohesion/coherence, and from Module 5 you should refer to items such as 'A Child's Crossed Words Puzzle', which have a specific language-acquisition content. Re-read the commentaries printed at the end of each module – they are examples of the kind of informed analysis and discussion that you need to produce for yourself.
AO4 apply and explore frameworks for the systematic study of language at different levels, commenting on the usefulness of the approaches taken (5%)	Show you can identify the most appropriate linguistic ramework to apply to a given text.	Try to carry in your head the kinds of questions relating to discourse structure, cohesion, exis, semantics, phonology and graphology.

For the Language Acquisition questions you will need to:

Know . . .	Be able to . . .
The principal milestones in linguistic development, in terms of: • pragmatics/language functions • phonetics • lexis/semantics • syntax/morphology.	Describe and analyse examples of child language data precisely and accurately, using the appropriate framework and terminology.
The issues surrounding the question of 'stages' of language development.	Analyse data with an open mind.
The principal theories that attempt to explain the process of acquisition, i.e. Behaviourist, innateness, cognitive and social.	Relate your analysis of specific examples of child language to these theories, and explain how they might explain the linguistic data you are presented with.
The relationship between spoken and written language and how this helps to explain the process of learning to read and write.	Comment precisely and in an informed way on data relating to children's early reading and writing.

As this module is designed to assess the knowledge and skills you have developed over the whole AS/A2 course, it may be useful to consider those aspects of the previous five modules you will need to draw upon, directly or indirectly, in Module 6:

Preparing for the synoptic module

Module	Skills/knowledge
1	Applying analytical frameworks; varieties of English including regional and Standard English, grounds for comparing, grouping and contrasting texts
2	Analysing language in relation to social contexts, using research findings, issues of power and gender; conversational analysis
3	Working with genres
4	Applying appropriate analytical approaches to a variety of linguistic data
5	Synthesising and re-casting texts of various kinds

Commentaries

Activity 1. First discussions

A: at first, a child's needs are fairly basic – nutrition, comfort and security just about cover everything. Parents rapidly learn to recognise the repertoire of cries and other sounds with which an infant communicates its basic needs. However, as a child grows older, its needs become more sophisticated – a loud yell may do to let mum know you're hungry, but to request those particularly tasty dinosaur-shaped chicken nuggets may demand the subtleties of language! As we will see in the following section, children also graduate beyond the basic biological needs to more social requirements for which an increasingly accomplished command of language is necessary.

B: an unfamiliar language strikes us as a continuous stream of unintelligible sound. It is difficult to determine the boundaries between words, and even if we begin to recognise certain sounds that sound like words, and recur frequently, we then have to try to guess their meaning from the context in which they are spoken. As for the grammar, it is difficult to know where to start, especially if it is a language very different from English. It might appear that things should be even more difficult for a child, as s/he has no other language to compare things with. Yet some academics do believe that in some ways even the smallest infant is better equipped than an adult to undertake this process of deciphering, as you will see later.

C: it is tempting to consider some languages more difficult than English, either because there seem to be more endings (or inflections) to learn, or because the pronunciations seem more difficult. However, the fact is that children the world over do seem to achieve approximately similar levels of competence in their mother tongue wherever they happen to be born. There may be some differences in the degree to which aspects of the written language are learned, however.

D: the answer is, of course, that all of these do seem to play a part – but the relative importance of each remains a matter for considerable debate among researchers and academics. This controversy will be investigated later in this module.

E: clearly, children learn to understand speech, and speak for themselves, first; this is a natural process that occurs in just about any circumstance into which a child is born. However, reading and writing come later, or, unless actively taught/learned, not at all. Our preoccupation with literacy is a relatively recent phenomenon; until the twentieth century, the human experience of language was overwhelmingly spoken. There may be some similarities, however, in the process of learning that takes place – this will be considered later in this module

Activity 2. A language taxonomy

Even the most basic inventory would include the following:

Phonology	Lexis and semantics	Grammar: morphology and syntax	Pragmatics	Orthography and graphology
Recognise, distinguish and produce and combine the phonemes of English. Recognise the meanings of and articulate words	Recognise and produce vocabulary (a working stock of 15,000 words should do to start though this can rise to 50,000).	Recognise and understand the semantic and grammatical function of English morphemes. Produce grammatically	Understand the ways in which social contexts contribute to meanings. Understand the codes that apply in different social situations.	Recognise and reproduce the letters of the alphabet in lower and upper case. Understand and apply the correspondences between letters/

and sentences with appropriate prosodic features (stress, intonation, pitch, timbre, etc.).	Understand and apply the morphological principles of word building (e.g. that *walked* = *walk* + *ed*). Understand and apply the denotations, connotations and register of words. Recognise appropriate contexts in which specific registers are used.	appropriate forms to express person, tense, etc. Recognise and understand the underlying rules of English syntax. Produce phrases and sentences that observe these rules.	Understand the ways in which social contexts contribute to meanings. Understand the codes that apply in different social situations. Understand and apply the rules of conversation in a variety of contexts. Understand and apply the principles that make for cohesion in different types of discourse.	combinations of letters and phonemes. Understand and apply the different conventions that apply to written language, including the use of punctuation conventions.

Activity 4

The function of the first utterance may seem to be simply the satisfaction of biological need – for food – though the word 'please' is more than is strictly needed for this.

The doctor's enquiry is a predictable request for information, and you might expect the conversation that follows to be a more or less factual exchange about the patient's complaint. However, a very similar utterance made in a different context has a quite different function – the second 'how are you' here is not necessarily a genuine request for medical information but has a fundamentally social or phatic function, assisting the business of human interaction.

The teacher's request does seem to have a very practical purpose – getting someone else to do something you require – but this is also bound up with the need for comfort (perhaps the teacher is feeling cold) and even social niceties (the use of Michael's first name and *please* help soften the command). Note also that it is softened by being framed as an interrogative rather than an imperative.

Finally, the declaration of enthusiasm for Westlife's latest is primarily a statement about the speaker's self – his/her enthusiasms, preferences – and identity. Much of the language we use in social situations at least partly serves this purpose.

Activity 5

A Big Mac and regular fries is certainly **instrumental** but includes *please*, which has an interactional function. The doctor's greeting combines **representational** (requesting information) and **interactional** elements (*Hello . . .*), whereas the businessman's greeting is mainly the latter. The teacher's request is both regulatory and instrumental, and the politeness strategies it features have an **interactional** function. The Westlife fan's comment is both **personal** and **interactional**.

Activity 6. Developing language functions

At 15 months, Harry has a limited vocabulary in adult terms, but he clearly uses a single word (*dada*) to perform different functions here – in Dore's terms, the first could be labelling or a greeting; in Halliday's, interactional or possibly representational. The second *dada* must either be labelling or greeting, whereas *Hardy!* is most likely labelling. However, in the absence of lexical or grammatical precision, Harry may be varying his intonation according to function.

In practice, early functions are likely to be confined to the first four in Halliday's list. When Hannah is 20 months old, her vocabulary has become considerably extended and she is sometimes combining two lexical items. The syntax is generally recognisable, and we can say that the beginnings of sentence construction can be found here. For all their limitations, the two-word utterances can express a variety of meanings and functions. *Daddy hat* is still labelling but is doing more than naming, as it attributes possession. *Juice* is a request (instrumental function in Halliday's terms), but now refers to an object not physically in view. *Nice teddy* may be a piece of interactional behaviour and *all gone* a more sophisticated piece of labelling, identifying as it does disappearance and non-existence.

At the age of $2^1/_2$, not only does Harry have a much wider vocabulary, but he has also begun to use the basics of sentence construction in his two-, three- and four-word utterances. This enables him to be more precise and expressive in his language functions. The request for information (*where red car?*) takes him into the realms of the representational, and he is no longer relying on intonation alone for questioning, as he uses the appropriate question word *where*. However, he has yet to acquire the complete syntactic structure of *where is the/my red car? Ron play Harry car* is a request for an adult to join in playing (regulatory function), more precise and less context-dependent than similar requests at an earlier age, but still lacking the appropriate modal structures used in adult requests.

By the time Hannah is $3^1/_2$, more or less fully-formed sentences and a wide vocabulary combine to serve a wide range of functions, from the personal (*Look at me, mummy!*) to the imaginative (playing at being a Power Ranger) to the heuristic (*That doesn't go there*). Instrumental requests are now formed using modal politeness (*Can I have . . .*), and even protests are now being constructed with appropriate negative syntax (*I don't want play that game . . .*).

Activity 7

The forms of these requests gradually become less context-dependent – *dada* depends very largely on contextual and gestural information, but with the emergence of a basic syntax (*Daddy drive car . . . I want Daddy drive car*) greater explicitness and precision are possible. However, *I want* is, in adult terms, very blunt; the last two versions show not only the acquisition of syntactic structures such as question forms and politeness strategies, but also the pragmatic awareness that such strategies can be more effective than direct requests in achieving the desired result.

Activity 9. The evidence

(a), (b) and (g): overgeneralisations (and semantic overextensions) suggest the child is doing more than imitating, as they illustrate the application of the child's own provisional grammar to the language, and are forms of language that they will not have heard any adult speak. The genetic predisposition to find patterns must be triggered by exposure to the right kind of stimulus, however – e.g. adults using language in which /d/ usually indicates past tense, and the fact that overgeneralisations eventually disappear also illustrates that imitation of adult models is part of the process.

(c) and (d): Genie is cited as an illustration of the 'critical period' theory (proposed by the biologist Lenneberg) whereby the language acquisition device only operates at its most effective during a particular phase of development. However, it might equally be argued that Genie's deprivation of social interaction, and isolation from other kinds of cognitive development, were so damaging that her subsequent failure to acquire language completely was not surprising. The development of creole languages among children who invest their parents' pidgins with complex structures seems to support the innateness idea, not only as it is a positive illustration of the 'critical period' idea, but because they are actually creating grammatical structures even where they didn't exist in the adult speech the children are 'imitating'.

(e), (g) and (h): the nature of the mother's expansions of her child's speech indicates that adult carers instinctively help to reinforce children's learning by providing implicit corrections. This may suggest that social interactions have more importance than Chomsky seemed to suggest. However, the child's response (or lack of it) to these corrections (as in the 'rabbits' example) can sometimes be explained by Chomsky's ideas (the child holds firmly to her current grammatical hypothesis); nevertheless, at some point children *do* seem to learn from these adult interventions and amend their grammar accordingly.

(f) and (i): there is evidence here for the biological innateness of the process; it may also be the case that language development is an aspect of the broader cognitive development which is also biologically programmed, provided the child is exposed to the right kinds of stimulus in his/her environment. Item (j) reminds us that *mere* exposure is not enough – without the socially interactive dimension, language acquisition does not occur.

Activity 10. Learning to read

Some of the main elements of the reading process you might have considered are:

- the eyes need to learn to follow a line of text smoothly from left to right and from top to bottom. This in itself is no simple feat of physical coordination, and young readers may use a finger to help focus the eyes on a line of text
- recognising the shapes of letters and words. This is complicated by the visual similarity of some letters (b/d, v/w, u/v etc.), some variations in forms of print (a or ɑ, for example) and the differences between lower- and upper-case forms
- recognising correspondences between these shapes and the aural experiences of language. This may be at the level of individual graphemes and the sounds they represent (i.e. *b* usually corresponds to the sound /b/). This is of course complicated by the fact that English is not a purely phonetic writing system. There is also the need to recognise that some pairs of letters don't correspond to two separate sounds at all, but are to be read as a single sound (= **digraphs** such as *ch*, *th* and *sh*)
- recognising that in English, the same graphemes can correspond to different phonemes and vice versa. So, for example, the sound /i/ can be variously expressed as *P**e**te*, *f**ee**t*, *f**ea**t*, *encyclop**ae**dia*, and the grapheme *c* can correspond to the phonemes /k/ (in ***c**at*) and /s/ (in ***c**inema*)
- matching words recognised on the page with words and meanings contained in the memory
- recognising syntactic units (e.g. phrases, clauses and sentences) and decoding their grammatical structures
- retaining an understanding of the first part of a sentence in the memory until the end
- recognising textual 'signposts' and other indicators of textual cohesion (see Module 4, pp.21–23)
- checking understanding against real-world knowledge (i.e. asking 'Does my interpretation of this text make sense?'). For example, if the passive structure of the sentence *the cake was eaten by Mary* confuses us and we are tempted to imagine the bizarre possibility that the cake is eating Mary, a 'reality check' should kick in to alert us to our misreading.

Activity 13. Writing for children

There is a steady increase in the amount of text on a single page from the single sentences of *The Toys' Party* to the extended paragraphs of *Pol and Pax*, marking a graduated decrease in the amount of visual contextualisation provided for the meanings in the text. Lexically, we note a gradual increase in the range and length of words (only 26 words are used in *The Toys' Party*, of which only seven consist of two or three syllables). Only the past tense and plural suffixes *-ed* and *-s* are included, and many of the words (*wanted*, *put in*, *Kipper*, *was*) are repeated to consolidate learning, notably the irregular unmarked past-tense form of *put*. After the initial *Kipper*, the pronoun *he* is sustained throughout to demonstrate prenominalisation.

The words are phonically predictable (e.g. *milk*, *jam*, *toys*) but some do seem to be designed to teach the 'magic e' effect – note the recurrence of the *-ake* cluster =/eIk/) in *cornfl**ake**s*, *c**ake*** and *b**ake**d*. They are all frequently used and consist entirely of concrete nouns within the same semantic field (foods) and people (*Mum*, *Kipper* and *nobody*). All of the actions and objects referred to in the text are represented in the illustrations.

Sentences are simple, active and very short – either three or four words long – and repeat three basic syntactic structures. These are: subject-verb-object (*he got his toys*, *he wanted a cake*), the verb 'be' and its complement (*Mum was cross*, *Kipper was sorry*), and the subject-verb sentence *Nobody wanted to come*. Note how the syntax of the repeated *he put in xxx* has been altered from the more common *he put milk in*, presumably to preserve the predictable sequence of subject-verb-object and avoid the potentially confusing split that occurs in phrasal verbs such as *put in*. The text also demonstrates the way *wanted* can be followed either by a noun-phrase object (*a party*) or an infinitive intransitive verb (*to come*). Otherwise, the verbs (all four of them) are all in the simple past tense.

The plot formula of *The Pirate Adventure* is a common one in children's narratives – going through a door/gate/wardrobe/tunnel into a different world may remind you of *Alice in Wonderland*, *The Lion the Witch and the Wardrobe* or *Tom's Midnight Garden*. The range of the vocabulary is a little wider; it is still mainly concrete (names and objects), though with some adjectival pre-modification (*little house . . . magic house . . . magic key*) and expressions of attitudes (*I don't like . . . we don't like . . .*). We also see the introduction of the comparative morpheme *-er* (*smaller and smaller*) and words from a semantic field away from the domestic environment (*sand*, *sea*, *pirates*). A wider variety of phonic patterns is illustrated within the text – *like* and *look* are contrasted (phonetically they differ only by the one central vowel) whereas *look* and *book* illustrate a similar pattern. Readers also need to recognise that *c*, *ck* and *k* can represent the same /k/ sound (in *magic*, *lock* and *key*) and that the *ey* in *key* is the same sound as the *ea* in *sea*.

One striking development is the introduction of dialogue, the appropriate punctuation conventions and the inverted forms *they said* and *said Chip*. This entails recognising the switches in narrative point of view from first to third person. Within the narrative and dialogue, the sentences remain simple and fairly short but you will notice a contrast of simple and progressive past tense forms (*Biff was looking . . . they looked . . . the magic was working . . . the windows were glowing*) and a number of extended and phrasal verb phrases (*looking at*, *came to play*, *began to glow*).

The setting of *Pol and Pax* is even further from home and features a further extended lexical range. More of the text refers to things not present in the illustration – the planet itself, its ring and its moons are not shown, and this lexis seems to presuppose some knowledge from the semantic field of astronomy. The text also introduces some lexical inventions – *shills, skimps, scrums*, *straps*, *stocks* and *stinks* take their place alongside the more familiar *shark* – a text at an earlier stage would probably have confined itself to the hyponym *fish*. The text is encouraging children to enjoy the potential for playfulness in language whilst at the same time presenting a variety of phonic patterns. The words are close relations of words they may know like *shells* or *shrimps* and the recurrence of similar clusters of consonants here (*sh*, *sk*, *scr*, *str*, *st*) enables children to practise the recognition and articulation of the same clusters they will meet in ***sh**oal*, ***sk**irt*, ***scr**amble*, ***str**etch* and ***st**ation*. It still largely avoids phonically unpredictable words, but words like *wriggled* and *caught* require the visual identification of non-phonetic word shapes.

Sentences are considerably longer here and include some compound (*they eat a slice of brain food . . . and this makes them as clever . . .*) and complex (*they wanted to see which of them could catch the strangest fish*) structures. Here, note the way *which of them* functions as both the object of the first clause and the subject of the second – a considerable syntactic challenge to the reader. There is also a wide range of verb tense constructions, past (including *neither of them had seen*), present and future, simple, progressive – but passive forms are still avoided.

Activity 15. The writing process

The list of skills involved in the process of writing can seem formidable. They include:

- holding and controlling the pen
- correctly forming the shapes of letters, both lower and upper case
- later, learning to produce **cursive** (joined-up) script
- selecting appropriate words and using appropriate graphemic combinations to spell them
- spacing words appropriately on the line/page
- understanding and applying principles of sentence construction
- understanding and applying the conventions of punctuation
- planning sufficiently far ahead to construct coherent sentences and texts
- learning and using forms and conventions for genres of writing such as letters, reports, stories etc.
- using the skills of reading to monitor and correct the writing as necessary.

Activity 16. Children's writing

The story about a witch and her lion uses the conventional 'once upon a time' opening and consists of several episodes culminating in a distinct 'ending' in which the witch is left alone. Cohesion is produced more by repetition of *the boy*, *the witch*, etc., than by pronouns and the very staccato feel of the succession of short phrases is a result of an absence of connecting words. Where they occur towards the end (e.g. *but*) they do not always function logically. The text is well controlled, mechanically, as it follows a fairly straight line from left to right and top to bottom, with appropriate spaces between words (though *upon* is represented as two words) and letters approximately scaled. There is some upper/lower case confusion with forms of b/B e/E l/L, though the majority of words use appropriate lower-case formations with Y being formed entirely above the line.

When it comes to spelling, there is the consistent application of some phonemic correspondences, even when these are in adult terms 'incorrect.' *Wich* is a plausible spelling of *witch* and may be a visual hybrid of *which* and *witch*. What seems to be the current hypothesis behind the writer's representation of the sound /k/? In every case – *ckasl* (castle), *ckam* (came), *wock* (walk), *lickt* (liked), *ckrid* (cried), *ckolde* (cold), *ckudnt* (couldn't) and *bicks* (because) – s/he opts for the **-ck** digraph. Such forms as *ckasl* and ckam are clearly *not* due to an imperfect attempt to imitate the word visually, but the result of creative overgeneralising analogous to that found in spoken language acquisition. Later, the writer will refine the hypothesis 'the sound /k/ is always represented by -ck' as s/he deduces that ck- never represents this sound at the beginning of a word in English.

Other trends can be noted: one group of errors is associated with the unstressed vowel schwa (as in *app**le**, cast**le**, litt**le*** and *wom**a**n*). Schwa, of course, has no single corresponding letter in English; as it is unstressed, the writer's apparent rule – ignore the schwa – has a certain logic! Many spellings suggest the writer is creatively applying the phonemic correspondences s/he already knows – *statid* for *started*, for example – but a smaller group (*org* and *orgug* for *orange, Sirh* for *Sarah*) suggest s/he is trying to recall the visual shape of the whole words rather than encoding the word phonically. This relates interestingly to the phonics/whole-word debate about reading discussed on pp.173–175 above.

The vocabulary is a mixture of the domestic and the fantastic, with *witch*, *castle* and *lion* belonging to a rather different semantic field from *apple*, *orange*, etc. Mostly, the writer has already started to structure his/her writing into short, simple sentences and has understood that full stops are used to mark sentence ends. There seems to be some dialectal influence behind the use of *were* for *was*.

b. Changing English

- Getting started: (a) perpetual change
  (b) the changing lexicon
- A brief history: how language has changed
- The nature of language change: some linguistic issues and controversies
- Data for analysis
- Preparing for the examination
- Commentaries

1. Getting Started: (a) perpetual change

You should first refer back to the following sections of previous modules, which relate to the nature of change in language:

'Our disappearing dialects' (AS Module 1, pp.40–41)

'Why Proper English is No Longer a Shore Thing' (AS Module 2, p.66)

'The origins of Standard English', (AS Module 2, pp.72–73)

Activities 11 & 12, The history of the English language, (A2 Module 5, pp.97–100)

The extracts from Jean Aitchison's 'The Language Web'; the *Young Guardian* article 'A language all of its very own'; the extract from Baugh and Cable's *A History of the English Language*; and 'Language Change' from David Crystal's *Encyclopaedia of The English Language* (A2 Module 5, pp.105–108).

Language change is a fact of life. As the world in which we live is constantly changing, no one should be surprised that a living language such as English will also be subject to perpetual flux and reinvention. You don't have to look (or listen) very far to bump into the reality of linguistic change; you may cringe at the pronunciation of BBC newsreaders from the 1940s and 50s, smile at the 'hippy slang' of the 1960s generation, be daunted by the apparent old-fashioned formality of a Victorian newspaper, be baffled by the alien-looking text in a 300-year-old document, or even become irritated by the latest piece of American slang to be adopted in the UK.

One of the major themes of your AS/A2 English language course has been the sheer variety that occurs in language use at any given moment; this teeming, simultaneous multiplicity of language is known as **synchronic variation**. From out of these different forms emerge the changes which affect languages over time – **diachronic variation**.

This process might be compared with the process of evolution and natural selection in the natural world: at any given time, for example, some horses may be taller than others, or have different-sized tails, but over time, some of these features will come to dominate the species, whereas others will tend to become rare, and so the species as a whole gradually changes in appearance. So with language, you can observe among English speakers at any given time a thousand variations in phonology, lexis, semantics and grammar, and then try to trace which of these take root and influence the development of the language over time.

This final section of this module will start to investigate in more detail the nature of language change, and suggest some explanations for how it occurs. As with the Language Acquisition section, this part of the course is designed to be **synoptic**, and to enable you to bring together all the relevant linguistic knowledge and understanding you have previously acquired. Once again, this book can only realistically aim to get you started; it will, however, try to provide the stimulus and the analytical frameworks that will enable you to carry your investigations further. This will involve carrying out some of your own research of *primary* materials (i.e. language data) and also reading some of the academic secondary sources recommended in the Further Reading list on p.244.

As with similar investigations into different aspects of language acquisition, it may be possible to submit an investigation in this area as a language investigation for Module 4.

In the course of your English Language studies throughout your AS and A2 course, you will already have become aware of some issues related to language change. Although you may not have paused very long to consider these in depth, you will already have met some aspects of this topic in the passages referred to above. This section will begin, therefore, by reviewing what you have already discovered about language change from your previous language studies.

ACTIVITY 1. REVIEW

As well as looking again at the passages suggested above, think back over the work you have done in your AS and A2 courses, and the different linguistic materials you have encountered. Make a note of how any of this material sheds light on these key questions about language change, and suggest your first responses to them:

- What are some of the ways in which English has changed?
- Which aspects of language are subject to change over time?
- What are some of the influences that cause change to happen?
- In what ways does change in language reflect *social* factors?

Compare the outcomes of your discussions with the commentary on p.232.

As with the Language Acquisition part of this module, as you encounter different kinds of linguistic data you will need to use the appropriate analytical frameworks to ask the right questions at each linguistic level:

- **phonology**: how has the sound of English changed?
- **graphology/orthography**: how have the print, punctuation and spelling conventions changed?
- **lexis**: how has the vocabulary of English changed?
- **semantics**: what changes have taken place in the meanings of words and constructions?
- **grammar:** how have the morphology and syntax of English changed?
- **pragmatics**: what changes have taken place in the way English speakers use language in different contexts?

A good starting point is one that is perhaps the most immediately observable of all of these – the ways in which new words and meanings are constantly entering the language.

ACTIVITY 2. CHANGE IN ACTION

Language change is not just something that happened in the past; it is happening now, all around us. For example, the following list of the most current teenage slang is based on a list compiled by the editor of *J17* magazine, on the basis of interviews with and letters, emails and text messages from people aged 12–18 in January and February 2001. It was published in the *Observer* on 18/3/01. One or two extra items have been added.

Carry out a classification exercise on this data (as in 'Sifting, sorting, and counting', Module 4, pp.13–14) and try to suggest what this selection of items reveals about how, and why, language change occurs.

Teenspeak: The Definitive Lexicon 2001

Anchor: a nuisance of a brother or sister who stops you going out with your mates (also **rugrat, anklebiter**)

Bling, bling: extravagant jewellery as worn by Madonna, Puff Daddy, etc.

Bo: exclamation of encouragement or mark of approval (*He is totally bo!*)

Boyf: **abbreviation for boyfriend**

Bone: to have sexual intercourse

Bothered: sarcastic expression at end of sentence to show indifference (also *Whatever!*)

Bowl it around: to swagger around in a macho style

Brad Pitt: (rhyming slang) – expression of disapproval

Britney Spears: (rhyming slang) – beers

Busted: caught out

Cane: to beat, out-class

Choccy: delicious, tasty (but not necessarily like chocolate!)

Diss: to criticise or attack

Fine: sexually attractive (also *fit, tick, da bomb, breakers*)

Get hold of: to form an amorous/sexual relationship

Gun: to slag off

Heavy: term of approval for something fashionable (also *mint, hectic, rough, phat, quality*)

Honey: an attractive girl

Hottie: a fit boy, also a hot flush

Innit/Isit: rhetorical question tag

Johnny no-stars: thick person

Minger: unattractive person

Mobie: mobile phone

Muppet: stupid person

Rents: parents

Rinsin': a good piece of music

Selecta: disc jockey

Slayer: an assertive female

Swerve: to change plans at the last minute

Scatty-yatty: unattractive female

Wack: false or insincere

Wallace and Gromit: (rhyming slang) – vomit

What's happenin?: greeting (also *Wassuupp?*)

Compare your suggestions with the commentary on p.232.

Another striking example of very recent language change in action has been the development of a distinctive style of text messaging by mobile-phone users and e-mailers. This is a classic example of technological constraints and opportunities spawning linguistic creativity.

ACTIVITY 3. TEXT-MESSAGING

Listed below are some items included in The Wicked Book of txttlk *(Buster Books, London, 2001).*

(i) Test your own knowledge and understanding of this style of language by 'translating' the text messages.

(ii) Using these examples, and your own experiences of text messaging, now try to define the 'grammar' of text-messaging, that is, the underlying rules that enable people to create and interpret new messages in this format.

Express your grammar as a series of rules a new text-message user could follow, and use any linguistic terminology that helps to define these precisely.

(iii) Try to suggest some of the reasons why this new linguistic code has arisen in the way it has. What has influenced its development?

Text-messaging

CMB	BTDT	ETA	BCNU	B4	
ChlYa!	CUL8r	F2T	IC**WenUXMe	NI	PAW
RUUp4It?	WsUuuuu?	:-)	:'-D	:-W	>;-)

Compare your results with the commentary on p.233.

(iv) Now carry out your own survey of text messages received by a sample group of phone users. How accurate a representation of the *real* language of text messages is the data offered above?

Activity 4. School Rules

By contrast with the previous examples of contemporary language change and innovation, consider the following text, which in the nineteenth century laid down the professional responsibilities of the teachers at Bury Grammar School.

As you examine the text, note down the various ways in which the language of this document differs from what you might expect to find in a similar document today.

Dureing all such time, Jorden the Master to be present in the Schole with the Usher, and to teach all such good Authors as are usually taught in other schools for the better education of youth. The Master & Usher shall not be absent from the Schole dureing the times aforesaid, nor withdraw themselves from thence, but only for, & upon honest necessary & reasonable occasions. And my order further is, that the Master and Usher shall not be absent from Schole above three days at once upon necessary busynes, except they obtaine the special License of the trustees or the major part of them, and so, that the Master & Usher be not absent at one and the same time.

I order that all the Scholars shall be obedient to all good and lawful Statutes now by mee made or hereafter to be made, touching the good Government & ordering of ye Schole . . .

Dureing all such time, Jorden the Master to be present in the Schole, with the Usher, and to teach all such good Author as are usually taught in other Schools for the better Educati- on of youth.

Compare your analysis with the commentary on p.234.

Activity 5. Investigating language change

These introductory activities should have begun to raise a number of questions about our language and how it has developed. As with Language Acquisition, the best way of extending your knowledge and understanding in this area is to carry out your own investigations. These will be most fruitful if you study a limited number of comparable texts from different periods. i.e. a *diachronic* analysis. You will need to collect some good data and support your analysis by doing some appropriate background reading. This could, but need not, entail looking at pre-twentieth-century texts; even texts produced within 40 or 50 years of each other can reflect significant sociolinguistic changes.

The following list of suggestions offer some possible starting points, which could also become appropriate language investigations for Module 4:

Some possible diachronic investigations

Topic	Sources
The language of children's books written at different times in the past	Primary schools and libraries – as well as your own collections.
Newspaper and magazine articles/ features written at different times; advertisements	Local libraries/archives will usually have a considerable archive of local and national newspapers. Secondhand bookshops and antique shops often have early twentieth-century magazines. You may need to make an appointment with your archivist to gain access to some of these materials – but it is worth it.
Personal diaries and letters	You may come across personal collections of these. If using published collections, try to find examples of facsimile reproductions.
Instructions and advice	Museums/libraries may have examples of Victorian cookbooks, guides to household management and other official notices.
Institutional language	Take photographs of sets of signs and notices of various kinds. National Trust properties etc. may have pre-twentieth-century examples.
Lyrics of popular songs	Collections of First World War, Victorian or older songs can be found in most libraries/bookshops.

Getting Started: (b) the changing lexicon

You may find it helpful to review the section on Morphology in Module 4, pp.33–35 before working through the following section

The perpetual flux of words and meanings in English is, perhaps, the obvious starting point for an investigation of language change. Although it is difficult to define precisely and accurately the sheer size of the vocabulary available to speakers of English, some estimates suggest it is anything up to a million words. As we will see later (see pp.213–214), throughout its history, English has not only 'borrowed' words extravagantly from other languages but has constantly re-combined and recycled them to create new meanings.

Dictionary writers (or **lexicographers**) try to keep track of this process by recording the appearance in the language of new words, or new usages for old ones (see the *OED*, below, pp.215–220). At the close of the twentieth century, in preparation for a new Millennial edition of their dictionary, Collins published a list of entries whose first recorded use in English spanned the century, and which seemed, in their judgement, to be characteristic of the year in which they were cited. A selection of those from 1950 onwards is reprinted below:

discotheque	stoned (drugged)	yuppie	compact disc
rock and roll	psychedelic	Rubik cube	VAT
test tube baby	teddy boy	acid house	Solidarity (Polish Trade Union)
Blairite	Catch-22	road rage	AIDS
PEP	laser	glasnost (policy of openness in government)	
Lego	workaholic	silicon chip	clone (of mobile phone fraud)
lunar module	crop circle	hovercraft	Ceefax
punk rock	Mexican wave	ethnic cleansing	
Alcopop	National Lottery	information superhighway	

Activity 6. Words of the twentieth century

(i) Suggest which decade (1950s, 1960s, etc.) you think each of these words/phrases were recorded in, noting down the reasons for your suggestions as you do so.

(ii) As with the Teenspeak examples above, this selection illustrates a number of areas of life which are important sources for new words and phrases. Suggest what these are.

(iii) Suggest which of these words you think may *not* be in current use in 50 years' time, and why not.

(iv) The data also illustrates some of the most common ways in which new words/phrases are constructed. Identify examples of each of the following:

- use of acronyms
- new meanings/uses for existing word/phrase
- combination of existing word into new phrase
- re-combination of morphemes/syllables from existing words to make new ones
- direct borrowing from another language
- brand name or personal name
- phonetically playful or catchy coinage

Gains and losses

Although the vocabulary of English has expanded enormously, it is not all one-way traffic; as many new words and phrases enter the language, others gradually slip out of common use, as the following letter to a local newspaper in Middlesbrough laments:

Slang is Slung

I started school in the '20s, leaving in the mid-'30s, living in the country when dialect was stronger than today. Words which were in use when I went to school one never hears used today.

[. . .]

When going to play rounders, one would shout out 'Bags I piesy' if they wanted to be the first at throwing the ball, when going to play cricket one would shout 'Bags I fuggy' meaning the first to bat, to 'kep' the ball was to catch it.

In spring, the village pond had frogs-fry on, frogs-spawn; tadpoles were called bull-eeads, robins were shufflewings and the snipe was ally sloper, the woodpecker was a yffle. At dusk there was the 'flitter-mouse' common bat, while the 'devil-screamer' swift flew overhead.

When out bird nesting and you found a nest with fledglings in, they were called 'gollies'. When flown they had 'fliged'. If you were stung you had been tenged. An 'otch'n' was the hedgehog, the donkey a 'fussack'. The common poppy was 'cup-rose', foxglove 'floss-docken','aigs' berries on the hawthorn.

If it was balm or lown there was no wind, hills were brant, not steep. Horses working the land left hoof marks, these were called delfs.

When anyone fell down, they had gone a pirler, 'meg' was one penny, 'binger' was half a cigarette. Rind on bacon was 'swoth', bent was 'kessen'.

ACTIVITY 7. DIALECTS IN DECLINE?

(a) The previous activities looked at some of the reasons why new words and meanings enter English. This time, suggest the possible causes, social or linguistic, of this alleged decline in dialect usage.

(b) If the anecdotal evidence of this letter is true – and there is some research evidence to support this view (see AS Module 1, pp.40–41, 'Our disappearing dialects') – consider whether it is something to be deplored, welcomed, encouraged or resisted.

Compare the outcomes of your discussions with the commentary on p.236.

A brief history

Before going any further, you do need to consolidate your previous knowledge about the longer-term story of the development of English. You need to do so because:

- it is in itself a fascinating story
- it reveals a lot about how, and why, language changes
- it helps you understand why English is what it is today
- it will help you make sense of texts written in the past
- it will prepare you to comment in detail on texts that you will meet in the examination.

What's more, although it can sometimes be tempting to focus on the obvious lexical and semantic changes in language, it is also important to be aware that *all* aspects of language are subject to change.

The full story of the history of English has been very well documented elsewhere, and what follows in the table below is a brief summary. You are strongly urged to refer to any of the following texts to extend the depth of your studies:

A. Baugh and T. Cable, *A History of the English Language*

David Crystal, *The Cambridge Encyclopaedia of the English Language*, (Part 1, The History of English)

Dennis Freeborn, *From Old English to Standard English*

Robert McCrum et al., *The Story of English*

ACTIVITY 8. RESEARCH AND EDITORIAL WRITING

As you carry out your own personal wider reading on this topic, you can also practise the editorial writing skills that you are developing for Module 5.

Choose one or more of the following subjects:

- the linguistic consequences of the Battle of Hastings in 1066
- the Middle English period
- the invention of printing and the emergence of Standard English
- changes in the sounds of English
- early modern English and the language of Shakespeare
- the growth of the English lexicon
- the spread of English in the nineteenth and twentieth centuries.

Then choose one of the following formats in which to re-present the information you gather:

- a wallchart for display in your study area
- an article of about 1,000 words to be inserted into a popular dictionary, or
- an illustrated presentation for interested adults/students.

(*This would also be a useful Key Skills Communication opportunity.*)

Time	Social, political, cultural and economic influences	Major linguistic developments	Examples
Pre-1st century AD	Britain inhabited by Celts, or Britons	People spoke varieties of Celtic languages, the roots of Welsh, Scots Gaelic, Irish, Manx and Cornish.	Partly as a result of what happened to the Celts later (they were displaced by the invading Anglo-Saxons), relatively few Celtic words survive in modern English. However, numerous place-names (Penrith, Leeds, York, Thames, Avon) remind us of our ancient roots.
1st–5th centuries	The Romans occupied mainland England	There was some limited influence from Latin on the native languages during this period. Some Latin words have survived, but the major Latin influence on English was to come much later.	Many place-names, such as Manchester, Lancaster, Chester and Worcester, derive from this period. A few other words of Latin origin which survive, such as *street*, *port*, *wine* and *wall*, may also date from this period.

5th–8th centuries	Invasions of the Germanic tribes (Angles, Saxons and Jutes) Christianity adopted (587)	The Celtic language was displaced except in Wales, Scotland, Cornwall and Ireland. **Old English** developed from the Germanic dialects of the invaders, which varied according to where the different tribes settled. This was the true beginning of English: many of the basic grammatical words (*the*, *in*, *was*, etc.) and many everyday nouns and verbs derive from this period. The Latin alphabet was adopted and Latin was used by the educated elite and in church.	**Old English** A considerable body of literature from this period survives. It is very foreign to modern eyes, and requires special study to understand it, as in this example from the poem *Beowulf:* Hwaet we Gar-Dena in geardagum, Peodcyninga prym gefrunon Hu da aepelingas ellen fremedon. *So the Spear-Danes in days gone by* *And the kings who ruled them had courage and greatness.* *We have heard of those princes' heroic campaigns.* (Translation by Seamus Heaney)
8th–11th centuries	Viking invasions	The Vikings' language (Norse) was close enough to the Anglo-Saxon of the inhabitants to allow communication between the peoples. The Vikings took over many of the Anglo-Saxon kingdoms, particularly in the north and east of the country.	Many Norse words have passed into standard English – *get*, *take*, *angry*, *awkward*, *they*, *she* – and even more have survived in the dialects of the north where some pronunciations and grammatical forms of dialects are also Scandinavian in origin.
11th–14th centuries	1066: the Normans invaded, led by William the Conqueror Norman French and English co-existed	Following the Norman invasion, there was a French-speaking power base – the court, the church and major landowners were mainly French-speaking, while the populace spoke English. During the twelfth century English was more widely used by the upper classes and in 1362 was used for the first time at the state opening of parliament. By 1425 English was used universally in speech and writing.	This was the beginning of the **Middle English** period; there was an inevitable flow of vocabulary from Norman French (itself heavily based on Latin) into English. English not only survived but was enriched by the language of the invaders. This period also saw the loss of many Old English word endings (inflections), many of which were replaced by the prepositions *by, with, from* etc. Much Middle English literature survives and is reasonably accessible to patient modern readers. This period also saw the beginnings of a major change in English pronunciation: the Great Vowel Shift.

15th–17th centuries	Printing invented (William Caxton set up his press in 1476) Many Greek and Latin texts were translated into English	There was a gradual acceptance of a standard form of English, made necessary by the increasing dissemination of printed materials.	**Early modern English** In the period 1500–1700 many more words entered the language than at any other period. New words were needed for new concepts and an influx of Latin and French words resulted. This period of world exploration also brought words from the languages of Africa, Asia and the New World. The Great Vowel Shift was completed – and the pronunciation of English began to stabilise. This was also the age of Shakespeare, himself a great coiner of words.
18th–19th centuries	The search for a standard, pure form of English	Attempts to define the vocabulary and grammar of English led to the establishment of prescriptive ideas about correctness. Non-standard varieties were viewed as inferior; Latin was upheld as an ideal language and a model for English dictionary writers and grammarians tried to lay down rules for correct usage.	This was the age of the dictionary, when writers tried to 'fix' spellings and meanings. 1721 Nathaniel Bailey's *Universal Etymological Dictionary* 1755 Samuel Johnson's *English Dictionary* 1762 Robert Lowth's *Short Introduction to English Grammar* 1762 Lindley Murray's *English Grammar.*
19th century–present	The expansion of British and American English	In the nineteenth century, rail travel, colonial expansion, the spread of literacy and education and the printed word extended access to standard and written forms of English. Electronic media extended this process in the twentieth century; meanwhile, American economic and political power succeeded that of the British Empire to ensure the spread of English as a world language.	American English was starting to become noticeably different from British English. English continues to absorb loan words from languages across the world. Grammar and pronunciation see few major changes, but in the late twentieth and early twenty-first centuries, a drift towards more colloquial and casual styles of language in many contexts reflects major social changes. American English increasingly influences British English and English worldwide.

ACTIVITY 9. TEXT CHRONOLOGY

Reprinted below is a selection of texts produced at different times. For the purposes of this exercise, facsimile reproduction of the original texts has not been used. As you will see, they all raise questions about aspects of English usage.

Using the table, along with your own further reading as a guide, try to place these in chronological order, and try to assign to each the century in which you think it was written.

Make a note of the various clues in each extract which help you place it.

Then compare your suggestions with the commentary on p.237.

1. The work of this society shou'd be to encourage Polite Learning, to polish and refine the English Tongue, and advance the so much neglected Faculty of Correct Language, to establish Purity and Propriety of Stile, and to purge it from all Irregular Additions that Ignorance and Affection have introduc'd . . . . I wou'd therefore have this Society wholly compos'd of Gentlemen . . . .
2. Some seke so farre outlandishe Englishe, that the forget altogether their mother's laguage. And I dare swere this, if some of their mothers were aliue, thei were not able to tell, what thei say, & yet these fine Englishe clerkes, wil saie thei speake in their mother tongue, if a man should charge them for couterfeityng the kynges Englishe. Some farre iorneid ientlemen at their returne home like as thei loue to go in forrein apparell, so thei wil pouder their talke with oursea laguage.
3. It is surely undeniable that standards at the BBC have fallen woefully when we are routinely subjected to virtual illiterates bombarding us with the sloppiest clichés, Americanisms and bad grammar. There was a time when the BBC could take pride in presenting its viewers and listeners with the best possible models of English. Sadly, no longer. The proliferation of audience participation shows – the pursuit of the insignificant by the inarticulate – reveals the desperate impoverishment of our once-noble native tongue. Dreary Birmingham accents and lazy northern bluster – you got it. Bad grammar and sloppy, inexpressive vocabulary? You got it. No dumbing down? Come off it!
4. If an academy should be established for the cultivation of our stile, which I, who can never wish to see dependence multiplied, hope the spirit of English liberty will hinder or destroy, let them, instead of compiling grammars and dictionaries, endeavour with all their influence, to stop the licence of translatours, whose idleness and ignorance, if it be suffered to proceed, will reduce us to babble a dialect of France.

How English has changed: some frameworks for analysis

This section will look in a little more detail at some of the principal changes that have occurred, and continue to occur, at each linguistic level of English. This provides a basic descriptive summary of these changes and the frameworks within which you can start to analyse the data you gather. As you examine each of them, start to consider the question of what might have *caused* them to occur, which is the theme of the next section.

Phonology

You have already seen how slight but distinct changes in the pronunciation of English can occur and start to spread through the language. The sociolinguist William Labov famously recorded such a change taking a place over a relatively short period in the American resort of Martha's Vineyard (see: 'Why Proper English is No Longer a Shore Thing', AS Module 2, p.66), and showed how this was the result of social tensions and processes. Even in the relatively short time that broadcast media have been available, we can observe the difference between the 'marked' RP of the newsreaders of the 1940s and 1950s and the more neutral, 'unmarked' RP of today. The greater acceptance and fashionability of regional accents in the media may also reflect a more democratic, less formal society.

Small-scale phonological changes are difficult to map and record – especially as the era of recorded sound only goes back a hundred years or so. Nevertheless, it is easy to see that such apparently small changes have, over a long period of time, amounted to a transformation in the sound of English. In the absence of tape recordings we have to rely on written evidence of what English sounded like in previous centuries.

ACTIVITY 10. SOUND DETECTIVES

How would you use written texts to draw conclusions about how pronunciations may have differed in the past? Suggest the kinds of evidence which might be most useful.

Compare your thoughts with the commentary on p.238.

Some principal changes in English phonology

1400–1600	*The Great Vowel Shift* In 1400 English vowels would have sounded very different from the way they sound now: *time* would have sounded more like *team*, *see* like *say*, *fame* like *farm* *so* like *saw*, *do* like *doe* and *now* like *noo*. Over a couple of hundred years these vowels changed to something approaching the pronunciations we know today.

1600–present	Some lesser changes in vowel sounds occurred, and there was the gradual disappearance of the /r/ sounds in words like *far*, *horn*, and *horse* – except in some regional accents. The notion of **Received Pronunciation** emerged in the nineteenth/twentieth centuries.
Current developments	Accent styles now fluctuate in popularity; transatlantic influences and 'Estuary English' spread as RP styles become less marked. The stress in words like *con**tro**versy* (or ***con**troversy*) continues to be unstable.

Spelling

The modern preoccupation with 'correct' spellings is a relatively recent phenomenon. Indeed, differences in spelling conventions are very often the most immediately obvious thing about a text from a previous century. In the pre-print era when literacy was much less common, there was no fixed system and in the handwritten manuscripts that survive, words are spelt according to regional pronunciation and personal preference.

So the development of printing brought dilemmas aplenty to printers; texts from the fifteenth–seventeenth centuries show many internal inconsistencies, with the same word often being spelt differently within the same text. It was the gradual acceptance of the authority of dictionaries in the eighteenth century that led to the ultimate fixing of spellings.

Unfortunately, these fixed spellings were not the result of a single consistent system. Modern spellings show evidence of previous pronunciations, for example, the silent *gh* in words such as *night* would have represented a pronunciation similar to that found in the Scottish word *loch*. In the word *name*, the final *-e* represents the schwa sound the word originally had. Other words reflect their origins rather than their pronunciation – the *ps-* in *psychology*, for example corresponds to the Greek letter ψ rather than any English pronunciation of /p/.

Some changes in English spelling

Pre-15th century	No consensus. All texts were handwritten and reflected regional pronunciations.
15th–18th centuries	From the spread of printing, the momentum towards Standard English expressed itself in the dictionaries of the eighteenth century, which attempted to fix spellings.
18th century–present	Notions of 'correct' spellings now firmly embedded – even when they reflect pronunciations that vanished long ago. Some spellings reflect the origins of loan words e.g. *ph-* is used for /f/ in many Greek-derived words like *physics*. The American dictionary of Noah Webster (1828) tried to rationalise spellings along more phonetic lines, and the writer G. B. Shaw proposed a radical redesign of the English alphabet – to no effect.

Some recent American influence in words like *jail* (c.f. English *gaol*) and *program* (c.f. English *programme*).

Graphology and orthography

Even relatively recent texts, such as personal letters or diaries written in the early twentieth century, can reveal that handwriting styles have changed; look further back into the nineteenth century or earlier and such differences become even more marked. Similarly, the conventions used by printers have changed, as at first the use of lower- and upper-case letters, or of various fonts, or of different kinds of punctuation developed in a fairly haphazard way.

ACTIVITY 11. LOOKING AT PRINTED TEXTS

Summarised below are just a few of the more notable changes in graphology and orthography since the sixteenth century.

You need to make use of your local reference library/archive, and ask about facilities for requesting access to texts printed before 1900. You will usually have to identify some items from a catalogue, and fill in a request slip to view the documents.

Look for examples of these orthographic changes in practice, and for any other noticeable variations from modern printing.

u/v	In pre-seventeenth-century texts, these letters were either interchangeable, or used according to whether they occurred at the beginning (*v*) or elsewhere in a word (*u*). Only later did they come to represent the vowel *u* and consonant *v*.
y/i/j	The use of *y* or *i* to represent the sound /i/ varied considerably in the period before the eighteenth-century dictionaries tried to stabilise practice. The letter 'j' was originally a variation on 'i', so many words spelt today with *j-* are found to have an initial *i-* in many texts from the seventeenth century and earlier.
s/ʃ	The practice of using the extended (ʃ) form of the sound /s/ when it occurred in the middle of words persisted well into the eighteenth century.
Upper- and lower-case conventions	In the seventeenth century upper-case letters were often used for *all* nouns as well as at the beginnings of sentences, but the eighteenth-century grammarians restricted their use. Some uncertainty and variation of practice remains today.

Punctuation marks	Pre-sixteenth-century texts are punctuated (or 'pointed') very differently: a single stroke (/) known as the **verigule** sometimes did the job of a full stop or comma; in the sixteenth century and afterwards full stops served as commas. Colons, semi-colons and speech marks only started to appear during the early Modern English period.

Lexis and semantics

The history of English has allowed it to absorb vocabulary from many different sources – its basic stock of Germanic words has been successively added to by Norse (Viking) French, Latin, Greek, other European and later worldwide languages. What is the point, though, of having several different words for the same thing? The answer lies in the tendency of language as a system to avoid any such redundancy and to create useful distinctions. Some would say that there is, in fact, no such thing in English as a pure synonym; if a word enters the language which has a similar meaning to one that already exists, one of the words will either die out, or shift its meaning/connotation to enable new distinctions to be made.

ACTIVITY 12. SEMANTIC DISTINCTIONS

Consider the following sets of near-synonyms which reflect three different sources of English lexis.

Try to define (a) the different connotations that these semantically similar words have come to assume and (b) the distinctive character, or 'feel', of the three sets of words.

Anglo-Saxon	French	Latin
kingly	royal	regal
ask	question	interrogate
rise	mount	ascend
time	age	epoch

Compare your results with the commentary on p.238.

Lexical invasions and borrowings

It is impossible to adequately summarise the endless tides of new lexis which have flooded into English across the centuries. What follows is a very basic indication of some of the major trends.

Pre-1066	A mixture of Anglo-Saxon and Norse words formed the basic stock of English, with a sprinkling of Celtic and Latin.
Middle English period	A massive influx from French and (directly or indirectly, Latin), especially in the areas of law, government, religion and science.
Early modern English period	The explosion of scholarship accelerated this trend – but the pursuit of trade and exploration also led to the assimilation of words from many other sources – notably Italian, Spanish, and non-European languages.
1800–present day	The expansion of the British Empire brought English speakers into direct contact with many languages worldwide, and the vocabulary similarly expanded to accommodate words of Australian Aboriginal, Native American, and Asian origin (to name but a few).
Current developments	As English is adopted as a world language, it continues to develop its own identity in different regions, both giving English words to other languages (a process which is not always welcomed!) and taking them in return.

Semantic change

The appearance of a new word in a language is, of course, only the beginning of the story. Once it becomes part of the currency of the language, the meanings and applications it has for speakers can shift dramatically. Therefore, when reading a text from the past, you may think you recognise a word but may actually misunderstand the sense it conveyed when it was written.

The various kinds of semantic change are summarised below:

Broadening	The meanings of a word gradually extend to a wider sense than the original meaning.	*Holiday* originally meant a holy day, to mark a religious festival. As such days were often the occasion for relaxation and merry-making, the word gradually came to lose its religious connotations. The practice of taking one or two weeks off work, perhaps to travel to a resort to relax and enjoy oneself, is largely a twentieth-century concept, but this has now come to be the primary sense of the term.
Narrowing	Precisely the opposite of broadening – here, the meaning gradually becomes more specialised or specific.	*Meat* (see Activity 13 below).

Amelioration	With this process, a word with very severe or even taboo connotations and use gradually becomes less pejorative and milder in its sense.	The word *naughty* originally meant someone who possessed nothing but by the sixteenth century was applied to a wicked or evil person. Today it has a much milder application, and a phrase such as *What naughty man is that?* in a seventeenth-century text, may elicit laughter from the uninformed!
Pejoration	The exact opposite of amelioration: words with neutral or even positive connotations gradually come to acquire pejorative associations.	*Villain* and *churl* both once described agricultural workers of very low status, but without any suggestion of criticism. Interestingly, both gradually came to acquire negative connotations (as in *churlish*) just as the word *peasant* has almost come to do.
Register drift	A word that is thought of as slang can eventually gain acceptance as respectable; conversely, some respectable words can drift towards the fringes of acceptability.	The word *fag*, in the sense of a nuisance or something tiring, occurs in many eighteenth-century sources as acceptably 'standard' English. To describe something as *a bit of a fag* in the later twentieth century, however, was to head towards the region of slang.

Etymology and using the Oxford English Dictionary

The study of the origins of words, and the ways in which their uses and meanings have changed, is known as **etymology**. As a student of language change, it is important for you to be able to use etymological information to illuminate both the meanings of individual texts and to study the principles of language change outlined above in action.

Your principal resource for this kind of work is the *Oxford English Dictionary*. This should not be confused with the various smaller dictionaries which carry the word 'Oxford' in their title; the *OED* (as it is generally known) consists of some 18 large volumes of small print in thin paper (or, thankfully, a CD-ROM).

The reason the *OED* is such a huge document is that it attempts to be an extraordinarily comprehensive record of English vocabulary. It contains:

- an entry for every known English word in general usage, as well as entries for many that are not
- definitions covering all known meanings of these words, both current and historic
- pronunciations and spellings (with variations if they exist) of each word
- compounds and derivations from each word

- the origin of each word, where this is known
- dated quotations illustrating the different meanings of the word at different times in its history.

Activity 13. Using the *OED*

(*i*) *Reproduced below is just part of the entry for the word* meat *taken from the CD-ROM version of the* OED.

Note the format of the entry:

1. pronunciation and word class
2. variant historic spellings
3. origins (OE = Old English/Anglo-Saxon)
4. earliest recorded meaning (1.a.; food in general)
5. dated examples of this meaning
6. later meanings and examples (note that different meanings may, of course overlap and be in use at the same time).

The story of the change in the meanings of *meat* is a good example of semantic narrowing. Use the information in the *OED* entry to complete the table above by telling the story of this narrowing process.

① Headword, modern spelling, pronunciation (in IPA) and word class (n = noun)

② Variant forms/spellings found in sources

meat (mi:t), *n.* Forms: I mete, mæt(e, mett, 2–8 mete, 3 mæte, 4–5 meite, mett, meyte, 4–6 meet(e, met(te, 4–7 meyt, 5 maite, mate, meett, (*pl.* meyttes, -is), 5–7 meate, meit, 6 *Sc.* meitt, 5– meat.

③ Possible origins in other languages (OE = Old English/ Anglo Saxon)

[OE. *mete* str. masc. = OFris. *met(e, meit,* OS. *meti* masc., *mat* neut., OHG. *maz* neut., ON. *mat-r* masc. (Sw. *mat,* Da. *mad*), Goth. *mat-s*: –OTeut. types **mati-z, *mato-*, prob. repr. an original neuter **matoz-, -iz-*:–pre-Teut. **mados-, -es-*, perh. f. root **meþd-* to be fat: see MAST *n.*[2]

The LG. and Du. *met* minced meat (whence Du. *metworst,* G. *mettwurst* sausage) is prob. unconnected; cf. med.L. *matia* pl., tripe.]

④ Numbered meanings/ senses – earliest first

I. a. Food in general; anything used as nourishment for men or animals; usually, solid food, in contradistinction to drink. Now arch. and dial.

green meat: grass or green vegetables used for food or fodder (see GREEN *a.* 4). See also HARD MEAT, HORSEMEAT, WHITEMEAT. ***meal of meat, meal's meat***: see meal *n.*[2] I e.

a900 tr. *Bæda's Hist.* v. iv. (Schipper) 568 He eode on his hus & þær mete [*v.r.* mæte] þyȝede.

⑤ Citations of word used in this sense – in chronological sequence (a = ante/before) c = circa/around

c975 *Rushw. Gosp.* Luke xii. 23 Sawel mara is ðonne mett.

a1050 *Liber Scintill.* xlvii. (1889) 153 Nys rice godes meta & drinc.

c1175 *Lamb. Hom.* 135 Ne sculen ȝe nawiht ȝimstones leggen Swinen to mete.

c1200 ORMIN 3213 Hiss drinnch wass waterr aȝȝ occ aȝȝ. Hiss mete wilde rotess.

a1240 *Lofsong* in *Cott. Hom.* 205 Ich habbe i-suneged ine mete and ine drunche.

a1300 *Cursor M.* 898 Mold sal be þi mete for nede.

c1380 WYCLIF *Wks.* (1880) 206 Alas, þat so gret cost & bisynesse is sette abouten þe roten body, þat is wormes mete.

c1440 *Pol. Rel. & L. Poems* (1903) 185 Thy mete shall be mylk, honye, & wyne.

1477 NORTON *Ord. Alch.* v. in Ashm. (1652) 76 Without Liquor no Meate is good.

1578 LYTE *Dodoens* ii. xlvi. 205 These kindes of lillies are neither used in meate nor medicine.

1623 COCKERAM ii, *Meate of the Gods*, Ambrosia, Manna.

1693 TATE in *Dryden's Juvenal* xv. (1697) 378 Who Flesh of Animals refus'd to eat, Nor held all sorts of Pulse for lawful Meat.

1775 JOHNSON *Journ. W. Isl.* 86 Our guides told us, that the horses could not travel all day without rest or meat.

1794 C. SMITH *Wanderings of Warwick* 66 Sending out women and children, after a hard day's work, to collect meat for the cattle.

1819 SHELLEY *P. Bell* vii. v. 4 He had..meat and drink enough.

1844 STEPHENS *Bk. Farm* II. 709 Meat is then set down to them on a flat plate, consisting of crumbled bread and oatmeal.

1893 Stevenson *Catriona* xxi. 253 When..my father and my uncles lay in the hill, and I was to be carrying them their meat.

1902 *Daily Chron.* 12 Dec. 5/6 Imports of fruit and other choice green~meat.

(meaning 1b. edited out here)

c. Proverbs and phrases.

Citations of figurative idiomatic uses

a1529 SKELTON *Col. Cloute* 450 Swete meate hath soure sauce.

1546 J. HEYWOOD *Prov.* (1867) 8 God neuer sendth mouth, but he sendeth meat.

1597 SHAKES. *2 Hen. IV*, ii. iv. 135, I am meat for your Master.

1616 T. DRAXE *Bibl. Scholast.* 127 One mans meate is another mans poyson.

a1623 FLETCHER *Love's Cure* iii. ii, What's one mans poyson, Signior, Is anothers meat or drinke.

1749 FIELDING *Tom Jones* xi. viii, My lady is meat for no pretenders.

1809 MALKIN *Gil Blas* x. ix, Why must one man's meat be another man's poison?

1853 Mrs. GASKELL *Cranford* xv. 296. After that she acknowledged that 'one man's meat might be another man's poison'.

1902 J. CONRAD *End of Tether* xiv, in *Youth* 370 One man's poison, another man's meat.

1905 A. BURVENICH *Eng. Idioms* 240 It is nuts to him; meat and drink to him, viz. the very sort of thing he likes.

1914 G. B. SHAW *Misalliance* 17 Whats one woman's meat is another woman's poison.

1929 J. B. PRIESTLEY *Good Companions* i. iii. 82 She had a trick of repeating phrases, raising her voice the second time, that had been meat and drink to mimics at Washbury for years.

a1930 D. H. LAWRENCE *Phoenix* (1936) 701 In the free, spontaneous self, one man's meat is truly another man's poison. And therefore you *can't* draw any average..unless you are going to poison everybody.

1937 PARTRIDGE *Dict. Slang* 515 *Meat, the nearer the bone the sweeter the*, a..low catch-phrase applied by men to a thin woman.

1939 F. THOMPSON *Lark Rise* i. 20 In spite of their poverty and the worry and anxiety attending it, they were not unhappy, and, though poor, there was nothing sordid about their lives. 'The nearer the bone the sweeter the meat', they used to say.

1939 N. MARSH *Overture to Death* xxii. 254 I'm no psycho-analyst, but I imagine she'd be meat and drink to any one who was.

2nd meaning obs = obsolete

† 2. A kind of food, an article of food, a 'dish'. white meat, an article of food made with milk. Obs. (Cf. bake-meat, milk-meat, sweet-meat.)

Citations – note date of final entry as evidence of obsolescence

c897 K. ÆLFRED *Gregory's Past. C.* xliii. 318 Ða mettas be God self ȝesceop to etonne ȝeleaffullum monnum.

c1200 ORMIN 11540 þatt time þatt himm ȝet wass ned To metess & to drinnchess.

1340 *Ayenb.* 51 A god huet we hedde guod wyn yesteneuen and guode metes.

c1374 CHAUCER *Boeth.* ii. met. v. 35 (Camb. MS.), They heldyn hem apayed with the metes þat the trewe feeldes browten forth.

c1470 HENRY *Wallace* iii. 315 He..Maide him gud cheyr of meyttis fresche and fyne.

1519 *Interl. Four Elem.* (Percy Soc.) 34 Of all metes in the worlde that be By this lyght, I love best drynke.

1565 COOPER *Thesaurus, Coccetum*, a meate made of honie and popie seede.

1598 FLORIO, *Geladia*,..the meate we call gellie.

1613 PURCHAS *Pilgrimage* (1614) 200 They must not vse the same knife to meats made of milk, which they vsed in eating flesh.

1667 PEPYS *Diary* 2 Sept., In discourse at dinner concerning the change of men's humours and fashions touching meats.

1726 SWIFT *Gulliver* iv. vi, He desired I would let him know, what these costly meats were.

fig.

1601 B. JONSON *Poetaster* v. i, Shun Plavtus and old Ennivs; they are meates Too harsh for a weake stomacke.

3rd meaning – the modern sense of the word

3. a. The flesh of animals used for food; now chiefly in narrower sense = BUTCHER'S MEAT, FLESH n. 4, in contradistinction to fish and poultry. Also, local U.S., confined to certain types of meat, usu. pork.

dark meat (U.S.): 'all the meat of chickens and turkeys, except the breast and wings, these being called light meat' (Webster *Suppl.* 1880).

Citations of word used in this sense

13.. *E.E. Allit. P.* B. 637 þe burne..by þe bred settez Mete.

c1460 FORTESCUE *Abs. & Lim. Mon.* x. (1885) 132 In Fraunce the peple salten but lytill mete, except thair bacon.

1590 SHAKES. *Com. Err.* ii. ii. 57 *S. Dro.* I thinke the meat wants that I haue. *Ant* . . . What's that? *S. Dro.* Basting.

1656 STANLEY *Hist. Philos.* viii. (1701) 298/1 He Water drinks, then Broth and Herbs doth eat, To Live, his Scholars teaching, without Meat.

1727 ARBUTHNOT *Tables Anc. Coins*, etc. xviii. 190 The *Vectigal Macelli*, a tax upon Meat.

1793 BEDDOES *Sea Scurvy* 59 Considering fresh meat, or the muscular part of animals, chemically, I [etc.].

1828 LYTTON *Disowned* Introd. 8 And, harkye, Bedos..if you eat a grain of *meat* I discharge you. A valet, Sir, is an ethereal being, and is only to be nourished upon chicken!

1832 J. K. PAULDING *Westward Ho!* I. 124 Nothing is called meat in these parts but salt pork and beef.

1845 C. M. KIRKLAND *Western Clearings* 93 Venison is not 'meat' to be sure, in our parlance; for we reserve that term for pork, *par excellence.*

1856 'Stonehenge' *Brit. Sports* 182 Thickened milk and broth, the latter with the meat of the sheep's head broken up in it.

1881 *Daily News* 16 Sept. 5/4 Wild ass and antelope meat are also brought in for sale.

1883 C. A. MOLONEY *Fisheries W. Afr.* 56 The cleaning, pickling, and drying process only requires ten days, when the fish, sometimes two or three inches thick in the meat, is ready for export.

1891 *Fur, Fin & Feather* 182 A bearskin is worth $5 to him..besides, he likes the flesh if meat (i.e. pork) is 'skeerse'.

1902 *Dialect Notes* II. 239 *Meat,* bacon always understood.

1903 *Ibid.* 320 *Meat,..*pork. Not often applied to beef, mutton, etc.

1927 *Ibid.* V. 469 *Meat,..*ham; –used only of the hog.

meaning of plural form of the word — b. pl. Different kinds of meat.

citation of this

1693 CONGREVE in *Dryden's Juvenal* xi. 22 In Shambles; where with borrow'd Coin They buy choice Meats, and in cheap plenty dine.

1841 LANE *Arab. Nts.* I. 110 And took to him wine to drink, and boiled meats.

1902 *Westm. Gaz.* 4 June 7/3 Within a fortnight the price of meats all over the country will be reduced.

Compare your explanation with the commentary on p.239.

(ii) Find out if your school/college library/resources centre has either the printed or the CD ROM version of the *OED*. Your local reference library will almost certainly have one.

Carry out a similar study of the ways in which the meanings of the words below have changed:

fancy genius housewife melancholy nice quick

Grammar

The story of the development of English grammar is worthy of a book of its own – students are referred again to standard reference works such as Baugh and Cable (see Further Reading, p.244). However, it may be useful to summarise briefly some of the principal lines of development here:

Old English	Old English was highly inflected; i.e. grammatical relationships were expressed not by word-order but by changes in word-endings. Some of these inflections began to disappear as a result of contact with Norse.
Middle English	This process continued; word-order became the main method of expressing subject-verb-object relationships.
Early Modern English	During this period there was a surviving distinction between the second-person singular pronoun *thee*, *thou*, *thy*, *thine* and the second-person plural *ye*, *you*. The plural form of *you* also denoted formality or respect. This distinction only survives today in some rural dialects. The second-person pronoun had its own distinctive verb ending *-est*, so we find *I go* but *thou goest*. The third-person singular also had a verb ending which we do not use today: *He goeth* is now *He goes* – *-eth* has been replaced by *-es*. Some formerly irregular verbs (e.g. *dove*, past tense of *dive*, and *clomb*, past tense of *climb*) became regular (i.e. *dived, climbed*). Double negation (e.g. *I cannot go no further*) was common and questions could still be asked by inverting the pronoun and the verb, as in *Why look you so pale?* However, the use of the auxiliary *do* form *Why do you look . . . ?* was becoming increasingly common. The range of verb tenses and the use of modal verbs expanded.
1800–present	Although very similar to twenty-first-century English, nineteenth-century grammar did differ in some respects. Some verb tenses (and auxiliary verbs) were used rather differently and there were some different prepositional uses.
Contemporary development	The gradual disappearance of *whom* as the object form of *who* in informal contexts continues the historic process of inflection loss; recent appearances include the intransitive use of *Enjoy!* and the football commentator's present perfect tense used for narratives (*He's put a cross in and he's put it into the back of the net*).

Activity 14. The language of Shakespeare

Reprinted opposite is the opening page of Shakespeare's play *Twelfth Night* as it appeared in the First Folio edition of 1623. Use your own wider reading (including reference to the *OED*) along with the information in the tables above to carry out a detailed analysis of the ways in which language has changed since the play was published.

Remember to focus on:

- graphology, orthography and spelling
- lexis and semantics
- syntax and morphology.

Pragmatics, attitudes and style

Along with the purely linguistic aspects of language, the way it is used in society, and its speakers' attitudes towards it also change over time and reflect all sorts of social and cultural developments.

The question of what is unacceptable or offensive in language is very sensitive to social values and priorities. In a highly religious society, for example, the strongest taboos may be blasphemy: references to God and Christ were, in earlier centuries, scandalous in the extreme. Sexual and lavatorial language have become less taboo in our own century as social attitudes towards personal frankness have relaxed. More recently, however, we have become more acutely aware of the offence caused by racist and sexist language which would have been acceptable to earlier generations.

In more general terms, the later part of the twentieth century saw a tolerance of more informal and colloquial styles of language; as our former insistence on rigid codes of social behaviour (in dress codes, or dining-table etiquette, for example) has slackened, so styles of language in what would once have been seen as formal contexts have become more informal, and more like feigned casual speech.

255

Twelfe Night, Or what you will.

Actus Primus, Scæna Prima.

Enter Orſino Duke of Illyria, Curio, and other Lords.

Duke.

IF Muſicke be the food of Loue, play on,
Giue me exceſſe of it: that ſurfetting,
The appetite may ſicken, and ſo dye.
That ſtraine agen, it had a dying fall:
O, it came ore my eare, like the ſweet ſound
That breathes vpon a banke of Violets;
Stealing, and giuing Odour. *Enough*, no more,
'Tis not ſo ſweet now, as it was before.
O ſpirit of Loue, how quicke and freſh art thou,
That notwithſtanding thy capacitie,
Receiueth as the Sea. Nought enters there,
Of what validity, and pitch ſo ere,
But falles into abatement, and low price
Euen in a minute; ſo full of ſhapes is fancie,
That it alone, is high fantaſticall.

Cu. Will you go hunt my Lord?

Du. What *Curio*?

Cu. The Hart.

Du. Why ſo I do, the Nobleſt that I haue:
O when mine eyes did ſee *Oliuia* firſt,
Me thought ſhe purg'd the ayre of peſtilence;
That inſtant was I turn'd into a Hart,
And my deſires like fell and cruell hounds,
Ere ſince purſue me. How now what newes from her?

Enter Valentine.

Val. So pleaſe my Lord, I might not be admitted,
But from her handmaid do returne this anſwer:
The Element it ſelfe, till ſeuen yeares heate,
Shall not behold her face at ample view:
But like a Cloyſtreſſe ſhe will vailed walke,
And water once a day her Chamber round
With eye-offending brine: all this to ſeaſon
A brothers dead loue, which ſhe would keepe freſh
And laſting, in her ſad remembrance.

Du. O ſhe that hath a heart of that fine frame
To pay this debt of loue but to a brother,
How will ſhe loue, when the rich golden ſhaft
Hath kill'd the flocke of all affections elſe
That liue in her. When Liuer, Braine, and Heart,
Theſe ſoueraigne thrones, are all ſupply'd and fill'd
Her ſweete perfections with one ſelfe king:
Away before me, to ſweet beds of Flowres,
Loue-thoughts lye rich, when canopy'd with bowres.
Exeunt

Scena Secunda.

Enter Viola, a Captaine, and Saylors.

Vio. What Country (Friends) is this?

Cap. This is Illyria Ladie.

Vio. And what ſhould I do in Illyria?
My brother he is in Elizium,
Perchance he is not drown'd: What thinke you ſaylors?

Cap. It is perchance that you your ſelfe were ſaued.

Vio. O my poore brother, and ſo perchance may he be.

Cap. True Madam, and to comfort you with chance,
Aſſure your ſelfe, after our ſhip did ſplit,
When you, and thoſe poore number ſaued with you,
Hung on our driuing boate: I ſaw your brother
Moſt prouident in perill, binde himſelfe,
(Courage and hope both teaching him the practiſe)
To a ſtrong Maſte, that liu'd vpon the ſea:
Where like *Orion* on the Dolphines backe,
I ſaw him hold acquaintance with the waues,
So long as I could ſee.

Vio. For ſaying ſo, there's Gold:
Mine owne eſcape vnfoldeth to my hope,
Whereto thy ſpeech ſerues for authoritie
The like of him. Know'ſt thou this Countrey?

Cap. I Madam well, for I was bred and borne
Not three houres trauaile from this very place:

Vio. Who gouernes heere?

Cap. A noble Duke in nature, as in name.

Vio. What is his name?

Cap. *Orſine.*

Vio. *Orſino*: I haue heard my father name him.
He was a Batchellor then.

Cap. And ſo is now, or was ſo very late:
For but a month ago I went from hence,
And then 'twas freſh in murmure (as you know
What great ones do, the leſſe will prattle of,)
That he did ſeeke the loue of faire *Oliuia*.

Vio. What's ſhee?

Cap. A vertuous maid, the daughter of a Count
That dide ſome tweluemonth ſince, then leauing her
In the protection of his ſonne, her brother,
Who ſhortly alſo dide: for whoſe deere loue
(They ſay) ſhe hath abiur'd the ſight
And company of men.

Vio. O that I ſeru'd that Lady,
And might not be deliuered to the world

Y 2 Till

Activity 15.

To see this process in action we have only to consider the following two texts aimed at young female readers, written 70 years apart.

Compare and contrast the different ways language is used in them, and suggest what developments in language use they illustrate.

(a) Editorial from J17

Wanna know what your future holds? Our free Halloween destiny guide will fill you in. It told me I'm going to be famous for 15 minutes, I'm an OK snog (phew!), and I've got a personality like Prince William. One is not amused!

And if that ain't spooky enough for you, then check out our spellbinding chat with three real-life witches (p44), the oh-so-ironic scary movie quiz (p30), and J17's coolest, vampiest style tips ever. Batwing sleeves? Yes, please!

And just to prove that not all boys in masks are psychos, we bring you a gorgeous Slipknot poster (p120). Robbie's on the reverse side if you're feeling squeamish...

Have a good 'ween!

Sophie

PS Look out for J17's fab new stationery range on sale now in WHSmith's!

(b) Extract from *The Girl's Own Annual* c. 1920

THE EDITOR Writes:

On the Call to the Individual

While I am not one of those pessimistic people who complain that peace-time is worse than war-time (because I know that it is not), I cannot ignore the fact that the present days are very difficult ; and most of my readers will agree with me that the attitude of a large section of the community towards labour, social, and moral questions is most unsatisfactory, and calculated in some cases to ruin the nation as a whole unless some definite check be forthcoming.

So much has already been written on such subjects as the laxity in the matter of morals ; the iniquity of wholesale strikes ; the emptying of the churches ; and the curse of " ca'canny," that it is useless to discuss these problems any further, unless one has a workable solution to offer. Every house-mistress knows without my telling her, that very few of the workpeople who enter her doors do anything like a real day's work for the high wages they receive ; that the striker is the very embodiment of selfishness, since he hits untold numbers of his fellow-men and women for whom there is no strike-pay available ; that the world seems to be in a seething ferment, with greed running riot and moral depravity utterly unashamed.

Compare your analysis with the commentary on p.239.

The nature of language change: some linguistic issues and controversies

In this section, you are advised to consult the following texts:

J. Aitchison, *Language Change, Progress or Decay*

J. Aitchison, *The Reith Lectures 1996*

D. Crystal, *The Cambridge Encyclopaedia of the English Language*

Shelley Martin, *Language Change*

T. Pyles and J. Algeo, *The Origins and Development of the English Language*

In some ways, language change is like a rumour, a joke, or a spontaneous chant that breaks out in a football crowd. It is difficult to see how and where it originates, and even harder to see how it spreads so rapidly. Of course, not all jokes, rumours or chants take off in this way – have you ever tried starting one? So another question is why some do, and others don't.

Your consideration of language change began by considering the link between the variation in language at a given moment (synchronic variation) and variation over time (diachronic variation). As you saw when you looked at the evolution of the meanings of *meat* (see pp.216–220, above), these are connected, because when you look at all the synchronic variety of English, you know that some of these forms (lexical, phonological, or grammatical) will grow and take off, entering popular usage, whereas others will either die away or remain on the fringe of English, either as dialect or slang. As there is no single authority that decides which words/forms should survive in English, and which should not, in order to understand why the language has developed in the way it has, you have to look at a mixture of social and linguistic factors.

Activity 16. The causes of language change

It is helpful to consider the causes of change under two headings

Sociolinguistic explanations for language change:

- the impact of new technologies, intellectual and social activities, and attitudes
- the influence of particularly powerful groups in society
- the importance of language as an indicator of personal and social identity.

Linguistic, or **systemic** explanations for language change:

- the need for any language to work efficiently
- the tendency for English to become increasingly regular.

Look back over your previous explanations of all aspects of language change. In what ways do any of the causes listed above illustrate these factors?

Compare your thoughts with the commentary on p.240.

Attitudes towards linguistic change

Although change in language is inevitable, this has not prevented some users of English from trying to pin down and fix aspects of usage, nor has it excluded others from protesting about and resisting aspects of change. In fact, one of the unchanging aspects of language seems to be that at any given moment, some people will be convinced that things are on the slide and that civilisation as they know it is threatened because of some perceived deterioration in the standard of contemporary usage.

In very broad terms, this perpetual debate is a dispute between those who adopt a **prescriptive** approach to language use, and those who take a **descriptive** stance. If the eighteenth and nineteenth centuries were the high-water marks of prescriptivism, the later part of the twentieth century saw a shift in a more permissive and descriptive direction.

The two positions can be summarised as follows:

Prescriptive	Descriptive
Standards of usage should be maintained; proper pronunciation, usage of words and correct grammar are all essential for the precise communication and expression of meanings. We should therefore be watchful for and resist any change that represents a decline from these standards.	A language tends to develop naturally; it will always change, and it will always tend to meet the communicative needs of the people who speak it, as these inevitably change. At any moment there will be many potential changes in usage: some will die away, but others will take off, and it is futile to seek to prevent this.
Dictionaries and grammar manuals (such as Fowler's *Modern English Usage*) lay down the rules of language that should be followed: 'This is correct English; deviations from this are incorrect.'	Such manuals can only ever record (a) the way words are being used at a particular time, and (b) the judgements of a consensus of speakers at a given moment. Some of these standards are arbitrary and elitist. As language is organic, and is constantly changing, dictionaries and grammar books are out of date as soon as they appear. Standards of correctness are determined not by academic linguistic authorities ('top down') but by the broad mass of speakers ('bottom up').
Some aspects of modern speech reveal a decline in standards: sloppy speech, too much slang, an increase in swearing and bad grammar. These are unnecessary and threaten the quality and effectiveness of language.	Language change is healthy and necessary; a language will always change to reflect speakers' needs. It is more relevant to talk about 'appropriateness' than 'correctness'. Social expectations, not linguistic truths, determine what style of language is acceptable in different social situations.

ACTIVITY 17. LINGUISTIC AUTHORITY

The question of authority in language is a slippery one. Discuss the following aspects of this topic in groups:

- What sources of linguistic authority do we turn to for clarification of a grammatical point or the meaning/spelling of a word?
- Where has their authority derived from?
- Are our ideas about 'correct' usage of language democratic (i.e. do they reflect what most speakers actually understand and do) or elitist (i.e. are they imposed by an intellectual/institutional elite?)
- Is a dictionary such as the *OED* prescriptive or descriptive in its approach?
- What about smaller dictionaries which have to decide which words/meanings to include, or leave out?
- If you are told that some aspect of your use of English is 'wrong', what is your response?
- From your wider reading, find some examples of modern English usage which some prescriptive critics have attacked.
- In some countries there is an official organisation whose role is to lay down rules about usage (e.g. the Académie Française in France). Would such an institution be a welcome or useful one for English speakers? Discuss the pros and cons.

Data for analysis

This section suggests some texts for you to continue and extend your investigations of language change.

(a) Examine the advertisements and feature opposite. They appeared in an American newspaper, the *St Louis Post-Dispatch*, in 1912. In what ways does this data provide evidence of language change during the twentieth century?

You could extend the investigation by collecting a sample of similar features from more recent newspapers, either American or British.

(b) Examine the following advertisements for medical products which appeared in . . . .

Compare their use of language with that in similar advertisements from a more recent publication.

ADVICE ON

Love and Courtesy

Written for the Post-Dispatch

By BETTY VINCENT.

"Winning Him Back."

SOME of you ask me a question which women have been asking for a great many hundreds of years, and which I rather fancy they will keep on asking even after they get the vote.

Stripped of non-essentials, it goes something like this: "A young man used to act as if he cared about me. Now he stays away, although we are not angry. But I love him, and how can I win him back?"

My dear, you CAN'T. Perhaps that seems cruel to you, but the sooner you realize it the better. "Man is a giddy thing," says the most famous "bachelor gentleman" in literature. He's right about it, but it can't be helped.

If he wants to go and you try to call him back he will only despise or pity you. Your best plan is simply—to forget.

A Deceitful Suitor.

A. L. writes: "My fiance tells me he is getting $40 a week. But he keeps putting off our marriage and always has some excuse for not buying me an engagement ring. I think he is not making nearly as much as he says. Should my mother ask him about it?"

It would be better for you yourself to have a talk with him, and insist on perfect frankness in regard to his finances. He owes it to you, since he has asked you to marry him.

Forget Him.

B. C. writes: "I am fifteen and very much in love with a young man. I have written him many letters, but he does not answer them. What shall I do?"

Stop thinking about him. You are too young to be in love with anybody.

Propose.

L. G. Writes: "I have been paying attention to a young lady for six months and am convinced that I love her. Am I justified in telling her so?"

Certainly.

The First Kiss.

I. J. writes: "Is it proper for a girl to let a young man kiss her, if she knows he is very nice? They are not engaged."

A girl is supposed to keep her kisses for the man whom she loves well enough to marry.

Too Old.

W. E. writes: "I am in love with a widow eleven years older than myself. Do you think our marriage is likely to be happy?"

Such unions seldom turn out well.

Bad Form.

A. S. writes: "Is it a girl's place to hold her fiance's overcoat when he leaves after a call?"

It is not considered good form.

The Separate Home.

O. S. writes: "I am about to be married, and the young man insists that I live with his parents, who are well off. What do you advise me to do?"

Try to arrange for a home of your own. You will stand a much greater chance of happiness.

Foolish.

A. K. writes: "I have been corresponding with a young man whom I have never seen. He wants to come here, but my mother wouldn't let me marry him. Shall I go to him?"

Certainly not! And stop thinking of marriage in connection with a man you've never seen.

Press On.

B. L. writes: "I am very much in love with a young lady, but my chum is also paying her attentions, although she has not admitted caring for him. Would it be fair for me to press my suit?"

Certainly, as the young lady is not bound in any way to your friend.

FIND DEAFNESS CURED

ALFRED CROMPTON'S SPECIFIC FOR DEAFNESS is the best remedy out for this annoying complaint. One bottle has permanently cured. A trial is respectfully invited. Sold in bottles at 7½d, and 1s. 1½d. each, by Alfred Crompton, Druggist, Fleet Street, Bury.

–

[ADVT.]

THE GREAT BOTANIC REMEDY

DR. TORRENS' HERBAL PILLS. No words can convey an adequate idea of the wonderful and astonishing effects produced by using the above pills. If anything was wanting to prove the immense superiority of the botanic practice of medicines over all others, the great success of TORRENS' HERBAL PILLS would alone be sufficient. these pills never fail to give relief in all cases of gout, Jaundice, diseases of the liver, and the dreadful drain of diseases arising from dyspepsia or indigestion. Some idea may be formed of the immense number of testimonials of the value of these pills, when it is known that the following were communicated to the agent at Ripon all in one day:-

To Mr. Abbot: Stationer

Sir, – I have been ill about three years, not worth the ground I trod on. I was gradually sinking, but, hearing of Torrens' Pills, I was determined on trying them. I got one box, and found myself gaining strength; I took a second, and found I was getting a great deal better; I took a third, and now I am all right. I have every reason to praise Dr. Torrens' Pills. Please insert the above.

Mr. H. Masterman. Ripon.

(c) Look closely at the following items of public information, the first being a reward poster that appeared in Sussex in 1800 and the second an advertisement for coach services from Worthing to London. What do these documents reveal about the ways in which language has changed in the last 200 years?

FIFTEEN GUINEAS
REWARD.

WHEREAS on the 27th of NOVEMBER laſt, JAMES PAGE fraudulently obtained from Mr. HENRY FORD, of *Midhurſt*, Suſſex, Malſter, at Horſham Fair, a handſome GREY GELDING, about 15 Hands high, 8 or 9 Years old, blind of the near Eye, Tail nicked, Head and Legs newly trimmed, but not the Tail; had ſeveral Saddle Marks, and Hoofs a little broke;---had on a very good Saddle, the Letter R engraved on the two fore Buttons, an old double Girth, and a double reined Bridle, with double Bits and Curb Chain, all plated.

The ſaid Mr. HENRY FORD, hereby offers a Reward of TEN GUINEAS, and the *Petworth Proſecuting Society* FIVE GUINEAS more, to the Perſon or Perſons who ſhall apprehend the ſaid JAMES PAGE; to be paid on his Conviction.

The ſaid JAMES PAGE is 5 Feet 7 or 8 Inches high, rather ſtoutly made, about 29 or 30 Years old, of rather ruddy Complexion, light ſtraight Hair, rather rough Voice, with partly a Weſt Country Dialect, Walks upright, and has been a Soldier; had on a dark coloured dirty round Frock, with Silk Handkerchief round his Neck, dark coloured Worſted Stockings, Shoes tied with Leather Thongs, and a ſmall Hat flouched. By order of ſaid *Henry Ford* and the ſaid Society.

M. J. DAINTREY, *Clerk to the ſaid Society.*

Petworth, Suſſex, Dec. 2, 1800.

VERY
SUPERIOR AND FAST TRAVELLING
BY SAFETY COACHES,
TO
LONDON,

Shoreham, Brighton, Lewes, Newhaven, Horsebridge, Eastbourne, Battle, Dover, Arundel, Littlehampton, Bognor, Chichester, Emsworth, Havant, and Portsmouth,

FROM J. SNOW'S SPREAD-EAGLE AND UNIVERSAL COACH OFFICE,
No. 20, SOUTH STREET, WORTHING.

TO LONDON,

THE SOVEREIGN and ACCOMMODATION, Safety Coaches, every Morning, at NINE o'Clock, to the Spread Eagle, Gracechurch Street, CITY, and Spread Eagle Office, 220, PICCADILLY, corner of the Regent Circus, and next door to Webb's Hotel; from whence they return every Morning, at a Quarter before NINE.

Route—Through Horsham, Dorking, and Epsom.

Messrs. JOHN SNOW, HOWES, DAWSON, MITCHELL, HOLDEN, and W. CHAPLIN, Proprietors.

N. B. Parcels Booked to all parts of the Kingdom.

TO BRIGHTON,
PATENT SAFETY COACHES,

THE MAGNET, every Morning at Half-past NINE o'Clock, and returns from Brighton every Evening at FIVE.

THE ECLIPSE, every Evening at FIVE o'Clock, and returns from Brighton every Morning, at TEN.

The above Coaches go to the Spread Eagle Office, No. 18, Castle Square, Brighton, from whence the WONDER and HERO Coaches leave for HASTINGS every Morning (except Sundays) at NINE o'Clock.

TO PORTSMOUTH,

THE DEFIANCE through Arundel, Chichester, and Havant, every day at Half-past TWELVE precisely, and returns from the George Hotel, Portsmouth, every Morning at NINE o'Clock.

Passengers and Parcels Booked for the above Coach at the Norfolk Arms, Arundel, and the Dolphin Hotel, Chichester.

J. SNOW & Co. Proprietors.

County Fire and Provident Life Office.

The London Daily and Weekly Newspapers to be had at the above Office, as stated on the other side.

Preparing for the examination

Remind yourself of the Assessment Objectives in the grid on p.53 above, which equally apply to the 'Language Change' questions.

In addition, for the 'Language Change' questions you will need to:

Know	Be able to
The principal changes that have taken place in the development of English, at different linguistic levels (phonological, lexical, orthographic, grammatical, pragmatic).	Recognise in linguistic data evidence and examples of these various changes, and identify and comment on them using appropriate terminology, relating these given examples to your wider knowledge.
Some of the sociolinguistic and linguistic explanations of how these changes occur.	Relate evidence of language change in texts to underlying social and linguistic explanations.
Some of the arguments and controversies that surround some aspects of language change.	Understand and evaluate the different attitudes expressed towards language change.

Commentaries

Activity 1. Review

We can sum up the learning points from previous modules as follows:

Language change point	Source
The earliest known languages spoken in the British Isles were Celtic, whose descendants survive today in the form of Welsh, Scots and Irish Gaelic, and Cornish.	A2 Module 5 pp.106–107, 'A Language All of its Own' and Baugh and Cable
First the Romans (55BC onwards) and then the Anglo-Saxons (up to AD1000) helped shape what became known as English.	Module 5 pp.106–107, 'The Dawn of English'
Until the emergence of an accepted form of Standard English from the fifteenth century, different dialects were spoken. This important development was partly due to technological (the invention of the printing press) and social factors. The power and prestige of those who spoke the East Midlands dialect ensured that this was the dialect that became accepted as 'correct' English.	AS Module 2, pp.72–73
The pre-eminence enjoyed by English in the world today is a result of political and economic factors – first, the extension of the British Empire, and in the twentieth century, the power of the USA.	AS Module 2, p.73
Observable changes in accent can take place over a relatively short period of time, and are closely related to questions of social class and identity.	AS Module 2, pp.66–67
Linguistic change is constant and inevitable, but can also be the subject of complaint and controversy.	A2 Module 5, pp.105, 107–108 Jean Aitchison and David Crystal

Activity 2. Change in action

Every generation creates its own distinctive slang which expresses a new identity and effectively distances it from its older predecessors. Much of this slang will be very short-lived, being surpassed by the next generation, and will gradually fade from the speech of those who currently use it. However, one or two items may end up having a longer lifespan, or may in time even drift into the mainstream of Standard English.

In any event, the examples in the list represent many of the ways in which new words and meanings do emerge in English. In terms of the sources and subjects referred to, several items reveal a distinctively topical influence, and many others embody references to different aspects of 'teen' culture, notably dance music, a cult TV programme (*Buffy the Vampire Slayer*) and even working in McDonalds (*Johnny no-stars*). Technology, generally an important source of new words, is represented here only by *mobie*. Terms of approval and disapproval, and terms connected with sexuality are also strongly represented.

In terms of the linguistic construction of the items, you may have grouped together the phonetic abbreviations (*boyf* and *rents*), and the phonetically playful *scatty-yatty*. The ending *-ie* or *-ey* (as in *mobie*, *choccy* and *hottie*) is commonly used to abbreviate or familiarise items (as it does in nicknames, for example). Some items use rhyming slang, which embody cultural references (*Wallace and Gromit*, *Britney Spears*, *Brad Pitt*). In others, some important trends are illustrated; words are sometimes adapted from one word-class to another (so *gun*, which began life as a noun, becomes a verb) and others undergo various kinds of semantic transformations. So, *anchor* and *gun* are both used metaphorically and *choccy* is extended to mean not just 'chocolate' but, by implication, 'as delicious as chocolate' (see 'Semantic change', pp.214–215).

Activity 3. Text-messaging

(i)

CMB:	Call me back
BTDT:	Been there done that
ETA:	Estimated time of arrival
BCNU:	Be seeing you
B4:	Before
ChlYa!:	Chill ya
CUL8r:	See you later
F2T:	Free to talk
IC**WenUXMe:	I see stars when you kiss me
N1:	Nice one
PAW:	Parents are watching
RUUp4It?	Are you up for it?
WsUuuuu?:	What's up?

The symbols at the end of the list have been termed *emoticons* – i.e. icons which express the emotions of the sender. The ones here are:

:-)	(smiling)
:'-D	(crying with laughter)
:-W	(I'm lying)
>;-)	(I've just had an evil thought)

(ii) A grammar of text-messaging

- reduce the message to essential, meaning-carrying words by using ellipsis and/or elision
- spell most words using essential consonants only
- use phonetic spellings and short homophones only
- where possible, use common idiomatic phrases which can be initialised as **acronyms** (e.g. ETA)

- use upper case to indicate the initial letter of each word, lower case only for any subsequent letters included; there is no need for spaces
- use numbers where they equate phonetically to phonemes in your intended message (e.g. 1 = *-un,* 8 = *-ate* etc.)
- use the sounds of letter names to represent combinations of phonemes (e.g. CU = *See you*)
- use graphic symbols and punctuation marks to create icons (e.g. *** = *stars*, :-) = *I am smiling.*

(iii) Text-messaging offers the opportunity of much cheaper communication than conventional phone calls – so economics, as usual, has a lot to do with it. The price of this economy is the restriction in terms of speed of use – the mechanics of mobile phone keypads makes the entry of individual letters awkward and time-consuming, so users try to reduce the number of digital elements required. The solutions users have created to this problem typifies the linguistic creativity of all speakers as it utilises the available means to produce new forms of language that are nevertheless rule-governed and therefore intelligible to other users familiar with the code. You can probably recognise here a process similar to that which characterises children's language acquisition.

Another important practical aspect of text-messaging is the confidentiality it offers. Like other types of slang or code, it seems partly designed to exclude possible eavesdroppers and restrict intelligibility to those in the know, as typified by the example PAW (= *parents are watching*).

Activity 4. School rules

At first glance, you are most likely to notice the forbidding graphology of the text. The relatively high density of text on the page and the unfamiliar fonts of the characters remind us that these visual elements are as subject to change as our vocabulary. The same is equally true of handwriting, with differing styles being favoured in different periods. Then on closer inspection, you will note the apparently eccentric spellings, both inconsistent (different spellings of *school* in the same passage) and different from modern practice (*during*, *busynes*, *obtaine*). Upper case letters are used in places where we would not use them today (*Authors*, *Usher*). The meanings seem mainly consistent with modern usage, but what was the function of an Usher in a school? Nowadays, we only expect to find them in courts, churches and theatres.

However, as you try to read the text, what you are really likely to be struck by is the extreme formality of tone and the convoluted syntax. We still expect formal documents to be formal, but this text contains words such as *aforesaid*, and *thence*, which tend only to be found in legal documents today. The long and complex sentence beginning with *And* – itself another departure from modern convention – adds to the formality. So perhaps it is not only the various separate elements of language that change over time, but also our sense of stylistic appropriateness.

Activity 6. Words of the twentieth century

(i) The first entries in the Collins dictionary were as follows:

1950s	1960s	1970s	1980s	1990s
discotheque stoned rock and roll teddy boy psychedelic Lego hovercraft silicon chip	Catch-22 laser lunar module	Ceefax punk rock test-tube baby Rubik cube workaholic VAT	Mexican wave acid house PEP compact disc AIDS glasnost yuppie Solidarity (Trade Union)	crop circle ethnic cleansing clone information superhighway National Lottery Alcopop road rage Blairite

In general, the exercise illustrates the degree to which language reflects all kinds of social, political and technological developments. *Workaholic* and *yuppie*, for example, give expression to the increased emphasis on work and professional advancement among young adults in 1980s Britain. You may, however, have been surprised to discover that *psychedelic* pre-dates the 1960s culture with which it is associated.

(ii) You will probably have noticed several items drifting from youth culture (especially from music) into mainstream language here – *discotheque* (and its later shortened form), *stoned*, *rock and roll*, *acid house*, etc. – and several others from wider cultural phenomena (the *National Lottery*, *Catch-22*, the title of Joseph Heller's novel). Various kinds of technological inventions and developments (*hovercraft*, *lunar module*, *clone*) are represented, as are the worlds of politics and economics (*VAT*, *PEP*, *glasnost*), whilst other words refer to specific events or social phenomena (the *Mexican Wave* first occurred – allegedly – at the 1986 World Cup).

(iii) It is likely that those terms that refer to a very specific context (*glasnost*) or short-lived culture (*teddy boy*) will be the first to drift out of use. We may still refer to rock and roll in 2001, but will we be talking about acid house in 2051? Words associated with specific technologies and/or products are also vulnerable: as soon as the product or technology becomes redundant, so do they. What future for the hovercraft or PEPs?

(iv) **Acronyms** such as *VAT*, *AIDS* and *PEP* become so well known that we often forget what the letters actually stand for. In the case of *laser* (Light Amplification by Stimulated Emission of Radiation) the use of lower case obscures the fact that it is an acronym at all. Technology and occupationally specific jargon are spectacularly fruitful producers of acronyms. *Yuppie* – young professional person – combines acronymy with the familiar that is so common in teen slang.

Many of the items in the list involve **new meanings/uses** being found for old words. Sometimes the new usage represents an extension of the word's original meaning to a new context – *clone,* for example, is extended from the genetic to the technical (as in copying the electronic identity of a mobile phone). Other examples show familiar words being combined to create new meanings (*acid house, compact disc* and its acronymic form, CD).

The list includes many examples of morphological recombination. This involves the transfer of a familiar prefix or suffix morpheme (e.g. *-craft* as in *aircraft, -ite* as in *Luddite,* or *alco-* as in *alcoholic*) to a new context: *hovercraft, Blairite, alcopop.* However, in this process, strange things can sometimes happen.

In the case of *workaholic,* the word is based on a false morphology: in *alcoholic,* only the *-ic* suffix actually means 'addicted to'; but in *workaholic, chocoholic,* and another adaptations the *ahol-* has been tagged on so that in practice, a new morpheme is born – *-aholic* now means 'addicted to'. (A similar process led to the creation of *hamburger, beefburger, cheeseburger* etc.)

In the case of *discotheque,* the suffix is even borrowed from another language (French, as in *bibliothèque*). Similarly, *psychedelic* draws on a foreign source (Greek) for both its constituent morphemes, *psyche* (originally 'breath' or 'soul', though commonly translated in English as 'mind') and the *delos* ('visible'). Both these morphemes have been used in the formation of related words like *psychotropic* or even *funkadelic.* Direct foreign imports include the names of the Hungarian mathematician Ernö *Rubik,* and *Lego,* which is derived from the Danish *leg godt,* or 'play well'. The tendency for phonetically catchy phrases to take root can be seen in examples like the alliterative *road rage* though it, too, has since spawned many spin-offs such as *air-rage*) and rock and roll.

Activity 7. Dialects in decline?

(a) Some of the underlying causes for the loss of the dialectal terms include:

- fewer people now have direct contact with the rural world that was the source of many of these terms
- the mass media of communication (and education) play a greater part in people's lives, and are unlikely to feature regional dialect usage, creating instead a tendency towards standardisation
- other kinds of non-standard speech may have taken the place of the ones that have been lost – perhaps ones that express a different, 'cooler' kind of personal or social identity for young people
- increased mobility means that fewer people grow up and go to school close to where they live, or in small communities where a dialect used to be spoken.

(b) As can be seen in the extracts on the opposite page, linguistic change can generate surprisingly strong feelings. The author of the letter seems to regret the passing of his/her dialect, and those who sympathise may nostalgically lament the passing of a remembered way of life that the dialect represents. You may think that increased standardisation is a good thing (clarity of universal communication, ease of understanding) or a bad one (loss of regional identity and of colourful linguistic diversity), depending on your point of view.

Activity 9. Text chronology

The extracts are ordered chronologically as follows:

(i) Extract 2: Thomas Wilson: *The Arte of Rhetorike* (1553)

Clues: spellings include a final *-e* in many words subsequently dropped, and the use of *i* for *j* and the *u* for modern *v* in *ouersea* and *loue*. Lexis is mainly recognisable, though some grammatical constructions (e.g. *like as their loue to go*) are now archaic. The contempt for *outlandishe Englishe* is a comment on the huge influx of loan words that were entering the language at this time.

(ii) Extract 1: Daniel Defoe, 'Essay upon Projects' (1667)

Clues: spellings are now (mainly) standardised in the forms we recognise, though 'stile' would now be 'style' and there is some unusual use of upper case. The apostrophe has now made an appearance. The preoccupation with polishing and refining the language is characteristic of this period.

(iii) Extract 4: Samuel Johnson, 1755 Preface to a *Dictionary of the English Language*

Clues: With the exception of *stile* and *translatours*, the spellings, orthography and punctuation are now in line with modern usage. The complex but precisely grammatical syntax of this long sentence is rather more formally constructed than the sort of thing you are probably used to. The word *suffer* is used in a sense ('allow', 'put up with') now seldom used, though it survives in the phrase 'to suffer fools gladly'. Note the familiar complaint about imported words!

(iv) Extract 3: letter to a newspaper, 1999

Clues: twentieth-century English lexis, spelling and grammar – though, perhaps with irony, the writer uses the non-standard form *You got it*, derived from a hamburger commercial. Note the semi-informal note in places – the shortened sentence *Sadly, no longer.* and the injunction *Come off it!*, which takes the text momentarily in the direction of spoken language. The phrase *dumbing down* seems to be a relatively recent acquisition, but the conservative concerns expressed (e.g. about the imported 'Americanisms') are centuries old.

Activity 10. Sound detectives

Perhaps the best evidence is to be found in rhyming verse, or song lyrics, where sets of rhyming words can be compared, and where regularity of rhythms can reveal shifts in the ways words are stressed. This kind of evidence reveals that in the poetry of the eighteenth-century writer, *tea* would have been pronounced 'tay', and *speak* rhymed with 'take'. This hints at another piece of evidence – spellings may hint at older pronunciations, and although we usually pronounce *-ea-* the same as *-ee-* in modern English, it seems to have formerly represented a sound rather closer to modern English 'ay' (/eɪ/).

Going further back into the substantial body of poetry that survives from the Middle English period and earlier enables experts to predict with some confidence the probable phonology of the time, and how it has changed.

Other evidence is taken from such sources as Christopher Cooper's *The English Teacher* (1687) which lists homophones, some of which remain homophones and others which have changed in pronunciation. For instance, *boil* was listed as having the same pronunciation as *bile*; *coughing* as *coffin*, *fight* as *fit*. Elisha Coles, in his *English Dictionary* of 1676, has, among more familiar homophones, the following: *ear* and *year*, *home* and *whom*, *leper* and *leaper*.

Of course, linguists are not just interested in individual words, but in how the whole system of phonemes in English may have shifted over time.

Activity 12. Semantic distinctions

Kingly implies a certain grandeur and majesty, but is, of course gender-specific; *regal* retains the sense of grandeur, but in a gender-neutral way, whereas *royal* carries fewer connotations, and is more simply a descriptive label.

Ask is a very basic concept; to *question* someone begins to imply the exertion of some pressure and suspicion, which the word *interrogate* takes one step further.

Again, the Anglo-Saxon *rise* is the basic, denotative word; *mount* is much more limited in use, and is a purely physical action (you can mount a horse, but you cannot mount to live again). *Ascend* takes us to a different level of formality.

If you say *That was before my time*, 'time' has a humble sense of 'a duration'; an *age*, however, has a grander and more historical sweep (as in the 'Age of Exploration'). An *epoch* assumes almost epic proportions, implying both a longer period and one of weighty or significant events.

Overall, then, Anglo-Saxon has been the bedrock of the language: everyday, unpretentious, often monosyllabic and basic. Informal registers (and colloquial speech) will still tend to include many Anglo-Saxon-derived words. This can be partly explained in terms of sociolinguistics – its history as the language of the people, as opposed to the aristocratic and learned French and Latin.

French-derived words tend to feel rather more sophisticated, less muscular; Latinate vocabulary still more so, polysyllabic, abstract, and likely to occur more frequently in literary, formal and legal registers of modern English.

Activity 13. Using the OED

The earliest meaning of *meat* (or *mete*) in Anglo-Saxon/Old English from 900 onwards was food in general. This sense persisted until the late nineteenth century and may linger in some dialectal use. The first kind of narrowing is in the meaning of a specific *kind* of food – apart from one very early example in 897, this seems to have started to appear from 1200 onwards. The final stage of the narrowing process is the appearance of the third, and principal modern sense, of butchered flesh, from 1460 (again, disregarding a very early reference). For 500 years, these meanings must to some extent have co-existed (*synchronic* variation) but over that period the third sense has gradually gained ground and is now the primary meaning (*diachronic* variation). However, vestiges of the older senses still survive today (see the 'S-curve' theory of language change, pp.240–241 below) in some idiomatic expressions.

Activity 15

The *J17* piece illustrates the pseudo-speech of much informal modern English. The phonetic *wanna* reflects the casual pronunciation of speech that might once have been termed 'sloppy', and the direct questioning/address of the reader, with the implied conversation of *Batwing sleeves? Yes please* reinforces this sense of colloquial intimacy.

The register is relentlessly casual throughout, with *OK* used as an adjective, *snog* as a noun and *phew* as an ironic editorial commentary. The non-standard double negative (*that ain't*) flouts conventional Standard English correctness, and there is a sprinkling of terms (*spooky, scary, vampiest*) which belong to a specific kind of 'teenspeak'. Note, the creating of the term *vampiest* by a typical means of lexical formation – transposing the superlative morpheme *-est* and the adjectival suffix *-y* to the noun *vamp*. The irreverent reference to royalty pokes fun at the very linguistic formality (typified by the impersonal pronoun *one*) with which the royal family (and the originator of the 'not amused' quotation, Queen Victoria) tend to be associated.

By contrast, the *Girls' Own Annual* piece avoids any informality or even a direct personal address. Instead, passive structures are used (*so much has been written . . .*) and the vocabulary is from a formal, literary register of Standard English with its abstractions (*the embodiment of selfishness*), formal and rhetorical righteousness, and its elaborately figurative flourishes (*the world seems to be in a seething ferment*). The social references are to *house-mistresses* rather than Robbie Williams, and the tenor of the article solemnly sermon-like; the grammatical structures *without my telling her* (c.f. *without me telling her*) might be thought pedantic today, and the text includes the same impersonal pronoun (*one has a workable solution . . .*) that was mocked by the *J17* writer.

The world has clearly changed much in the 70 years that separate these texts, and the use of language has changed with it.

Activity 16. The causes of language change

Technological developments can clearly have a major impact on the language, if they also significantly change our lives. The printing press was partly responsible for the requirement for Standard English, because it soon transformed our society from an oral-based culture to a highly literate one. Improvements in means of travel and communication contributed to this process. More recently, some would argue that the computer age is set to have a comparable impact, not just because of the hundreds of new words and meanings it has spawned, but because it is transforming the means with which we communicate (as with text-messaging). Other social and intellectual developments – travel, trade, the development of new areas of interests and knowledge, a more liberal climate in which traditional taboos are weakened – create the need for new kinds of expression. The history of English is also the history of its speakers, as each successive generation uses it to express and reflect its own experiences, preoccupations, values and concerns.

The success of a particular linguistic variation often seems to depend on the power or influence of those users who practise it. It was economics and political geography, not linguistics, that installed the East Midlands dialect as notionally 'correct'. These days, if the powerful broadcast media (such as the BBC) adopt a particular usage, it is more likely to achieve wide acceptance than if a group of students decide to initiate a new pronunciation or expression. However, as you saw in Module 2 of the AS book and Labov's Martha's Vineyard study, in which a non-prestige form of the local accent was seen to spread over a number of years among the island population in reaction to the American RP of holidaymaking outsiders, the covert power of some groups can also be influential. Language, it must also be remembered, is not just a means of communication, but a membership badge that proclaims people's identity and sense of belonging. So, the slang associated with youth cultures makes headway because it is accepted as fashionable by groups of young people who identify with those cultures; in this way, it may eventually 'graduate' into the standard language.

Some kinds of change are less easy to explain in sociolinguistic terms. The Great Vowel Shift, for example, is thought to be the result of the requirement within any phonological system for the various vowel phonemes within a language to be sufficiently distinct from each other to prevent confusion. So, if, for whatever reason, one vowel begins to resemble another, the second vowel will in turn change to preserve the difference between them. Similarly, the general drift within English grammar over many centuries has been towards regularisation. So, for example, we have now lost the past tense forms *dove* and *clomb* in favour of *dived* and *climbed*. We might call this a systemic change – the cause is part of the inherent linguistic regularity rather than the result of any obvious social pressure. This process is reflected in such things as plural noun forms too. For example, the old plural for *shoe* was *shoon*, that for *house* was *housen*, just as the plural of *child* is still *children*. These plural forms have been lost, except in some rural dialects, and the plural form is now in line with that which is most common – the addition of the *-s*.

Of course, some changes are short-lived; if the social grouping, experience or attitude that has produced them fades, then the language disappears as well.

This, after all, is the fate of much of the slang which is the linguistic equivalent of the ephemera, tiny insects with lifespans of a day or less. More influential and long-lasting changes, whether lexical, semantic, grammatical, phonological, orthographic or pragmatic, seem to follow an S-curve: that is to say, there is a 'gestation' period during which the new feature occurs in the speech of a small number of speakers. Then, if the sociolinguistic or systemic influences combine favourably, there is a point at which it starts to take off and spread rapidly through larger numbers of speakers, before 'levelling out' and leaving a small number of exceptions to the trend. This is what seems to have happened when the *-s* noun plural overtook the *-en* plural, leaving a small number of exceptions (*women*, *children*, etc.) which resisted the change.

Glossary

acronym word or phrase derived from or consisting of a series of initial letters

active voice (see also *passive voice)* form of the verb in which the agent of the action is also the subject of the verb

affix a meaningful part of a word (see *morpheme)* attached either to the beginning *(prefix)* or end *(suffix)* of a word

amelioration in language change, the process whereby a word gradually takes on more favourable connotations (see also *pejoration)*

anaphoric reference (see also *cataphoric reference)* any word/phrase in a text/discourse that refers back to something previously mentioned

auxiliary verb verb (such as is/have/can) used alongside a 'main' verb in the formation of tenses

broadening in language change, the process whereby the range of meaning of a word gradually extends (see also *narrowing)*

cataphoric reference (see also *anaphoric reference)* any word/phrase in a text that refers forward to what is to follow

cohesion (see also *anaphoric* and *cataphoric* reference): the interconnection (literally, 'sticking together') within a text/discourse

coherence (see also *cohesion)* the sense of a text/discourse 'flowing', following on logically and creating overall sense

coordination (see also *subordination)* the linking of clauses within a sentence, usually using the conjunctions 'and', 'but' and 'or'

deixis/deictic reference inexplicit reference (usually via *demonstrative* and other *pronouns)* within a text/discourse to things/people outside the text/discourse

demonstrative pronouns the class of words including *this, that, these, those*

diachronic variation variation in language over time

digraph combination of two letters that represents a single phoneme

ellipsis omission of one or more words in a phrase/sentence

etymology study of the origins and semantic development of lexical items

holophrase in child language, a one-word utterance that expresses a meaning equivalent to that of a whole adult phrase

language acquisition device the term used to describe the hypothetical genetic programming that enables humans to acquire language

longitudinal study in language-acquisition studies, the study of the language development of one or more children over a period of time

miscue analysis systematic study of the slips and errors made by a child reading aloud

modal verb group of verbs including *will, would, shall, must* and others which indicate degrees of certainty and other attitudes towards an action

morpheme smallest meaningful part of a word

narrowing (see also *broadening)* in language change, the process whereby the meaning of a word gradually becomes more restricted

object in clause analysis, the recipient of the action (see also *subject)*

overextension in the acquisition of semantics, the tendency of children to extend the meaning of a word beyond its adult sense

overgeneralisation tendency in children to over-apply a general grammatical rule

passive voice (see also *active voice)* form of the verb in which the receiver of the action is made the subject of the verb (e.g. 'the postman was bitten by the dog')

pejoration in language change, the process whereby a word gradually takes on less favourable connotations (see also *amelioration)*

phonemic transcription transcription (usually using the International Phonetic Alphabet) which attempts to represent accurately the pronunciation of phonemes by the speaker(s)

phonics in the development of reading and writing, the explicit teaching of letter combinations and their phonemic values

phrasal verb verb consisting of (usually) a 'main' verb + preposition

prefix see *affix*

subject in clause analysis, the agent of the verb (see also *object, coordination)*

suffix see *affix*

synchronic variation variation within language at any given moment

tags (either *question tags* or *tag questions)* short questions such as 'isn't it?', usually attached to the end of phrases/utterances

telegraphic speech in child language, speech that tends to include the 'content' words but omits unessential, grammatical words.

Further Reading

The key to success in your A2 examination is to extend and underpin your studies by making intelligent use of appropriate secondary sources. The study of the English language is a vast area, and what follows is a selection of the texts we feel students are most likely to find relevant and accessible. Some of them have already been referred to in the main body of the text.

Module 4. Language Investigation

Of course, the most appropriate reading will depend on your chosen topic, but the texts listed here offer valuable starting points and suggestions for approaches for a range of possible topics.

A. Goddard, *Researching Language*
C. McDonald, *English Language Project Work*

Whatever your topic, you are likely to find a useful source of reference in:

D. Crystal, *The Cambridge Encyclopaedia of Language*
D. Crystal, *The Cambridge Encyclopaedia of the English Language*

Grammatical issues are helpfully clarified in:
D. Crystal, *Discover Grammar* and *Rediscover Grammar*

Other useful sources include:

Butler, Bloomer and Trott, *Projects in Linguistics*
Carter and McCarthy, *Exploring Spoken English*
Hutton and Wainwright, *In Your Own Words*
D. Langford, *Doing Things with Words*
M. Sabba, *Focusing on Language*

Module 5. Editorial Writing

This practical test of your reading and writing skills is underpinned by an understanding of stylistics and textual cohesion and coherence. The following sources should prove useful:
U. Clark, *Stylistics*
I. Pople, *Discourse Analysis*
J. Shuttleworth, *Editorial Writing*
AQA Examiners' Reports

There is a great deal of material covering both the areas included in this module. The following is a selection of the texts you are likely to find in libraries or bookshops.

Module 6. Language Development

Language Acquisition

J. Aitchison, *The Articulate Mammal*
D. Crystal, *The Cambridge Encyclopaedia of Language,* Section vii, pp.227—248
D. Crystal, *The Cambridge Encyclopaedia of The English Language,* Ch. 23, 'Learning English as a Mother Tongue', pp.426—435
D. Crystal, *Listen to your Child*
F. Myszor, *Language Acquisition* (in the Living Language Series)
M. Donaldson, *Children's Minds*
J. Peccei, *Language Acquisition* (Routledge Workbook Series)
M. Lowe and B. Graham, *English Language for Beginners*
K. Perrera, *Children ~ Writing and Reading*
S. Pinker, *The Language Instinct*
G. Wells, *The Meaning Makers*

Language Change

B. Bryson, *Mother Tongue*
E. Camey, *Spelling* (Routledge Language Workbook)
D. Crystal, *The Cambridge Encyclopaedia of The English Language,* Part 1, pp. 4-115
D. Freeborn, *From Old English to Standard English*
S. Goodman and D. Graddol, *Redesigning English*
G. Hughes, *Words in Time*
D. Leith, *A Social History of English*
D. Leith et al., *English Language: History, Diversity and Change*
S. Martin, *Language Change*
T. Shortis, *The Language of ICT*
Trask, *Language Change* (Routledge Language Workbook)

Index

abstract concepts 176
acquisition process 157–165
acquisition stages 157–162
acronyms 233
active voice 32
adverbial phrases 27
affixes 34
ambiguities 70
amelioration 215
analogies 113, 135
anaphoric reference 22, 63, 142
assessment objectives
editorial writing 73
language development 147–148
language investigation 1, 45–46
auxiliary verbs 159, 164

behaviourist model 166–167
bound morphemes 34
brain areas 170

captions 116, 117–118, 146
cataloguing 82–83
cataphoric references 22, 63, 142
causes of changing English 226–227, 240–241
change in action 107–108, 199–200, 232–233
changing English 148, 196–231
attitudes 222, 224–225, 239
causes 226–227, 240–241
change in action 199–200, 232–233
diachronic investigations 202
dialects 205, 236–237
etymology 215–220
examination preparation 231
further investigations 228–231
grammar changes 221–222
graphology 212–213
great vowel shift 210–211, 240
history of English 205–210
investigating 202
lexical trends 213–214, 238
lexicon change 203–205
lexis 213–214, 238
linguistic variation 226–227, 240
nature of change 226–228
orthography 212–213
perpetual change 108, 197–202
phonology 210–211, 238
pragmatics 222, 224–225, 239
printing 212–213
punctuation 213
semantic change 213, 214–215, 238
Shakespeare's language 222–223
slang 204, 241
spelling changes 211–212
style 222, 224–225, 239
teenspeak 199–200, 232–233
text chronology 209–210, 237
text-messaging 200–201, 233–234
upper and lower case conventions 212
children's early speech 83–86
children's language acquisition 148–187
acquisition process 157–165
acquisition stages 157–162
behaviourist model 166–167
children's writing 183–187, 195–196
cognitive development 168
comparative study of many children 151
developing language functions 155–156, 191
early language skills 149, 188–189
established thinking 165–171
first 12 months 154–157
genetic argument 167–168
Halliday's taxonomy 153–154
interactional function of language 153
investigation 150–151
language acquisition device 167
language functions 153–154
learning to read 172, 192–193
learning to write 182–187, 195–196
literacy 171–187
one-word stage 157–158, 163
pragmatics 157
readability 175–177
regulatory function of language 157, 191–192
social function of language 153
social pragmatics of language use 169
sounds and spelling 68
sounds for communication 154
storytelling skills 161
taxonomy of language 150, 189–190
teaching reading 173–175
telegraphic stage 157–158, 164
textual difficulty 175–177
thinking and language 168–169
two-word stage 157–158, 163–164
writing for children 178–180, 193–195
writing process 183, 195
children's stories 47–49, 70–71
children's writing 183–187, 195–196
Chomsky, Noam 167
classroom discourse 12–13, 58–59
clauses, main and subordinate 28
closed questions 58
co-ordinating conjunctions 28
cognitive development 168
coherence of text 20–22, 63–65
cohesion of text 20–23, 63–65, 114–115
commentaries
editorial writing 132–146
examination technique 132
language development 188–196
language investigation 54–72
complex sentences 28, 177
compound sentences 28, 177
concrete objects 176
consonant harmony 85
correction by adults 170
creole 170
cross-references 89–92, 142
cursive script 196
cut and paste 114–115

dash 38
data
collection 8–9
organisation 13–14, 59–62
potential 10–13
presentation 113
validation 9–10, 55–56
deictic references 145
deixis 22
demonstrative pronouns 64–65
descriptive approach to language use 227
determiners 26
developing language functions 155–156, 191
diachronic investigations 202
diachronic variation 197, 226
dialects 205, 236–237
dictionary writers 203
discourse structure 19–22
double negation 221

early language skills 149, 188–189
editing 114–115
editing skills 103–108, 143–144
editorial writing 73–146
definition 73–79
editorial experiments 120–126
examination preparation 126–132
history of English 97–98, 140–141
new texts 93–120
producing a text 75, 132–133
skills 206–208
sources of text 76, 78, 133–134
tagging 80, 134
working with sources 79–93
egocentric speech 168

- ellipsis 29, 56
- ending 143
- **English language**
  - changes 107–108
  - history 97–100, 104–108, 140–142, 205–210
  - origins 106–107
- etymology 215–220
- Estuary English 211
- evaluation 86, 87–88
- **examination preparation and technique**
  - changing English 231
  - editorial writing 126–132
  - language acquisition 188
  - language development 187–188
  - pre-released material 126–127
  - synoptic module 188
  - time allocation 127–132
- exclamation mark 37
- extended noun phrases 69

- fact and opinion 87–88, 137–138
- false morphology 236
- figurative comparison 135
- figurative language 69
- footers 142
- forewords 142
- formulaic writing 72
- **frameworks**
  - application to data 18–19
  - choice of 38–40, 69–70
  - discourse structure 19–22
  - film previews 38–39, 69
  - graphology 23–24
  - lexis 29–33
  - morphology 33–35, 68
  - orthography 35–38, 68
  - phonology 35–38, 68
  - pragmatics 24–26
  - semantics 29–33
  - syntax 26–29
- free morphemes 34
- full stop 37

- genetic argument 167–168
- glossing 110–112
- grammar 159–160, 189–190, 198
- grammatical connectors 21
- grammatical control 70
- graphemic correspondence 172
- graphology 19, 23–24, 175, 189–190, 198

- Halliday's taxonomy 153–154
- headers 142
- headings 102, 116–117, 142, 145
- headlines 142
- headwords 135
- history of English language 97–100, 104–108, 140–142, 205–210
- holophrases 163
- homophones 238

- image to text ratio 102
- incomplete sentences 71
- instrumental element 190
- interactional function 153, 190, 191
- International Phonetic Alphabet (IPA) 16–18, 158, 171
- introductions 142
- investigating changing English 202
- investigation suggestions 7–9
- language acquisition 147–187
- language acquisition device 167
- language change 147
- **language development** 147–241
  - examination preparation 187–188
- language functions 153–154
- **language investigation** 1–72
  - analytical frameworks for language study 2
  - definition 2–5
  - language research project 3–4
  - marking scheme 53
  - science of language study 2
  - time planning 51–52
- **language research project**
  - annotating spoken English 15–17, 62
  - classroom discourse 12–13, 58–59
  - data collection 8–9
  - data organisation 13–14, 59–62
  - data potential 10–13
  - data validation 9–10, 55–56
  - frameworks applied to data 18–19
  - frameworks choice 38–40
  - investigation suggestions 7–9
  - newspaper reports 20–21, 63–65
  - preparation 5–45
  - presentation 41
  - radio news 22–23, 66, 94
  - report structure 42
  - researching the chosen topic 40–41
  - significant features 10–11
  - skills audit 6–7, 54–55
  - spoken English 15–17, 62
  - subjects for investigation 4–5
  - transcribing spoken English 15–17, 62
  - tutorial advice and record 43–44
  - write-up 41–43
- learning to read 172, 192–193
- learning to write 182–187, 195–196
- lexical connectors 22
- lexical range 70
- lexical terms 112–113
- lexical trends 213–214, 238
- lexicographers 203
- lexicon change 203–205
- lexis 19, 29–33, 70, 158–159, 175–176, 189–190, 198, 238
- logical connectors 21, 145

- main clauses 28
- material selection 96–98
- Middle English 221
- miscue analysis 181–182
- mismatch 159
- modal verbs 31
- morphemes 33–35, 68
- morphological recombination 236
- morphology 19, 33–35, 68, 175–176, 189–190, 198, 236
- motherese 169
- multiple sentences 28

- names 111
- narrowing 214
- need for language 152–157, 190
- negative reinforcement 166
- neologisms 70
- **new texts** 93–120
  - analogies 113
  - captions 116, 117–118, 146
  - closing 118–120, 146
  - cohesion 114–115
  - cut and paste 114–115
  - data presentation 113
  - editing 103–108, 114–115, 143–144
  - glossing 110–112
  - headings 116–117, 145
  - lexical terms 112–113
  - material selection 96–98
  - names 111
  - opening 118–120, 146
  - paraphrasing 108–110, 144
  - quoting 114–115
  - references 111
  - response to a commission 93
  - signposting 100–101, 142–143
  - spoken texts 102–103
  - style models 93–96, 139–140
  - stylistic features 109–110
  - summarising 108–110, 144
  - text formats 101–103
  - text structure 98–101
  - writing and rewriting 103–113
  - written texts 101–102
- newspaper reports 20–21, 63–65
- Norse 221
- noun phrases 26–27
- nouns 30

- offensive language 222
- Old English 221
- one-word stage 157–158, 163
- opening 118–120, 146
- orthography 19, 35–38, 68, 189–190, 198, 212–213
- overextension 159
- overgeneralisation 160, 192
- Oxford English Dictionary (OED) 215–220, 228, 239

- pair/group discussion 4–5, 54
- paralinguistic aspects of speech 16
- parallel identical sentence structure 70

paraphrasing 108–110, 144
parentese 169
passive voice 32
pejoration 215
persuasive texts 29
phatic function 190
phonemic correspondence 172
phonemic transcription 16
phonics approach to teaching reading 173–175
phonology 19, 35–38, 68, 158, 189–190, 198
phrasal verbs 32
Piaget, Jean 168
pidgin 170
positive reinforcement 166
post-modification 27
pragmatics 19, 24–26, 157, 160–162, 189–190, 198, 222, 224–225, 239
pre-modification 26, 69
prefixes 34
prenominalisation 63
present perfect tense 31, 221
presentation 41
printing 212–213
producing a text 75, 132–133
productive language acquisition 162
pronouns 22, 33, 145
prosodic aspects of speech 16
pseudo-speech 239
punctuation 37–38, 71, 184, 213
puns 70

quantifiers 26
question mark 37
question tags 58
quoting 114–115

racist language 222
readability 175–177
received pronunciation 16, 211
receptive powers of children 162
reduplication 163
references to names 111
referent 63
register 69
register drift 215
regulatory function of language 157, 191–192
repetition of word or phrase 22
report structure 42
representational element 190
representational language 163
response to a commission 93
reverse engineering 76
rhetorical devices 70–71, 184

schwa 17
second person pronoun 221
semantic change 213, 214–215, 238
semantic connectors 22
semantic distinctions 213, 238
semantic features 159
semantic understanding 173
semantics 19, 29–33, 70, 158–159, 176, 184, 189–190, 198
semicolon 38
sentence building
  combining clauses into sentences 28–29, 67
  combining phrases into clauses 27–28
  groups and phrases 26–27
sentences
  complex 28, 177
  compound 28, 177
  incomplete 71
  multiple 28
  parallel identical sentence structure 70
  simple 28, 176–177
sexist language 222
Shakespeare's language 222–223
shapes of words 173
signposting 100–101, 116, 142–143
simple sentences 28, 176–177
skills audit 6–7, 54–55
Skinner, B F 166
slang 204, 241
snytax 176–177
social function of language 153
social pragmatics of language use 169
sounds for communication 154
sources of text 76, 78, 133–134
sources study
  cataloguing 82–83
  conflict 91–93, 138–139
  critical approach 80, 87
  cross-referencing 89–92
  evaluation 86, 87–88
  fact and opinion 87–88, 137–138
  summarising 83–86
  tagging 80–86
  understanding texts 86
spelling 184, 196
spelling changes 211–212
spelling, non-standard 70
spoken languages
  International Phonetic Alphabet (IPA) 16–18
  paralinguistic aspects 16
  phonemic transcription 16
  prosodic aspects 16
  received pronunciation 16
  transcripts 15–17, 62
spoken texts 102–103
sports interviews 31
storytelling skills 161
style 222, 224–225, 239
  features 109–110
  inconsistencies 133, 145
  models 93–96, 139–140
subordinate clauses 28
suffixes 34
summarising 83–86, 108–110, 144
synchronic variation 197, 226
syntactic structures 173, 184
syntax 19, 26–29, 70, 189–190, 198
synthesis 133

tagging 80–86, 134
taxonomy of language 150, 189–190
teaching reading 173–175
teenspeak 199–200, 232–233
telegraphic stage 157–158, 164
temporal connectors 64
text
  chronology 209–210, 237
  coherence 20–22, 63–65
  cohesion 20–23, 63–65, 183–184
  formats 101–103
  structure 69, 70, 98–101, 173
text-messaging 200–201, 233–234
textual difficulty 175–177
time planning 51–52
titles 142
topic-specific vocabulary 69
transcribing spoken English 15–17, 62
20th century English 203–204, 235–236
two-word stage 157–158, 163–164

unanswered questions 71
underextension 159
upper and lower case conventions 212

verb phrases 27
verb tenses 31, 71, 145, 177
verbs 31
verigule 213
Vygotski, Lev 168–169

whole word approach to teaching reading 173–175
word classes 30–33, 71
word selection 184
word-order 29
write-up 41–43
writing and rewriting 103–113
writing for children 178–180, 193–195
writing process 183, 195
written texts 101–102